The Evolutionary
Foundations
of Psychology

The Evolutionary Foundations of Psychology
A UNIFIED THEORY

Felix E. Goodson
DePauw University

HOLT, RINEHART AND WINSTON, INC.
New York Chicago San Francisco Atlanta
Dallas Montreal Toronto London Sydney

Copyright © 1973 by Holt, Rinehart and Winston, Inc.
Library of Congress Catalog Card Number: 73-8004
ISBN: 0-03-077615-5
Printed in the United States of America
34567   038   987654321

To the two finest psychologists I have known:
Melvin H. Marx
Kenneth S. Wagoner

Preface

This book represents an effort to develop an integrative theory of psychology. When I first planned it I was optimistic about the undertaking— because I grossly underestimated the time and labor that would be involved. I thought I could write it in two years; it has taken ten. Through these years I have been chastened by the sheer enormity of the task and humbled by finding myself well beyond my depth many times—perhaps because I have tried always to reach a little farther than my grasp.

What I have attempted to do is to examine the many dimensions of man's nature and to integrate them in a logically coherent system without viewing man in isolation either from the totality of his nature or from his environmental context. I have tried to clarify human hopes, desperations, purposes, and experiences of freedom without treating these notions as clichés.

In a real sense this book is aimed not only at psychologists but also at anyone who seeks deeper insight into his own nature, for it attempts a fuller view of man than has been acknowledged in certain contemporary theoretical systems.

Although the book was written primarily for readers already familiar with the basic concepts and problems of psychology, undergraduates and interested laymen should be able to follow the arguments, especially as much of the most technical material has been placed in separate and unessential sections at the ends of chapters.

My debts are so great that I cannot acknowledge all of them. I have shaped much of this material in the classroom, and many students have contributed both to the concepts and the structure that have emerged: especially Judy Diehl for her insight into the nature and function of the autocept, Peggy Gladden for her notions on the nature and function of apperception, Jo and Tom Tombaugh for criticisms that necessitated consideration of volitional behavior, Chris Wurster for work on language, and Steve Weber for his analysis of movement and depth perception.

Many of my colleagues have also helped generously in this endeavor. I am most grateful to Marvin Marx for his sharp questions and pertinent criticisms and to Kenneth Wagoner, who participated in the discussions that led to this work and paved the way for me to pursue it by arranging grants and special classes. The criticisms of Mike Silver and Bob Garrett forced me to question my basic assumptions again and again and the encouragement of Harry Hawkins and Carroll C. Pratt provided inspiration to keep me going. I owe special debts to George Morgan, who contributed much to the organization and clarity of the entire manuscript; to Albert Reynolds and Forst Fuller and Preston Adams for evaluating those notes on the implications of evolutionary theory; and to Elmer Klempke for his careful scrutiny of sections dealing with the issues related to the philosophy of science. Theodore Newcomb made many suggestions that strengthened both the logic and the expression of many arguments. Harold Proshansky has done much to improve the clarity, continuity, and style of the manuscript. Finally it was Jeanette Ninas Johnson who tied it all together, both in terms of style and in tightening the logic of many of the arguments.

Although what I owe to earlier thinkers will become clear in the course of the argument, I want to acknowledge here the principles discovered by Charles Darwin, from which the specifics of my theory are frequently derived.

Finally, in any project of this kind, there is always one person who deserves more gratitude than does any other. In this instance, it is my wife Cheryl, who served as constructive critic, lucid interpreter of my frequently tangled grammar, and unerring corrector of incorrect spelling, yet still found time to do research and to write many of the notes.

Greencastle, Indiana
April 1973   F.E.G.

Contents

x   Contents

1

Some Basic Principles

We do not know by what process life first emerged upon the earth or in what form. It may have resulted from an interaction of conditions so rare as to lie at the most extreme levels of probability; or the circumstances may have been so common that life emerged in many places and in many forms simultaneously. Furthermore, we can only surmise the degree of qualitative change between the inanimate and the animate. Perhaps the first sign of life took the form of proteins so primitive that they can be called "living" only with caution; but it could also have been sudden and dramatic.

Why is there no evidence that new forms of life are still emerging directly from the context? Despite prolonged and continuing efforts to find such evidence, there has been no success. It is possible that life is still "becoming" but that the process is too obscure to be captured by our blunt techniques. More likely the circumstances appropriate to the emergence of life are no longer present: As the earth has cooled or the atmosphere has changed, or electrical disturbances have altered, the felicitous moment has passed. Or perhaps the very emergence of life itself brought conditions inimical to repetition of the event; the essential gaseous balance may have been disrupted, or the stamp of hunger with which nature marks its creatures may ensure that all those primitive prototypes at the threshold of life are devoured, even as they struggle, by those already on the other side. It is even possible that the specific flight of

1

meteorites that some believe may have "seeded" the earth was unique and that all life has spread from this initial accident. From this welter of speculation the reader can take his pick. We choose to follow A. I. Oparin (1953) in accepting the notion that the environmental ingredients that once were propitious are simply no longer present. Experimenters who have demonstrated that proteins, however primitive, can be created when electrical charges are sent through primitive atmospheres add some weight to this view.[1]

Although we cannot answer questions about the beginnings of life, we can infer something about the surrounding circumstances, both of those beginnings and of subsequent evolution. Our earth, then as now, was a perpetual flux of energies. The first "unit" of life was surrounded by this pressing, vibrating, radiating, chemically reacting manifold; it arose within this maelstrom of forces and continued to exist only because some kind of adaptation to these forces was possible. The story of man's evolution is in the manner in which through countless ages the process of natural selection has been determined by reactions to these energies. As evolutionary products of a particular type of environment, men bear the imprint of this environment in the various processes and structures that constitute their beings. This observation raises certain basic questions: Can we not gain insight into the nature of any organ or process by examining the environmental circumstances that produced it? More specifically, can we not gain understanding by inferring the adaptive contribution of a given structure or process to survival?

It is our view that such examination can tell us a great deal about the present attributes of organisms. We shall argue that a few simple principles were crucial to adaptation among the most primitive forms of life and that these same principles are still operative in the most complex evolutionary product: the human being.

The Relation between Organism and Environment

Our system is an extension of Charles Darwin's theory of evolution.[2] We assume that differential response to certain energies in the environment has been both essential to survival and the occasion for evolutionary change. Any organism will be found at any given time to reflect within its various attributes the characteristics of the context that shaped it: Every creature is thus, in a sense, representational of its environment. Even as we may infer the type of world from which an organism has come by a careful examination of its various attributes, so we may make valid inferences about the characteristics of an organism from an examination of the energies in the environment in which it has evolved.[3]

The human being thus has sense organs that tell him when molecules are moving either too rapidly or too slowly, when objects are too sharp or apply too much pressure, when subtle shifts in electromagnetic energy and the vibrations emanating from objects occur. In a very real sense the ability to discriminate effectively and to respond rapidly to such energy shifts is both the occasion for and the highest achievement of the evolutionary process. As the sense organs are "energy specific" as a result of the processes of natural selection, the other components of the organism are also derived from, and thus represent, the forces acting upon them. Gravity has manifested itself in a particular type of skeletal and muscular structure; atmospheric pressure and temperature have helped to determine the type of body covering.

This functional interrelationship between organism and environment is dramatically emphasized when man is exposed to an alien context. Consider the problems that must be solved before he can survive in outer space. Suddenly he is placed in a situation in which one of the major forces that has structured his body during the evolutionary ages is no longer present: Without the orientation provided by gravity, the problems of adjustment and perhaps even of survival become severe. In outer space man not only finds himself in circumstances where certain "primal molding forces" like gravity and atmospheric pressure are missing, but he also is exposed to new energies that may harm or destroy him. Protected from the effects of radiation, as he was during the evolutionary journey, man did not develop sense organs that would allow him to respond differentially to such energies. And, as man has evolved where oxygen was always plentiful, he does not have receptors that tell him when he is dying of oxygen starvation. In space, then, man must build extensions of his sense organs to allow differential responses to these alien energies and conditions, or he must armor himself against their effects. He must create artificial conditions that approximate those in which his species has evolved and that, as a function of natural selection, he essentially represents.

Functional Interpretation

The preceding discussion suggests in a general way the relations between man and his environment. Every species incorporates within its morphology and process systems the effects of thousands of generations of interaction with particular segments of the environment. There is thus a functional interrelationship between each creature and the context within which its progenitors evolved. If an attribute noted at any given evolutionary moment has remained within the species for an enduring period, it can be understood in terms of its adaptive function. Why? Because it was through its contribution (however slight) to adaptive facility that the attribute was incorporated in the species and retained.

During the discussion of organisms and their attributes that will be offered in the following pages, this functional perspective will be paramount. We shall always ask questions like "How did (does) this characteristic abet the organism in its struggle for survival?"[4] "In what way did (does) it contribute to

facility of response?" "How did (does) it make the organism a more efficient adaptor?"

This emphasis upon such functional interpretations rests upon one critical
assumption: that there is a direct and intimate relationship between human
understanding of any attribute and the discovery of its function. In this notion
we see a break from the commonly affirmed statement that science should
simply *describe* the various phenomena of the natural world. The adherent of
the functional perspective insists that a descriptive statement is not enough; it
is necessary, but not enough.

We can consider *any* characteristic of an organism within two frames of
reference. We can *describe* the attribute and its operation as objectively and
as precisely as possible. But we can also—and here is where the functionalist
places his emphasis—infer what the attribute *is for*. From a descriptive point
of view the lens of the eye can be defined as "a concave, oval-shaped piece of
cartilage"; a functionalist might say instead that the lens is "an organ that
allows the projection of a clear image upon the fovea."

Let us consider the aye-aye. This little nocturnal primate, native to Madagascar, is so unusual that taxonomists have had difficulty in assigning it to an
appropriate category; finally they have placed it in a pigeon-hole all its own.
It has a large bushy tail, large naked ears, teeth that continue to grow out as
they are worn off, and nictitating membranes that keep its nocturnally adapted
eyes wiped clean. But it is the aye-aye's hand that is most peculiar. It consists of the thumb and four fingers common to all primates; three of the fingers and the thumb are ordinary in appearance, but the middle finger is
extremely thin and looks something like a bent piece of black wire. These
descriptive statements fulfill the general requirements of scientific objectivity
and precision, but they merely whet the appetite. What about that third finger? It is here that functional interpretation can contribute understanding.
How does the thin, wiry finger of the aye-aye aid him in his struggle for
survival?

Let us make a hypothetical safari in search of the function of the third finger of the aye-aye. First, we must journey to Madagascar, then we must move
into the jungle at night, and there if we move silently and stealthily we may
observe a remarkable tableau: the aye-aye crouching near a half-rotten log, its
large naked ear glued to the wood, and its entire posture suggesting intense
concentration. Suddenly, we see the amazing finger in action, probing a small
hole in the wood and emerging with a fat grub. The "why" of the finger
becomes clear. As the aye-aye made the long evolutionary journey into a
tighter and tighter interrelationship between its process systems and its environmental niche, the finger reflected more effective adaptation, demonstrating this
interrelationship. From an evolutionary point of view, this adaptation is completely logical. If a species feeds primarily on grubs, those variations that abet
(however slightly) the ability to catch grubs will be retained; the long narrow
finger of the aye-aye is a direct expression of this selective circumstance.

Primitive Life and the Primal Environment

Previously we remarked that the principles that must have obtained when life first appeared and prospered can provide insight into its contemporary forms. In order to clarify this statement, we shall now try to infer the characteristics that even the most primitive forms of life must have demonstrated in order to survive. Then we shall try to extract certain principles that seem as fundamental to understanding man's most complex behavior as to explaining primitive life.

Although we know little about the specific origins of life, we can make two inferences, one about its constituent material and the other about the context within which it must have existed. First, regardless of the particular form or complexity of primitive life, it must have been constructed of protoplasm. This substance is the only form of matter in which life, whether plant or animal, is now manifested, and it seems plausible to conclude that it was the basic constituent of life from the beginning. If this conclusion is correct, we can make another critical inference about our first units of life. They must have been relatively vulnerable.

Second, unless the earth has changed remarkably since life first appeared, early life must have existed within a context of fluctuating energies. This inference also seems plausible. Energy shifts are in perpetual process on earth today, and they were likely present (in as great a variety and amplitude) when life began. We are now in a position to make a more general statement.

If such a unit of life was comprised of relatively vulnerable material and if it existed in a context of fluctuating energies (the extremes of which would often have been pronounced), then some method for reducing the traumatic effects of energy shifts was required for continued existence. That is, an organism composed of vulnerable material and existing in a context of fluctuating energy *must* have some means that will allow it to retain or regain a condition of relative balance within its body system if the life process is not to be disrupted. Certain techniques of maintaining or regaining equilibrium were thus essential to the continuing existence of primitive life. We believe that only two such techniques were possible and that their expression describes the two main lines of evolution.

First, an organism may maintain the equilibrium essential for existence by developing "armor" like the bark of trees, the fur of animals, the shells of oysters. This technique has been the predominant tangent taken by countless species. Probably more than 99 percent of all the creatures that have ever lived have developed it. The great coral reef off the coast of Australia attests that myriads have followed this line of evolution to the point of living death. Undoubtedly an armor component is intrinsic to the life process itself, for living requires a structure that is, at least to a limited degree, protective. But, as armor merely protects from energy flux, rather than allowing the use of such change for differential response, the greater the organism's reliance on it, the more inflexible the organism's adaptive potential will be. Even though structural armor is thus basic to the life process, its use in adaptation is essentially negative, for it imposes relative stasis upon the living things so endowed. This negative aspect can be more clearly recognized when we consider that the ultimate armor would protect the organism from the influx of any and all energy, a situation synonymous with not living.

Second, and far more important from the point of view of psychology, an organism may adapt to the energies imposed upon it by means of differential response. If a form of life, whatever its constitution, is to continue to exist in a context of fluctuating energies—some of which may be extremely disequilibrating in nature or intensity—it must be able to respond differentially to those energies. By "responding" we mean that it must in some fashion "draw away from" energies that are reaching dangerous levels, and by "differential" we mean that the response will be initiated by such harmful energy levels but *not* by those that are not harmful. Our primitive element must not only be able to respond to harmful energy, but it must also respond differentially to different intensities within a single energy dimension. We can surmise from an examination of contemporary one-celled organisms like amoebas or paramecia that such primitive differential responses may have been similar to the turgor or tropismatic reactions of these simple systems.

Let us examine more carefully our statement that the life element must draw away from harmful levels of energy. It is an inference from two interdependent facts: first, that there is a direct relationship between the proximity of an energy source and the intensity of the energy and, second, that any organism can withstand high energy levels better for shorter than for longer periods. The greater the deviation from the conditions optimal for life, therefore, the more rapid must be the alleviating response. A movement gradient can thus be predicted: The withdrawal response becomes less and less rapid as the level of energy imposed is reduced by increasing distance. The relative vulnerability of organic material allows us to make a similar inference about the *latency* of withdrawal behavior. Within the limitations imposed by the structure of the organism, the more intense the energy imposed, the shorter will be the latency of response.

If our primitive motile life element was constructed of vulnerable protoplasm, two gradients of behavior must have been present in its adaptive repertory. Although these gradients are inferred from a general examination of the processes that must have been requisite for primitive life, both are confirmed by observation of simple contemporary systems.

The movement away from potential trauma is only half the picture of primitive response. An organism cannot respond differentially without movement, and such movement itself requires the expenditure of energy. Furthermore, energy is required for maintenance of life, even in a completely quiescent state. Primitive life must therefore have been able to *obtain* energy from some source, but did this process also involve differential response? It could

be argued that energy might have been obtained from a source that was relatively constant in the environment: solar radiation, oxygen, or microorganisms
in water, thus obviating the necessity for differential behavior. The earliest
source of energy use very likely was of this diffuse type, requiring no movement from the organism. But differential response is implicit even in such passive reception. Unless there was some mechanism that permitted reception of
appropriate energy and rejection of what could not be used, the organism
would have been both overburdened and deprived of the energy essential for
response. Very likely the most primitive differential-response mechanism was
simply that of ingestion or noningestion.

Furthermore, as in every instance there would be a practical limitation on
the amount of energy that could be ingested at any one time, such an organism
would necessarily have had to respond differently when sated than when
depleted. A gradient of response can thus be predicted in which the speed of
ingestion decreases as a function of growing satiation, assuming that the physicochemical processes (whatever their specific nature) would operate gradually,
rather than suddenly.

Although such differential ingestion without doubt appeared early in the
evolutionary history of primitive organisms and still remains part of the
response repertory of every living creature, *approach* behavior of the entire
organism must have appeared at approximately the same time. For much of
the energy commonly used does not exist homogeneously within the environment but is unevenly distributed; other creatures are one of the most common
sources of food, and they occur as individual units. Gross differential responses
to them would thus be essential. Actually such responses represent very little
advance over the bare essentials necessary for life already discussed. They were
probably simple extensions of the ingestion behavior already mentioned, triggered and guided by similar physicochemical changes.

It seems likely that such differential approach behavior was initiated and
sustained by taxis changes produced by chemicals emanating from the energy
source. If so, an approach gradient would again be predicted since the amount
of chemical present would be proportional to the distance of the organism
from the energy source, if other variables are constant. The chemical emana-
tion that initiated approach activity would become more intense as a function
of increasing proximity, producing increasingly rapid movement.

We could also predict a response gradient as a function of the relative satiation of the organism. As energy was depleted, more rapid gross movement
toward the energy source would occur, and consumption would be more rapid
once the source had been reached, in parallel to the gradient for passive ingestion. From the point of view of adaptation, the emergence of such an approach
gradient would be expected, for a level of depletion that might be endured
without harm for a short time could cause damage or death if extended for
longer periods. Therefore, the greater the disequilibrium, the more rapidly the

organism must move. Such approach behavior (both ingestion and gross movement) would describe a gradient similar to the one predicted in the "moving
away" responses already discussed.

All early differential behavior was likely of the primitive turgor or taxis
variety observed in certain simple contemporary organisms. The general nature
of the negatively accelerated function predicted can be determined experimentally. Furthermore, through minute examination of the physicochemical
changes that occur in such organisms some understanding of the "mechanism"
that initiates and sustains both approach and avoidance behavior might be
obtained.

Statement of Fundamental Postulates

It is our belief that the mere existence of a motile life element presupposed the
demonstration of certain principles. If these first elements were constituted of
vulnerable organic material, differential response to energy shifts was essential
to existence, and more rapid responses to intense energy applications became
critical for survival. As such responses, and indeed all other life processes,
required energy, the organism must also have responded differentially to energy
sources; and, the greater the energy depletion, the more rapid must have been
the response. A condition of "minimal variation" must have been maintained
or regained; the greater the deviation from this condition, the more rapid must
have been the alleviating response.

Therefore the first motile life elements must have been simple, homeostatic,
negative-feedback mechanisms and, considering the contexts in which they
emerged, could not have been otherwise. We believe that differential response
to energy fluctuation is a requisite of evolution, as well as of survival, and that
all living organisms, from the simplest to the most complex, reflect more or less
elaborate variations of the simple principles described.

This discussion leads directly to a statement of the *fundamental postulate
of process*. The postulate is fundamental because it is presumed to apply to
every life process from the simplest to the most complex.

The Fundamental Postulate of Process

*All overt or covert activity serves the immediate function of impelling the
organism toward equilibrium.* This postulate is derived from the observation
that a condition of minimal variation must be maintained if life processes are
to continue undisrupted. It is thus derived from the most rudimentary conditions essential to even the most primitive life. There is also a *fundamental
corollary* to this postulate.

The Fundamental Corollary

*Within the limits imposed by structure and available expendable energy, the
more an organism deviates from equilibrium, the greater its compensatory*

activity will be. This corollary is based on the observation that greater deviation from optimal conditions for the continuation of life requires more rapid compensatory changes if life processes are not to be disrupted.

Implicit in both postulate and corollary is the assumption that the same processes that were essential to the existence of the first motile life elements remain essential to the most complex evolutionary products.

The fundamental postulate of process will be cited again and again throughout this book, for it is assumed to be demonstrated in all known examples of life. But, from a theoretical point of view, another postulate is equally important. The example of the aye-aye dramatically portrays the manner in which a given attribute evolves to reflect a particular adaptation circumstance. But the truly exceptional aspect of the aye-aye's finger is that as an adaptational device it is *not* exceptional. Any organ or process that has been retained by a species for an extended period can also be evaluated in terms of its adaptive contribution. The curious grassy material on the human head, the flappy pieces of cartilage called ears, the white protrusions from the gums are all functional characteristics and can be understood in terms of their adaptive significance.

This functional orientation is so basic to our theory that it is taken as given in our second fundamental postulate.

The Fundamental Postulate of Inference

Every nonintrinsic attribute that has remained characteristic of a species for an enduring period contributes (or once contributed) to the survival potential of the organism.[5]

This postulate has been critical to the development and integration of the theory to be presented here. It has provided the perspective that makes possible the derivation of many hypotheses from the theory. We shall refer to it frequently in different guises. Throughout the following pages it will serve as a unifying principle. It is so important that we must caution the reader against a common misapprehension: the notion that evolution somehow reflects some larger purpose or plan. The statement that "an attribute could not have come into being if it had not had adaptive function," is correct after the fact. But *no* attribute has ever appeared in order to fulfill the requirements of some teleological design. Attributes come into being by slow increments; each such increment remains with the species because it increases adaptive potential. Each attribute is a composite of many such functional increments that have occurred through chance and have been retained and integrated by the species because they have increased, even though slightly, the species' chances for survival.

As we follow the evolution of our hypothetical primitive form of life, we shall continually suggest how both fundamental postulates and the fundamental corollary have been manifested in each new attribute. We shall begin with a discussion of primitive motile life as a simple homeostatic negative-feedback system and explore more and more attributes until we have developed a hypothetical organism with all the characteristics of the human being. It should be emphasized that although something very like our outline must have happened, we do not claim that the actual process of evolution occurred in precisely the manner to be described. Rather, it is our intention to use this approach as a vehicle for developing a theory that will allow an integrated view of the disparate characteristics of human beings as a single comprehensive system. This statement of purpose has within it a problem which is inescapable and should be clarified at the outset. We call it the intrinsic dilemma.

How does one depict an organism consisting of many systems so related that a change in any one has immediate repercussions throughout all the rest by means of explanatory techniques based on categorization and then deal with such categories separately? The human being functions according to principles operating simultaneously, but the use and understanding of language are sequential processes. In an endeavor to explain we must begin at some particular point and continue as if each process under consideration were separate from those before and after. In the organism such processes as sensation, perception, apperception, motivation, and behavior are all dynamically and perpetually interdependent, yet we must use separate words in sequence and organize this book into separate sections in sequence. There is no escape from this dilemma. Fortunately, the reader's memory permits an accumulation of these categories that may be welded into a total view. We shall therefore make a systematic attempt to refer the reader backward and foreward to points pertinent to the particular section that he is reading and to point out critical relationships whenever possible.

Let us begin by re-examining the capacities and limitations of our primitive form of life as it has been traced so far and by considering how various attributes have allowed more effective adaptation to the environment.

Notes

1 Oparin (1953) has formulated an intricate theory of the process by which life first appeared on earth. It is impossible to accurately summarize this in a short space, but we would highly recommend its study by the interested reader.

Recently, M. Goulian, A. Kornberg, and R. L. Sinsheimer (1967) of Stanford University have been able to synthesize self-replicating deoxyriboneucleic acid chains *in vitro*, a process that has previously occurred only in living organisms. Using a DNA chain from infectious Phage O XI74 as a model, they combined the raw materials, including adenine, guanine, cytosine, and uracil, with a DNA polymerase (enzyme) previously developed by Kornberg; the result was new DNA chains identical to the model. Whether or not we define such elements as "living," there can be little doubt that an important step, both toward the creation of life and the validation of Oparin's theory, has been taken.

2 It is curious to trace what has happened to Darwin's theory since the publication of *On the Origin of Species* in 1859. Immediately a great gap in his basic premise was revealed: the unanswered question "What caused variations?" Darwin sought to mend the gap with J. de Lamarck's doctrine of acquired characteristics, but it was a poor patch, based as it is on the notion that experience

can somehow change the sex cells in the gonads. From 1890 to about 1930, the principle of natural selection lost its influence among scientists, just as it was being assimilated by the public. The saltationist interpretation that species can be established by gross mutation captured the scientific imagination, and natural selection, though not totally disregarded, was eclipsed by this more dramatic explanation of change. But the developing study of genetics, related research, and population statistics all combined to suggest that Darwin had written better than he knew. Ernst Mayr (1959) has suggested, in the opening address to the symposium honoring the 100th anniversary of publication of *On the Origin of Species*, that we have come full circle and are closer to Darwin's original conceptions now than at any time during the last century.

Evolutionary theory has, however, become more sophisticated. It has now been recognized that mutations are typically minute and may thus account for the variation that Darwin noted, that many such genetic mutations must occur before noticeable alteration occurs within a species, and that the adaptive contribution of any genetic change must be evaluated according to its integration into the total synchrony of a complex living system. A genetic change can be fortunate or not, depending upon other attributes, and can be beneficial in one genetic context but lethal in another. Evolution is a game of chance in which every card dealt changes the values of all the other cards and in which the environment may at any moment shift the rules. But natural selection serves as the ultimate judge of which hand wins and thus sets the course of all evolution.

[3]It seems strange that there is so little direct empirical support for a theory as widely accepted as that of Darwin. Three investigations have been conducted quite recently. The most famous and by far the most convincing is that of H. B. D. Kettlewell (1959) on industrial melanism. A certain species of moth *(Biston betularia)* grew rapidly darker during a period in which the trees of England were being blackened by industrial soot. Kettlewell surmised that this change was the result of natural selection occasioned by the fact that birds that normally feed on this moth could not easily see the darker members of the species. Kettlewell documented his theory by recording the recovery rates of both light and dark moths released in industrial and nonindustrial areas and found that the proportions of moths reclaimed after various lapses of time supported his notion. He photographed birds picking conspicuous individuals off trees while protectively colored moths remained unharmed nearby. He also included photographs in which dark moths melt into darker backgrounds and light moths are almost invisible in lighter contexts.

Another example of natural selection in process has been reported by R. F. Johnston and R. K. Selander (1964); it involved the ecogeographical adaptation of house sparrows. The investigators found a marked inherited increase in body weight in birds living in colder climates and more northern latitudes. There were also changes in color and length of the tarsus. All such changes had occurred within 100 generations after these birds were first imported into North America from England in 1852.

A third piece of evidence is reported by T. H. Hamilton (1967). In 1859, an auspicious date for evolutionary theory, a few rabbits were brought to Australia. By 1950 the population had increased to hundreds of millions, so that "rabbit inundation" seemed imminent. To combat this rapidly expanding population explosion a virus peculiarly effective against rabbits was introduced. But as the years passed the proportion of rabbits succumbing to the virus kept decreasing. Apparently those rabbits with slightly higher resistance to the virus were surviving and transmitting this attribute to their offspring. High death rates, up to 99.8 percent in the beginning, slowed with time, and this adaptation took place in approximately ten years.

Selective breeding, what might be called "unnatural selection," also provides indirect support for Darwin's theory. Horses have been bred for centuries, some for strength, some for beauty and speed. Dogs have been bred for many purposes: greyhounds for speed, other hounds for hunting, German shepherds for police and seeing-eye dogs. Their uses are almost as numerous as are the separate breeds (Scott and Fuller, 1965). Near the turn of this century a special type of pigeon, the trumpeter pigeon, was bred for an unusual type of cooing (Levi, 1951). Cockerels have been selectively bred for variations in the frequency and vigor of aggressive and sexual behavior (Wood-Gush, 1960). The roller canary has been bred for better song over so many generations that now its song is completely different from that of wild canaries (Marler, 1959). And, of course, everyone is familiar with the different types of cattle that we now have, including the Jersey and the Guernsey for milk, the Angus and the Hereford for beef. No one needs to be reminded of Hitler's eugenic plan for an Aryan super race.

Animals have also been bred selectively for experimental reasons. A. Manning (1961) worked with the fruit fly *(Drosophila melanogaster)*, and within seven generations of breeding for fast and slow mating, developed one line with a mean mating latency of three minutes and another with a latency of eighty minutes. H. Gruneberg (1952) has reported breeding generations of waltzing and circling mice. J. H. Bruell (1962) bred mice for speed in wheel running. G. E. McClearn (1959) also bred mice, for readiness to explore an open field. R. C. Tryon (1942) selectively bred rats to learn to run a maze more rapidly. C. S. Hall (1951), who worked with turkeys as well as with mice, has reported breeding the quality of wildness into these animals.

[4]The arguments against survival value as the sole arbiter of evolutionary change have taken at least three different tacks. First, there is that of complexity. Why would life take on more and more complex forms if survival value were the only force shaping evolution? Why not more toward simplicity rather than toward complexity? Especially as complexity inevitably (even according to the neo-Darwinians) increases the probability of breakdown in an organic system.

For one reason, simplicity has a built-in limitation. Even for life to exist and to continue, a minimum (a casual reading of Oparin's 1953 book will suggest that this minimum is considerable) of complexity is required. There is a definite limit to the extent that any organism can simplify and still fulfill the criteria for living. But there is apparently no limit in the other direction. Furthermore, as life becomes simpler the number of possible variations is correspondingly reduced: the base for variation is lacking.

But then, has life actually tended toward complexity? As complex organisms ourselves, we are more interested in complex organisms. If, however, we let numbers indicate the direction of evolution, we find that complexity has not fared so well. The ocean is filled with rudimentary creatures, and microorganisms that exist in teeming billions give further evidence of the extent of simplicity. Those who claim that life has moved toward complexity may simply be biased by their emphasis on man.

But why is there complexity at all? Each new attribute increases the probability that something might go wrong, so why not a return to the simplest expressions of life? Complexity without function is lethal; however, some few attributes simply add more to survival probability than they take away. And, once an attribute has been incorporated, the probability of new functional variation increases. The probability of new lethal variations increases also, but the workings of natural selection tend to eliminate them. Variations that occur to functional attributes, even though most of them may be detrimental, ultimately result in the selection of changes that increase adaptive potential. That is, once an attribute has been incorporated, detrimental variations tend to drop out but functional variations tend to be incorporated. Both complexity and greater adaptability occur as corollaries.

But why do some species become fixed at a rudimentary level and endure for generations without appreciable change? Does the evolutionary past of a species affect the direction and set the limits for further evolution? Apparently so. The more a species adapts to a restricted environment, the greater will be its tendency to remain fixed. Once the species has adapted to the restrictions, any variability may interfere with its close interrelationship with the environment. The likelihood that a given variation will be beneficial decreases, for it would interfere with the adjustment already made. The species would thus evolve toward fewer and fewer attributes and an even closer dependence on the stable environment. The simple organism may survive quite effectively in a simple environment with only minor changes, but its survival is restricted to this environment.

Another argument is that the notion of evolution through progressive adaptation is shot through with teleology, that some ultimate end is implied. Neo-Darwinian theory counters this argument with the claim that changes in evolution are occasioned only by the variables acting at each moment. Suppose that we found some round pebbles on the beach where a small river runs into the ocean. These pebbles have not always been round. They have been shaped by continual contact with other stones as they made their way downstream. Roundness was not a goal; there was no striving to reach the ocean. They were simply affected by the forces acting upon them at each moment. The same is true for organisms in the process of evolution: life may arise on a mountain and it may go toward an ocean, but there is no plan. The species present at any given moment in time no more reflect a plan than do the pebbles. But does this argument negate the existence of motivation and volitional behavior on the part of higher organisms? No, here we are speaking only of broad, evolutionary changes. We will deal with determinism and motivation later.

Finally there is the argument of tautology. Some critics think that neo-Darwinian theory involves an obvious piece of circular reasoning: The organisms that survive are the fittest, and the fittest are those which survive. Despite this circularity, the explanatory power of the notion is not weakened. Every statement has two different kinds of referents, the symbolic and the empirical, but symbolic circularity does not necessarily obviate empirical significance; nor does the observation that the fittest are those that survive a priori disqualify the statement that those that survive are the fittest. It does seem, however, that the phrase "survival of the fittest" is misleading. Survival of the *fitter* would be more accurate, for it emphasizes the notion that at a given evolutionary moment the attribute that abets survival is not necessarily either the most adaptable attribute possible nor does the adaptation ensure the fittest possible organism. It is simply the more adaptable attribute of those available at that moment that permits the organism as it is then constituted to make a better adaptation to its environment.

[5]This postulate seems obvious in the context of neo-Darwinian theory, for natural selection *is* selection according to relative adaptive function. But, despite common acknowledgment of the principles, many theorists apparently find it difficult to accept the universality of survival value as the only guiding force in evolution. A. Cronquist (1968), for instance, has suggested that certain evolutionary trends in plants seem to be selective, others more doubtfully so, and still others neutral or even mildly counterselective. Can this observation be assimilated to the basic tenets (mutation, selection, and incorporation) of Darwin's theory? The answer is "no," for the theory insists that the survival value of an attribute is the ultimate determinant of its incorporation, the sole arbiter of natural selection.

But then how do we explain the fact that so many attributes seem neutral and others even seem negative in terms of their contribution to survival? There seem to be three basic possibilities, each with ramifications.

First, it is possible that an attribute may be in the process of passing out of the species. The great majority of mutations are harmful, yet they may linger in a species for a while before they disappear. If we happened to look at one of these attributes and to surmise its adaptive contribution, we would obviously fail. An attribute may be passing because it is no longer functional. The horns of the caribou were once essential weapons against the great wolf packs of the north, but now the wolves are gone, and those heavy horns, attractive as they seem to hunters, have probably become a liability to survival. Any attribute that was once incorporated because of its survival value may become a liability when the effective environment changes. Furthermore, a functional attribute may be rendered extraneous or harmful by the development of some other attribute. To be functional any attribute must be synchronous with all the other attributes of the organism; a change in one may alter the contribution of another. Somewhere down the evolutionary path the ostrich moved "toward legs" and "away from wings," but wings may once have been its major instrument of locomotion. A candid evaluation now might judge them negatively.

Second, there is always the possibility that the investigator has made an error in observation or inference: that an attribute may actually have an adaptive function that he fails to see. An attribute may be so subtle or ephemeral in its effects that its contribution cannot be easily inferred. Consider the pineal gland. Scientists have puzzled over its function since Descartes mistakenly concluded that it was the organ of mind-body interaction; they had almost decided that it had no adaptive function. Now there is a growing body of evidence that it may respond to the amount of activity in the optic nerve and occasion compensatory changes in the production of sex hormones, which may in turn influence such diverse activities as migration in birds and the menstrual cycle in human beings. The pineal gland suggests another complication that may obscure the particular function of an attribute. Some attributes may not just disappear; they may literally shift functions. The pineal gland functions as a "third eye" in certain primitive amphibia, as an instigator of sexual behavior in many mammals, and as a governor of sexual development in humans.

The function of an attribute may also be difficult to recognize because it makes little or no contribution in itself but has catalytic or dampening effects on other attributes, sometimes at considerable functional distance. The function of the pituitary gland was difficult to determine because it seemed to make no contribution in itself. Now we know that it is the master gland, which determines the pace of the process in certain other glands. Indeed every organism is a complex system, with thousands of attributes in perpetually shifting dynamic synchrony. The function of many attributes may thus never be inferred in isolation from the operation of other attributes. Attributes are so interdependent that an alteration in any one may affect the adaptive contributions of the rest. And, of course, the degree of contribution, whether positive or negative, is always responding to changes in the environment! A slight alteration may move an attribute from the plus to the minus column and the reverse.

Third, it is possible that the investigator may be observing an intrinsic, rather than a basic attribute. If we were to try to determine the function of the whiteness of an elephant's tusks it is doubtful that we would ever arrive at a reasonable explanation. Every aspect of an organism, whether a "bit of bone or a hank of hair," must be constructed of some material with certain characteristics. We may designate such characteristics "intrinsic attributes." They are intrinsic simply because without them no attribute could exist at all. To try to determine the function of the whiteness of teeth or elephants' tusks, the softness of flesh, or the breakability of bones is futile. But it is often difficult to know whether a given attribute is intrinsic or functional. Brownness in eyes is functional because it provides greater resistance to the injurious effects of sunlight than do other colors, but if it were the only color available we would classify it intrinsic.

References

Bruell, J. H. Dominance and segregation in the inheritance of quantitative behavior in mice. In E. L. Bliss (Ed.), *Roots of behavior.* New York: Harper & Row, 1962.

Cronquist, A. *The evolution and classification of flowering plants.* Boston: Houghton-Mifflin, 1968.

Goulian, M., & Kornberg, A. Enzymatic synthesis of DNA. 23. Synthesis of circular replicative form of phage 0 X174 DNA. *Proceedings of the National Academy of Sciences of the United States of America,* 1967, 58: 1723-1730.

Goulian, M., Kornberg, A., & Sinsheimer, R. L. Enzymatic synthesis of DNA. Synthesis of infectious phage 0 X174 DNA. *Proceedings of the National Academy of Sciences of the United States of America,* 1967, 58: 2321-2328.

Greensburg, D. A. The synthesis of DNA: How they spread the good news. *Science,* 1967, 158: 1548-1549.

Gruneberg, H. *The genetics of the mouse.* The Hague: Nijhoff, 1952.

Hall, C. S. The genetics of behavior. In S. S. Stevens (Ed.), *Handbook of experimental psychology.* New York: Wiley, 1951.

Hamilton, T. H. *Process and pattern in evolution.* New York: Macmillan, 1967.

Kettlewell, H. B. D. Darwin's missing evidence. *Scientific American Reprints.* San Francisco: Freeman, 1959.

Levi, W. H. *The pigeon.* Columbia, S.C.: Brim, 1951.

Johnston, R. F., & Selander, R. K. Correlation between severe winter temperature and mean body weight for fourteen populations of the house sparrow, *Passer domesticus. Science,* 1964, 144: 548-550.

Manning, A. The effects of artificial selection for mating speed in *Drosophila melanogaster. Animal Behavior,* 1961, 9: 82-92.

Mayr, E. Where we are. *Symposia on quantitative biology.* Vol. 24. Cold Spring Harbor, N.Y.: Biological Laboratory, 1959.

Marler, P. Developments in the study of animal communication. In P. R. Bell (Ed.), *Darwin's biological work.* New York: Cambridge, 1959.

McClearn, G. E. The genetics of mouse behavior in novel situations. *Journal of Comparative and Physiological Psychology,* 1959, 52: 62-67.

Oparin, A. I. *The origin of life.* New York: Dover, 1953.

Scott, J. P., & Fuller, J. L. *Genetics and the social behavior of the dog.* Chicago: University of Chicago Press, 1965.

Singer, M. In vitro synthesis of DNA: A perspective on research. *Science,* 1967, 158: 1549-1550.

Tryon, R. C. Individual differences. In F. A. Moss (Ed.), *Comparative psychology.* New York: Prentice-Hall, 1942.

Wood-Gush, D. G. M. A study of sex drive of two strains of cockerels through three generations. *Animal Behavior,* 1960, 8: 43-53.

2

From Overt to Internal
Locomotion: An Overview

In this chapter we shall deal with the evolution of what may be called
"adaptation attributes." From our discussion will emerge the skeleton of the
theory to be treated more specifically in later chapters. It should serve both
as a basis for deriving and integrating principles and as a summary statement of
the general theory. The fundamental postulate of inference carries a heavy
burden in this development and should be kept in mind by the reader.

Within our frame of reference an adaptation attribute is a characteristic that
facilitates resolution of disequilibrium in the vulnerable material that constitutes
living organisms. It is not simply an organ or structure; rather it is a mode of
reaction that permits more rapid and effective adjustment to the environment.
Organisms that have reached approximately the same level of evolution (as
defined by response facility) can thus vary widely in size, shape, and structure.
Indeed, we may surmise that the workings of natural selection produce many
different creatures as each novel adaptation attribute evolves. In this chapter
we shall reexamine the evolutionary context in order to infer and describe the
functions of some basic adaptation attributes. Although there are many different kinds of living organisms, the number of adaptation attributes that have
been developed is remarkably small.

A brief summary of our discussion in Chapter 1 will help to clarify the concept of adaptation attributes, to suggest which one first appeared in the

17

evolutionary context, and to set the stage for discussion of the others. We recall that the first motile life element was required to demonstrate certain characteristics: It had to be able to move away from harmful energy sources and to move toward materials that could serve as sources of necessary energy; it also had to be able to respond *differently* to various types and levels of energy. Differential response, then, is a characteristic fundamental even to the most primitive motile life element,[1] fundamental in the sense that without it the element could not exist. We may consider such differential responsiveness the fundamental adaptation attribute. Indeed, the others that we shall discuss can be viewed simply as extensions of it as methods for implementing differential response. We turn now to describing these methods, beginning with the simplest and proceeding to the most complex.

Unidimensional Differential Behavior

Probably the most rudimentary form of differential behavior consists of responses to energies on a single dimension. As is well known, there is an inverse relationship between the nearness of an energy source and the amount of energy rising from it. It would thus seem reasonable to infer an early form of differential behavior that involved more rapid movement when closer to the source than when further from it. For example, an organism would move faster from heat when closer to it than when at a greater distance. The physicochemical changes initiating avoidance of slight increases of intensity on this energy dimension are the same (though less pronounced) as those occasioned by potentially more damaging levels.

The approach behavior discussed in Chapter 1 is also in its simplest form, unidimensional; the physicochemical changes underlying the responses occasioned by slight emanations from a food source are essentially the same (except in degree) as those occasioned by more concentrated emanations in immediate proximity to the primitive life.

We do not claim that an organism with the capacity to respond to only one energy dimension now exists or has ever existed, but we do insist that the unidimensional response is the simplest mechanism for differential behavior that can be logically deduced. Actually, even the most primitive life elements undoubtedly responded variably to several energy dimensions within their environmental context.[2]

Unidimensional behavior can serve as a basis for definition and clarification of certain concepts. Let us assume a hypothetical organism that can respond to fluctuations on only one energy dimension. In such an organism equilibrium would be defined as the condition obtaining until the response threshold had been reached. Minimum disequilibrium would be defined as the condition of the organism that exists when differential responses are initiated to increases of energy applications. Maximum disequilibrium is the condition when energy intense enough or energy shifts sudden enough damage the structure of the organism.

The postulate of process and the fundamental corollary of the theory are both explicable within the framework of unidimensional behavior. In our hypothetical organism movement would not occur until the point of minimum disequilibrium had been reached. According to the postulate of process, such movement would tend toward equilibrium because the induced responses would occasion movement away from the energy source. As there is an inverse relationship between distance from an energy source and energy received from that source, movement would soon place the organism beyond the point of stimulation; equilibrium would then be restored. The fundamental corollary is demonstrated by the speed or latency gradients proportional to the organism's distance from the energy source, the intensity of the energy, or the suddenness of its application. It should be noted that an energy change rarely occasions only minimum disequilibrium; more typically, it produces some greater degree of disequilibrium which initiates movement. One reason is that no organism is either perfectly sensitive or invariably reactive. In our example it has been assumed that the single dimension is potentially noxious. Parallel logic applies to the consummatory stimulus on a unitary dimension.

A variant of this type of behavior is immediately suggested. As a single energy dimension may encompass a wide range of intensities, it seems reasonable to infer that slight intensities on certain dimensions may produce approach responses, whereas greater intensities may produce avoidance behavior. As either extreme of a dimension like that between heat and cold is hazardous to living organisms, behavior must have been differentiated according to these two alternatives early in the course of evolution. This differentiation may reflect a relatively invariant relationship between the lower energy intensities on a potentially harmful dimension and the presence of food sources. Although we shall examine the use of cues in differential responses later, we can point out here that the presence of low intensity energy may serve to initiate approach activity, whereas higher levels can produce avoidance behavior. Euglena demonstrates this point: It moves toward a dim light source which is essential to photosynthesis but away from intense light that might be damaging. In each such instance a sort of behavioral fulcrum between the two types of response can be predicted and determined experimentally.

It should be noted that stasis at the fulcrum is actually a primitive form of "equilibrium," as we use the term in the postulate of process. The quiescence of an organism at that point demonstrates that equilibrium among all relevant factors has been achieved. According to the postulate, any deviation from this point will initiate movement toward it; according to the fundamental corollary, the greater the deviation, the more rapid such movement will be.

An organism with only this initial adaptation attribute would be extremely limited in its adaptability. It would be "bound" by the energy peculiar to a given dimension and unable to respond to changes in other dimensions. As there is often a narrow gap in space and time between slight and potentially dangerous levels of energy on a single dimension the "margin of safety" would be practically nonexistent. As the chemical emanations from energy sources decrease rapidly with distance, the "food finding" capability of such an organism would be extremely restricted. Sudden or extreme shifts of external energy or the absence of emanations from food material could cause the organism to perish. It seems obvious that the ability to respond to a cue rather than to the crucial energy dimension as such was a major advance in adaptability.

Using Cues in Differential Response

As we shall note repeatedly, continuity marks the development of adaptation attributes. Each new attribute in the hierarchy of adaptation represents only a slight alteration of a more primitive attribute and in turn provides the foundation for the next. The use of cues apparently followed this pattern. In its most rudimentary form it was only a minor extension of unidimensional behavior. In fact, the point at which cues were first used is impossible to guess. It could be argued, for instance, that this attribute is implicit in all unidimensional behavior and is exemplified in *any* response to nontraumatic intensities on a given energy dimension. Can we consider the amoeba's slow retreat from a dim light as an example of the use of cues? Certainly such behavior implies the capacity to respond to slight intensities, in themselves not damaging, in order to avoid energy levels that might be harmful. We might even argue that the most primitive unidimensional behavior involves the use of cues because both approach and avoidance gradients are implicit.

By "use of cues" we mean simply response to some change in energy on a dimension other than that directly representing the danger or the food material. What then is the most elementary example of the use of cues in differential response? We shall answer this question somewhat arbitrarily. We can begin by examining relatively nonspecific physicochemical mechanisms by which dimensions *similar* to the crucial one can initiate and sustain responsive behavior. When an energy shift on such a dimension occurs before appearance of the crucial dimension, the organism is abetted in avoiding harmful energy or in obtaining nourishment. As evolution progressed the use of more varied and subtle cues distinguished the more adaptable organisms.

The emergence of the use of cues as an attribute ensured a dramatic increase in adaptive potential. There can be little doubt that it was manifest in many different processes and organ systems (most of which have since disappeared) during the evolutionary journey. It still remains an essential characteristic of adaptive behavior whether simple tropisms or complex learning. Let us consider various types of the use of cues beginning with the simplest and ending with human behavior.

Innate Cross-dimensional Use of Cues

An energy dimension other than the critical one occasions disequilibrium and responsive behavior; this functional relationship between cue and response is transmitted genetically. An example is that of Venus's fly trap, a plant that closes the two halves of a barbed leaf in response to tactile stimulation (pressure changes), thus obtaining a source of energy. A more complex example is the migratory behavior of certain birds, for which a decrease in the hours of daylight serves as the cue. In both examples, the energy shift that initiates the response is on a completely different dimension from the critical energy sources which are to be avoided or approached.

The survival function of this attribute is considerable. Not only is the organism able to use more subtle and varied energy changes as the occasion for adaptive responses, but also the time interval between the energy shift and the behavior can be, at least in certain instances, fairly extended.

Innate use of cues across dimensions can be observed in many apparently diverse behavior mechanisms, from crude turgor responses to complex instinctive behavior. It should be noted that the adaptive function of such differential behavior arises from the occurrence of regularities in nature: Certain energy changes typically precede others in relatively invariable sequences.

Although this process permits greater facility in response, the organisms restricted to innate use of cues are still extremely limited in their adaptability. It is true that they are to some extent safe from the effects of harmful energies, but they are still bound by the cues that initiate and sustain behavior automatically. Their differential behavior is therefore stereotyped. If some new hazard impedes the normal sequence of cue and response, serious damage or destruction can result. Indeed, if circumstances have changed sufficiently, behavior triggered by the cue might lead to mass extinction of the species. If the islands to which the arctic terns migrate each year were to fall below sea level, the terns would die.

Innate use of cues across dimensions has been discussed in the current literature under such headings as "tropisms," "reflexes," and "instincts." Many common behavior mechanisms are hereditary in contemporary organisms.[3] Certainly we do not underestimate the functional value of such processes. As long as the environment remains relatively constant, they provide the most efficient modes of adaptation (in terms of time and energy required) that have evolved. Yet, because the circumstances of our environment are in continuous flux and energy changes do not follow one another with perfect regularity, inherited behavior mechanisms may become detrimental to survival.

So far we have dealt with the use of cues in adaptation to the external environment. As organisms are differentiated into organ systems with specific characteristics and functions, it follows that a similar adaptation process must necessarily occur in their internal environments. As a condition of "relative balance" is required among the process systems of an organism, several internal mechanisms must have cues to initiate activity toward equilibrium when imbalance becomes extreme. Such dynamic interdependence is common to all the organs and organ systems of living individuals, from the simplest cell to the total organism. If the saline content of even the simplest cell exceeds certain limits, compensatory reactions will restore the cell equilibrium (see note 1). Furthermore, when a particular physiological system deviates sufficiently from optimum balance, compensatory reactions may reverberate through functionally adjacent systems; if the disequilibrium continues or becomes more intense, the entire organism may become involved in the response. Cancer, for example, typically begins with a few cells, spreads through an organ, and then gradually invades the entire body.

The differential response mechanisms that accounted for the reactions of the first motile life to external energies and those presently responsible for the homeostatic characteristics of all living cells can be viewed as prototypes (and probably as evolutionary antecedents) for so called "self-regulatory systems" within the human body.

In our discussion of evolution from "life element" to "complex organism" we have considered only two adaptation attributes: differential responses to energy shifts on a single dimension and use of cues as a basis for differential responses. These behavior mechanisms are inherited, yet it is already possible to demonstrate the fundamental postulates of the theory: We can demonstrate the postulate of inference by the contribution of these attributes to survival and the postulate of process by the manner of their expression. The organism is constituted so that movement occurs only when there is sufficient deviation from equilibrium. Regardless of the form disequilibrium takes, the activity of the organism that it instigates whether overt locomotion or dynamic interchange among physiological systems does tend toward equilibrium. It is true, of course, that a given movement may increase disequilibrium in the immediate present, a point to which we shall return.

The fundamental corollary is also demonstrated by such behavior. The negatively accelerating curve describing negative feedback will be obtained whether we measure variation in the speed with which an amoeba approaches nourishment or the deceleration of the heartbeat in a more complex organism after severe exercise.[4]

We have suggested that most internal activity and much overt behavior are initiated and sustained by energy changes acting on inherited behavior mechanisms, and that an organism of great complexity and some adaptability could have evolved and continued to exist without going beyond this particular adaptation attribute. Yet organisms limited to such attributes would be greatly restricted in their survival potential. If the environment were altered sufficiently, this mechanism of adaptation might become the vehicle of destruction. An attribute that would allow the organism to change its responses in accordance with particular circumstances would be a major advance in adaptability.

Learned Use of Cues

Somewhere on the evolutionary path the organism developed the capacity to modify its behavior in response to particular circumstances. Following tradition, we shall call such changes in behavior "learning" and the process permitting these changes "memory," though both were undoubtedly primitive and incomplete at first.

This new attribute ensured the organism of a high level of efficiency. Whereas inherited behavior mechanisms allowed effective responses to environmental circumstances that remained constant during the evolution of the species, learning and memory allowed effective responses to circumstances of much shorter duration, perhaps only a small portion of the individual's life span. The organism could thus adapt to its ever changing environment, rather than being victimized by it.

An examination of the circumstances that contributed to the development of this adaptation attribute may provide some insight into the conditions surrounding the learning process. As we have previously mentioned, deviation from equilibrium may result from imposition of energy from an external source, depletion of energy available for life processes, or both. We have observed that differential behavior results when deviation from equilibrium is directed away from an energy source that is too intense and when it is directed towards material that can be used for energy. If learning is to function in adaptation, it must be related to these two conditions, which are fundamental to maintenance of equilibrium. When a cue consistently occurs before the appearance of either damaging energy or usable energy sources, the organism must be modified so that it can respond to this cue in the future.

Learning and memory freed organisms from the rigid behavioral straitjacket of inherited mechanisms. When even short-term consistency exists between the cue and the external energy shift or new energy source, effective behavior can occur without waiting for the crucial situation itself.

Secondary Adaptation Attributes

Only one primary adaptation attribute remains to be considered; we call it "internal locomotion." Before we can discuss it, however, we must examine certain processes that had to be present as precursors. For want of a better term, we call them "secondary adaptation attributes."

Sensory Input. Before learned behavior mechanisms could appear in the evolutionary hierarchy some input method other than that for innate behavior may have been necessary. Learning involves differential responses to cues that are generally more numerous and more fleeting than are those that initiate and sustain innate responses. What has been called "sensation" may have evolved simultaneously with the development of learning and memory processes.[5] Although this notion is extremely debatable, there should be little disagreement that sensation did become one of the primary channels for input of information about both external and internal energy shifts. That it evolved simultaneously with learning and memory and provided the basis for these processes seems a plausible deduction, however. Other input systems, as we shall see later, also emerged and continue to function, but none has allowed such effective integration in complex organisms as has sensation. The contribution of sensory input to behavior will be examined at length in Chapter 3.

Secondary Disequilibration Systems. The evolution of the use of cues introduces another problem. As energy shifts used as cues are without primary significance for adaptation (they themselves are neither dangerous nor energy sources), how do they activate the organism? Obviously, without motivation a cue would not alter behavior. When an organism experiences hazardous energy shifts or emanations from energy source material, this problem does not arise, for the sheer presence of the crucial circumstance provides the disequilibrium that occasions response. But this identification between critical circumstance and disequilibrium does not occur in the use of cues.

Some kind of secondary disequilibration system must have evolved concurrently with the emergence of the use of cues in order to elicit behavior. The most primitive examples of such systems were probably similar in many respects to the primary systems already discussed. That is, energy changes that were in themselves without immediate survival significance sufficiently resembled primary disequilibration systems so that the appropriate physicochemical changes would occur in response to them also. But, with the appearance of sensation and its implications for the use of more frequent and subtle cues, development of a more effective secondary disequilibration system was predictable. The cue must bring about changes within the organism that serve as the input to produce disequilibrium. But how? It is easy enough to talk about cues that occasion behavior towards or away from a stimulus but what powers such behavior? It seems likely that the disequilibratory significance of a given cue (at least for higher mammals) is derived largely from visceral changes. The means by which a previously neutral cue arouses visceral changes will be discussed in Chapter 5, and how the sensory input from them affects behavior will be considered in Chapters 6 and 7.

Although the major function of the input from visceral changes is to produce disequilibrium, it makes another contribution that, from an adaptation point of view, is almost as important. As we noted in Chapter 1, there is a relationship between the survival value of a response and the speed with which it is made: The more rapidly an organism can move away from harmful energy or toward an energy source, the more effective its adaptation to its environment will be. As physiological processes take time and rapidity of movement has adaptation value, we may infer that some emergency system had to evolve for quick operation in unusual circumstances, though remaining dormant otherwise. It might be objected that an organism remaining in a state of complete mobilization would be a more logical product of evolution, but sustaining total mobilization would require enormous amounts of energy and would subject the organism permanently to maximum stress.

From this discussion we may conclude that the processes traditionally subsumed under the label "emotion" have two important and interrelated functions: to lend disequilibratory significance to previously neutral cues and to speed responses.

Simplification Mechanisms. As evolution proceeded, the variety and refinement of cues that could be used for differential responses must have increased rapidly, making possible ever more subtle nuances in adaptive behavior. But more refined simplification mechanisms had also to emerge if complexity was not to expand to the point at which it would actually overburden the organism and cause its demise in the evolutionary struggle. There are three particularly important simplification mechanisms, all of which make vital contributions to adjustment and are therefore central to the development of psychology. We shall deal with each one briefly here and examine them at much greater length in later chapters.

The first simplification mechanism is *input fusion.* Most of the environmental circumstances important to the survival of complex organisms are signaled by changes in various energy dimensions. When there are sufficient receptors appropriate to such energy shifts, a wide variety of cues can be registered. A tiger can be heard or smelled; vision alone yields multiple cues to the animal's presence. The same is true of most situations critical to survival. A number of sensory components can signal their presence. The multiplicity of cues within modalities and the overlap among modalities ensure that discriminations will occur, but they add to the problem of complexity. Fusion permits partial solution of this problem, with a minimum reduction of critical information.

As the various inputs from a given environmental circumstance usually occur simultaneously, it seems that simultaneous presentation is the necessary condition for fusion. We shall discuss this process at length in Chapter 4, but its contribution to adaptation will be considered here.

Fusion frees the organism from having to respond to each bit of critical input by permitting it to respond to the circumstance as a whole. The presence of a tiger need not be registered separately by each set of sensory receptors furnishing information on shade, texture, sound, color, shape, movement, and so on. The simple phenomenological unity "tiger" can be registered through the fusion of all these components. Fusion thus simplifies the environment and markedly reduces the time required for effective responses. Its importance is demonstrated by the fact that most of the inputs characteristic of human beings consist of phenomenological wholes: We typically respond to books, trees, houses, and people, rather than to the multiple inputs that signify their presence. Following conventional usage, we shall call such fused representation "percepts."

Another kind of fusion produces what we shall call "motocepts." Every movement of an organism produces a variety of sensations through the kinesthetic receptors in muscles, tendons, and joints. As the input from relatively discrete movements nevertheless occurs almost simultaneously, the process of fusion can occur under these circumstances also. As we shall discuss in Chapter 7, such fusion is crucial in development of any given motor skill, for example, walking or typing.

Continual presentation of similar percepts or motocepts produces still another type of fusion, which is of equal or even greater importance. When similar phenomena are experienced repeatedly they become integrated into a general memory representation; for example, after experience of many houses, which may differ in certain respects, an effective summary becomes embedded in memory. This form of fusion not only reduces the number of items that must be encoded, it also lessens the complexity of later recall. Although this topic will be treated at length in Chapter 7, we note in passing that such fused memory representations underlie the development of concepts and are fundamental to language. Fusion thus greatly simplifies the organism's adaptation and markedly reduces the complexity of mechanisms for differential responses without appreciable reduction in efficiency.

Let us now consider a separate phenomenon, derived from input fusion, that has caused remarkable dissension among psychologists but must be included in any general theory if human beings are to be adequately understood. For want of a better term and for parallelism with the terms for other fusion mechanisms, we shall call it the *autocept*. Let us first consider how it develops and then suggest certain functions that it fulfills in the behavior of the organism.

As the phenomenon "tree" is derived from the simultaneous occurrence of sensory components (particular colors, shades, textures, shapes, and so on) and as the successive presentation of similar trees results in a memory representation that summarizes this diversity, so the autocept is derived from simultaneous and successive input components that permit an experience of self comparable to the experience of the tree.

The autocept makes a vital adaptive contribution similar to that of the percept. The inputs most immediately related to the welfare of the organism are summarized; the organism experiences itself as a unity which allows greater persistence and more consistently oriented behavior. For example, "threat" affects not one aspect but the entire organism, facilitating total and immediate response.

The self system also provides continuity and identity. How does a person know that he is the same individual that he was yesterday or for that matter a moment ago? Simply through sensory feedback from the continuing processes of his body that becomes familiar and engenders self-awareness much as certain other inputs engender awareness of thirst or hunger. But the most important function of the autocept is to provide an effective "need" system derived from the organism's total life experience.

The second simplification mechanism is *input constancy.* Although fusion of individual sensory elements into composites effectively reduces the sheer quantity of information bits experienced, an extraordinary complexity still remains. A particular item in the organism's environment is rarely if ever experienced in exactly the same way twice: There is no single retinal image that represents any particular object definitively. The size, shape, and brightness of each object vary with distance, angle of view, and amount of light reflected from it. Even though sensory elements are effectively fused into functional wholes, the organism must still respond to myriad versions of phenomenological unities. The same object may be presented from hundreds of different perspectives, each producing a different input. But, as a given item in the environment has essentially the same survival significance, regardless of the angle of its presentation, a simplification mechanism was likely to evolve. So called "perceptual constancies" provide the basis for vital simplification: Because of them, the organism need not react differently to the multitude of apparently different shapes, sizes, and brightnesses of a given item; it need react only to the sameness that persists despite the variations. Perceptual constancies simplify the organism's effective environment: A window remains the same regardless of perspective, and so does a tiger.

It may be objected that perceptual constancies provide simplification at the expense of information (that little retinal tigers seem harmless because of their distance, whereas big ones seem dangerous because of their proximity.) There is some truth in this objection. Some information *is* lost, but the adaptive contribution more than compensates for it. As we shall see in Chapter 4, other cues furnish the vital information about distance that differences in retinal size cannot contribute.

The third mechanism of simplification is *selection of input.* If two or more input components are imposed simultaneously, to which one does the organism respond? There must be some kind of selection. The simplest solution to this problem was without doubt occasioned by the fact that, as a unity, an organism can move in only one direction at a time; probably at first the direction was determined by a simple resolution of forces. When two negative energy sources at different locations are imposed on the amoeba, it follows the path that minimizes the combined effects of the negative energies. This resolution is probably effective for simple organisms, but for others the emergence of sense modalities and memory residuals multiplied immeasurably the number of information components pertinent to response. It was no longer sufficient simply to respond differentially to cues; it became necessary also to respond effectively to the specific input that was most crucial for survival at any given moment. Some process similar to "attention," as we presently understand it, had to appear if the organism was to respond effectively to myriad inputs. There had to be a central area accessible to material from both the various sense organs and from memory, yet behavioral integrity required that it be able to focus on only one bit of information at any particular moment.

The singleness of input focalization was a vital evolutionary requirement. Behavior would be completely chaotic and unadaptive if the organism were to react to every external and internal cue at once. Indeed it would resemble epileptic seizure more than adaptive behavior. Integrated behavior requires that the organism respond to only one bit of information at any given moment; effective behavior requires that the response be to that bit of information most crucial to the welfare of the organsim at any given moment.[6]

The mechanism by which materials from memory and sensation come into focus we call "apperception," following W. v. Wundt. It is automatic and, within the limitations imposed by structure (both innately determined and as shaped by experience), tends toward equilibrium. That is, of all the dynamically interacting "input components" potentially available from memory and sensation, those that are at any given moment most likely to facilitate restoration of equilibrium are most likely to be brought into focus.

As the most primitive selection mechanisms are homeostatic in nature, so we believe are the most complex. As human apperception is a continuous internal process, it too fits within the framework of the postulate of process. It can easily be imagined how the behavior of an amoeba caught within two fields of force will include those actions most likely to ensure equilibrium, but it is difficult to see how the complex process of human apperception is an extension of this same principle. We shall defend this view in Chapter 4.

So far in our tracing of evolution, guided by the postulate of inference, we have posited an organism with remarkable adaptive capacities. We have seen how the use of cues, facilitated by inherited mechanisms, has made possible effective responses to long-term environmental consistencies and how the development of learning and memory has permitted more subtle adaptations to short-term even relatively transitory contingencies within an individual's own lifetime. We have further observed how the use of more and varied types of cues presupposed the development of more refined sensory and retention equipment and necessitated the appearance of a process to allow the organism to respond to those bits of information from memory and sensation most pertinent to its immediate welfare. This study leads us to the third adaptation attribute that we shall examine.

Internal Locomotion

Let us reconsider the dual processes of learning and memory. It is assumed that in learning some change occurs in the organism as a result of its contact with its environment. This change is retained in memory, so that, at least theoretically, more adaptive behavior may result from encounters with similar environmental situations. It seems reasonable to assume that different kinds of retention systems may have developed and may still be represented among contemporary organisms. But, clearly, in most instances the retention system that most effectively represents the past experience of a given species should have the greatest survival value for that species. Ideally, it would make immediately available to the organism all pertinent information about a current situation and related past experiences. As such a retention system would have the greatest adaptive value, the direction of natural selection has been toward this theoretical ultimate in efficiency.

As organisms became increasingly mobile they came in contact with more and more of their immediate environment; an adequate system of retention thus meant essentially an "internalization" of that environment. Exactly how the "internalized world" was first represented is open to conjecture. Memory may have begun when the impact of energy on a primitive system produced some minimal damage that thereafter affected its behavior. But, after the advent of sensation as the major input mechanism, the memory "encode" (see glossary) apparently became similar to the stimulus itself. David Hume has often been quoted as remarking that there is a literal correspondence between the "world as experienced" and the "world as remembered."

The development of this internalized substitute world laid the foundation for the appearance of undoubtedly the most refined adaptation attribute yet evolved. Yet once again the continuity between adaptation attributes is evident. Covert locomotion, or "thinking," the logical next step, requires only a small extension of the learning-memory process already postulated. As soon as an internalized surrogate world came into existence, locomotion within it would have been predictable. Such internal movement, though requiring a small evolutionary step, represented a giant stride in adaptive facility. It permitted the organism to solve problems of great import to its survival without actually confronting the dangers.

The crux of our argument here is a parallel: External locomotion consists of that activity most conducive to equilibrium at a given moment, and internal locomotion operates on precisely the same principle. The postulate of process, that all activity, whether overt or internal, tends toward equilibrium, applies, whether the activity is behavioral, physiological, or what has been commonly called "psychological." Movement from one memory residual to the next is fully as automatic a process as is tropism in the moth or "choice" of the most equilibratory path by the amoeba.

"Thinking" can thus be defined as "the continuous process of apperception applied to the inputs from memory"; "sensing," on the other hand, is "the continuous process of apperception applied to inputs from the various receptor systems of the body." Actually the processes of thinking and sensing are functionally interrelated, for components from receptors and memory coalesce, and typically apperception shifts among them from moment to moment.

Although such functional coalescence is continual, there is a qualitative difference between the internal and the external worlds. From an evolutionary point of view, organisms that could not make this fundamental discrimination could not have survived; danger exists primarily in the external world, and the organism that tried to solve external problems by internal locomotion alone would probably soon serve as another organism's dinner. The ability to discriminate between the memory image and the sensory impression is thus essential to survival. What can happen to adaptation when the ability to discriminate between these two areas breaks down will be discussed in Chapter 8.

Before ending this chapter we must clarify certain issues that have continually intruded into the periphery of our thinking and undoubtedly that of the reader as well.

First, it may seem from the preceding discussion that a given adaptation attribute contributes only positively to differential responses and that its functioning can be legitimately evaluated apart from the total organism. Neither of these conclusions is correct. Regardless of the function of an attribute, its very inclusion in the process repertory of a species brings with it certain negative implications. No attribute can be incorporated without an increase in complexity, and complexity itself inevitably reduces ease of adjustment. The question is, Does the increase contribute more than it detracts? If so, it is a functional attribute, and this net, rather than absolute, functional value is the condition of its incorporation, which suggests that the adaptive contribution of a given attribute cannot be determined in isolation.

The organism is a totality comprising many organs and organ systems working in dynamic synchrony. The functional value of a single attribute depends not only upon its own contribution but also upon the synthesis of this contribution with those of other parts of the system. A student once asked, If the length of a frog's leg is a functional attribute, why did not the legs of frogs simply keep growing longer and longer? The answer is obvious: Not only does such an attribute bring increased complexity, but also, to be efficient, it must be integrated into the total system. Legs can grow only as long as the growth contributes more to survival than its complexity subtracts. This judgment must depend upon how the particular length of leg is integrated into the total frog. Years ago Leonardo da Vinci remarked that man "will not invent anything more economical, or more direct than nature, for in nature's inventions nothing is wanting and nothing superfluous." Nature does provide the most efficient adjustment with the least complexity, but the contribution of each attribute can never be understood in isolation and must always be considered as part of an integrated whole.

A second question that may have troubled the reader involves our method of developing the argument of this chapter. He may well say, "Come on, now, you can't really insist that your conclusions are completely derived from a logical deduction of what must have happened in the course of evolution.

Surely a good part of your reasoning was influenced by prior knowledge of the very attributes that you have so laboriously deduced." The accusation is valid, but the objection is not. Certainly a person freshly arrived from Andromeda could not simply examine our world and infer the inevitable emergence of a human being, let alone the attributes that we have described. That our inferences, though logical, are also based on accumulated empirical knowledge hardly constitutes a basis for criticism; indeed, it furnishes more reason to consider them seriously. As the reader is also a product of natural selection and exemplifies within himself the claimed principles and attributes, he provides a third informal check, derived from continual questioning: "Is that really how I work? Is this a valid description of that dynamic totality that I call 'myself'?" We think that it is.

A much less complex problem involves a possible inference from our sequence of chapters. The journey from original life element to complex organism may seem to have followed iron rails, its course fixed beforehand and man's appearance predetermined once life had first appeared. We do not share this point of view. It seems, rather, that man is the outcome of a remarkable number of adventitious events. If the evolutionary clock were turned backward 2 or 3 billion years, it is quite unlikely that man would evolve at all. There have been too many tangents in evolution, too many fortuitous circumstances to permit assumptions of inevitability. But, improbable as the eventuality may seem in retrospect, man *did* appear, and his appearance was "lawful." It is not our task to demonstrate the circumstances that may have made the emergence of man necessary; we shall simply explain the functional contribution of those attributes that both define him and permit his existence. We can hold the view that man is both a "lawful" outcome of natural processes and a manifestation of laws without accepting the restrictive notions of predestination or the circumlocutions of teleology.

Summary

Our skeletal model is thus complete. We have tried to trace the emergence of adaptation attributes from the initial motility of the most primitive organisms to the internal mobility of the most complex. Behavior began when a primitive life element, forced by necessity for survival to maintain or regain a minimum balance in its process systems, came to respond differently to energy shifts on a single dimension. With the advent of innate use of cues across dimensions (as in tropisms, reflexes, instincts), the survival potential of the life element was increased. The capacity to change as a result of its own experience (combining learning and memory) then allowed still more effective resolution of disequilibrium. We then found it necessary to infer the emergence of a secondary disequilibration system (emotion) that would provide the basis for response when the crucial circumstance itself was not imposed. Some kind of input (sensation) that could effectively represent the multiple energy shifts that serve as the basis for secondary cues was also necessary. But the use of such cues introduced burgeoning complexity requiring simplification mechanisms (like input fusion, constancies, and apperception) to ensure that the organism would not be immobilized by the sheer multiplicity of information bits received. Finally, we have observed the emergence of the "highest" adaptation attribute—that of internal locomotion (thinking)—and have surmised something about its contribution to adaptation.

Throughout this argument we have emphasized the continuity between the emergence of these adaptation attributes, showing how each must have been but a slight extension of the one before it and how even a slight change in process allowed a remarkable increase in response facility.

In the following chapters we shall consider the various traditional areas of psychology, indicating how the basic postulates and the basic corollary can serve as the apex of structure integrating and lending meaning to much of the traditionally diverse subject matter. No attempt at an exhaustive review of available empirical data will be made. Only certain pertinent findings will be considered. Furthermore, though a number of testable hypotheses may be framed as the argument proceeds, there will be no intensive effort to indicate the full measures of the theory's generative power.

We shall attempt only to chart the evolutionary path that we have haltingly indicated, leaving the reader—indeed, we hope encouraging him—to make his own forays into the dim hinterland from which our species emerged. It is in this same hinterland that the bases for human individuality must be sought. The path itself will seem strangely familiar and, we hope, inviting.

Notes

1We psychologists, enamored of the notion that differential behavior occurs as the total rat, chimpanzee, or man adjusts to his environment, are somewhat surprised to discover that it is actually a process occurring in *every* living cell, whether in isolation or in a complex body. Every cell is a homeostatic system that must maintain an appropriate balance among essential constituents if it is not to perish. When one essential element falls below its optimal concentration within the cell, compensatory activity within the membrane (differential behavior) brings about a return to the proper proportions. How differential behavior occurs has been the subject of some research and much speculation during the past few years. Two fundamental processes—passive and active transport through cell membranes—account for it. Passive transport can be explained easily: Vital substances are simply gradients of concentration, electrical potential, or both. Active transport is mystifying however. The cell must maintain in concentration proportions of certain components *different* from those in the fluid outside the cell. Some process must therefore work *against* both the concentration and potential (electrical) gradients to restore essential levels within the cells. As H. Holter (1961) has put it, active transport moves "uphill," against the forces of passive transport; it must therefore involve expenditure of energy generated through the cell's metabolism. For example, if the concentration of sodium within a cell falls too low, some kind of differential response mechanism in the membrane acts to take sodium from the environment, even though the concentration of sodium in the cell may already be far higher than in the liquid surrounding it. How does this response operate? According to one model developed by T. J. Shaw and reported by Holter (1961), there are carriers specific to each constituent of the cell; they transport the necessary components through the membrane when the internal concentration becomes too low. But what activates such carriers? How do they "recognize" their particular substances, and how do they carry their burdens "uphill" against the gradients? The notion of carriers thus does not solve the problem; it simply pushes it back a step. (A. K. Solomon (1962) has even suggested that the term "active transport" is a tacit admission of ignorance and that once the mechanism of differential response is understood the concept can be dropped from our vocabulary.)

Regardless of the mechanism by which differential response is accomplished, every living cell is capable of it and this capacity has without doubt been innate since life began.

[2]Certainly the simplest of all contemporary organisms is capable of responding to multiple energy dimensions. Several behavior patterns enable protozoans to respond efficiently to light, heat, and chemical gradients. For example, when *oxtricha* moves into an extremely hot area, it stops, backs, turns, and proceeds anew. It repeats this behavior until it finds an acceptable climate. Its course is directly away from the heat. No moves are made while conditions remain the same or improve. The amoeba also demonstrates effective escape behavior. It prefers darkness and when a weak light is shone on it as it feeds, it ceases to ingest. When the light is increased to a dangerous level it spills out already ingested food and swims away. H. S. Jennings (1906) discovered in his work with the stentor that the same external stimulus does not always elicit the same reaction: A cloud of carmine particles can produce as many as five different reactions from the same individual. If the stentor is unable to escape the unwelcome stimulation, it contracts itself into a tube; as a last resort it may abandon the tube shape and swim away.

The food-finding behavior of these small animals is another area of investigation. When an amoeba touches an edible tidbit (Allen, 1962) it reacts within less than a second, shooting out a hyaline cap (a watery cap formed from the cytoplasm in the forward area of the pseudopodium) to trap the food. The *Actinophrys sol* (Hall, 1964) has on its pseudopodia a sticky substance to which food adheres; the food is then shifted by means of protoplasmic flow to the surface of the captor's body, a food cup is extended to enclose it, and a food vacuole is formed. The tentacle of suctorean ciliates apparently reacts to specific substances in the cortex of pellicles of their prey. The sucker digests the prey in the zone of contact, and protoplasm flows down the inner tube of the tentacle. A process similar to drinking has also been reported in *Amoeba proteus* and other protozoans (Hall, 1964).

The causes of position changes in protozoans have also been studied. E. P. Lyon (1905) has suggested that position changes are responses to stimulation from substances of varying densities such as iron powder.

[3]Sometimes these inherited behavior mechanisms are both dramatic and remarkably specific in their functioning. Many species of birds have innate fears of the shape of hawks. Fireflies apparently have particular codes of flashes to

identify members of the opposite sex of their own species (McDermott, 1917).
A red spot on the bills of certain gulls is the primary pecking target of the
young; a peck on the red spot stimulates regurgitation in the parents and hence
feeding of the young (Tinbergen and Perdeck, 1950). The male silkworm can
respond to only one odor, and, as might be expected, that odor signifies the
presence of the female (Schneider, 1957). The peculiar chemical composition
of a stream apparently provides the homing cue for the salmon (Hasler, 1960).
To mark the direction and location of a food source, a certain species of fire
ant leaves a volatile chemical trail (which is dissipated in about two minutes
and thus prevents confusion once a particular food source has been eliminated)
(Wilson, 1962). In all these examples and many more that could be offered,
the cues have been related to some survival need of the species for so many
generations that they now occasion automatic responses.

[4]Implicit in the fundamental corollary of the theory is the notion that there
should be a direct correspondence between the imbalance in any physiological
system and activity designed to return the system to equilibrium. And indeed
this relationship could always be demonstrated if *both* the given system and the
equilibratory behavior could be isolated. But these requirements are difficult to
meet: A number of mechanisms may intervene between the activity and the
reestablishment of physiological equilibrium. For instance, several physiological
processes (such as chewing, salivation, swallowing, and digesting) are typically
interposed between the overt response to food deprivation and the eventual
elimination of hunger. To complicate matters even further many variables may
alter the curve obtained: the presence or absence of social stimuli, the palata-
bility of the food, experience with food, and the relative balance within other
systems. Also as achieved homeostasis in different systems often involves simultaneous or overlapping behavior, determination of the precise effect of a given
deprivation on behavior is doubly difficult.

Despite these problems, several empirical studies have confirmed the fundamental corollary. When crucial nutrients are removed from their diets, certain
organisms will even change their food preferences in order to regain balance.
A rat that has been subjected to adrenalectomy, so that it will require abnormal
amounts of salt, and then deprived of salt, will seek extremely low concentrations of salt in water to which an ordinary rat will not respond and will drink
great amounts of it (Richter, 1942). Cafeteria studies of human infants, which
permit babies to select their own diets from a large variety of food (Davis,
1928) have revealed a close relationship between particular deprivations and
compensatory activity, and as the child grows older the rapid disappearance of
this ability to compensate indicates the influence of cultural variables on predicted negative feedback. Rats are also subject to loss of body "wisdom"
through development of food preferences that override specific deficits. A. E.
Harriman (1955) found that rats that had been frequently exposed to both
sweet (glucose) and salty solutions failed to make the necessary compensatory
responses after adrenalectomies. They invariably chose the glucose and died.

In lower organisms fewer steps intervene between the deficit and the equilibratory activity; a clearer demonstration of the corollary can therefore be
given. In a sea anemone *(Anemonia sulcata)* deprivation lowers the threshold
for the eating response, whereas satiation raises it (Pantin, 1950). Reduced
glutathione, a substance typically present in the fresh body fluids of organisms,
is discharged along gradients from wounded tissue, and its dissipation apparently
stimulates compensatory searching behavior in *Hydra* (Loomis, 1955).   B.
Tugendhat (1960) found that the rate at which the deprived stickleback eats

worms starts high and then decreases gradually to satiation. D. R. Evans and L. B. Brown (1960) found that the eating threshold in the blowfly remains high for a time after feeding and then is gradually reduced to a level at which eating is resumed. E. Stellar and J. H. Hill (1952) found that in rats there is a relationship between level of thirst and both the duration of drinking bouts and the intervals between them. F. E. Goodson, M. G. Hermann, and G. A. Morgan (1962) found a negatively accelerated relationship between the rate of water intake and the time from the onset of drinking. A similar relationship was found by P. Marler (1956) in a study of aggression in the chaffinch: When two birds feeding in a cage were gradually moved closer together, the probability of a fight increased on an accelerating curve as satiation approached.

These studies are merely a sample of those that demonstrate homeostatic behavior. There are others, however, that have shown no negative feedback relationship between deficit and compensatory action: The functions may take the form of straight lines or erratic cycles. Much research with careful controls and exceptional isolation techniques will be required before the general application of the negative feedback corollary can be finally established empirically. Every scientific law requires that extraneous variables be controlled before it can be demonstrated empirically, and the negative feedback corollary is no exception.

[5]Although we have no way to determine when organisms first acquired sensation, there is some evidence that sense receptors, especially those responsive to light, developed early in the evolutionary journey. Light is a prerequisite for photosynthesis and thus the basis for most life as we know it; nearly all plants and animals are sensitive to light. By some unknown process (G. Wald, 1959) light forms the terminal high-energy phosphate bonds of adenosine-triosphate (ATP), which acts as a principal energy carrier in the cell. This process neither requires nor produces oxygen and is therefore called "anaerobic." Before the earth's atmosphere contained a large proportion of oxygen, this process could have produced large quantities of ATP, thus supplying energy for organic synthesis. "Preliving anaerobic organisms" would thus be predicted to be sensitive to light.

It would thus have been logical for the prototypical sense organ to have been the eye. *Euglena*, a genus of protozoans, has a flattened area of reddish pigment in the cytoplasm called the "stigma" or "eyespot." This light-sensitive structure in some unknown way serves to orient the organism toward suitable light sources. Variations of this kind of stigma are found in other types of protozoans (Hall, 1964).

Only three of the eleven major animal phyla have developed well-formed (image-resolving) eyes: the arthropods (insects, crabs, spiders), the mollusks (octopus, squid), and the vertebrates. According to Wald (1959), all three are types developed entirely independently. There seems to be no anatomical, embryological, or evolutionary connection among them. At three points in evolution, the (image-forming) eye has developed quite independently. All photoreceptors (in plants and in animals) have one feature in common, however: the use of carotenoids to mediate excitation by light. Plants manufacture their own carotenoids, but animals must consume vitamin A.

R. L. Gregory (1966) considers development of the eye as such to have begun with photoreceptors recessed in pits, which protected them from the surrounding glare and enabled them to detect moving shadows. One living creature, the nautilus, still has this type of eye. The primitive eye pits were subject to blockage and injury from particles; the next development was probably therefore a transparent protective membrane. The limpet eye still exemplifies this type.

In time this membrane thickened enough to form a crude lens. No animal's eye has ever overcome the need for periodic washing. Tears perform the same function once performed by the sea.

The earliest kind of eye preserved as a fossil is that of the trilobite, a creature that lived more than 500 million years ago; it was essentially the same type of compound eye that modern insects have.

S. C. Ratner and M. R. Denny (1964), in discussing the further evolution of the eye, have claimed that, as we move up the phylogenetic scale from the higher invertebrates, there seems to be no marked improvement in discrimination of brightness. Primates have better acuity than lower mammals do. Form vision is present in all vertebrates from fish to primates, though in the lower forms of invertebrates (except for the octopus) it is absent or minimal.

Not much has been written about the evolution of the other senses, but Ratner and Denny (1964) have reported that fish hear through the lateral line system which developed from tactile organs, and that this system is the precursor of the mammalian auditory system. (The lateral line system is a line of receptors running down the body of the fish; it is sensitive to vibrations and pressure changes.) R. J. Pumphrey (1940) observed that many insects have auditory organs but that they are very insensitive to changes in the frequency of sound. That insects do hear is, however, evidence of the very early evolution of audition. D. R. Griffin (1962) found that many fish have sensitive receptors lining olfactory pits in their heads; water circulates through the pits as the fish swim about.

[6]Quite early in the course of evolution the problem of information overload must have introduced a critical survival dilemma: The more information bits that were available, the bigger was the problem of selecting those inputs appropriate to each adaptation. Apperception (see glossary for a full definition) was the focusing mechanism that permitted the ultimate resolution of this dilemma in the human being and probably in certain other mammals. But the problem of stimulus selection is omnipresent in all forms of life, for certain energy shifts are inevitably more important for survival than are others. Hundreds of different "stimulus selector" mechanisms were no doubt tried and discarded along the way, but many functional ones must have been integrated into the repertories of living species. When a given configuration of stimuli achieved preeminent status in the adjustment repertory of a species, it was because it represented circumstances crucial to the survival and evolution of that species.

Of course, the most fundamental kind of stimulus selection is the simple ability of an organism to respond, however slightly, to a given energy shift. That there was response at all shows that particular fluctuations were important to the survival and thus to the evolution of the species. Functional dominance of certain dimensions over others, as indicated by hypersensitive ears, eyes, or olfactory mechanisms, is further evidence of a kind of stimulus selection. But we are concerned here with what Jennings (1906) has called "representative stimuli," stimuli that have become a kind of shorthand for certain critical environmental circumstances. As examples, let us consider again (see notes 3, 4) the responses of *hydra* to reduced glutathione, of certain birds to the hawk shape, and of gull chicks to the red spots on the parents' bills. Such selectivity is also demonstrated in many species of birds that respond in specific ways to songs of their own species (Thorpe, 1958) and in male mosquitoes that respond sexually only to the particular wingbeat frequencies of females (Roth, 1948). This latter mechanism is not perfectly adaptive, for young male mosquitoes may occasionally be sexually molested simply because their frequencies fall within the same range as those of nubile females.

In note 3 we mentioned the peculiar responsiveness of the firefly to the flash code of its own species. Certain fish have similar signals for identifying members of their species; for example, there is a black spot on the dorsal fin of *Prisella riddei* which is essential for recognition and thus for the formation of schools (Keenleyside, 1955).

Movement of an object of appropriate size is perhaps the most widely effective stimulus. Dragonfly larvae will snap at any object of appropriate size moving nearby (Baldus, 1926), and so will many species of spiders (Bristowe, 1941), the ordinary toad (Eibl-Eibesfeldt, 1952), certain snakes (Russell, 1943), and frogs. Indeed, such is the compulsion of frogs to snap at small moving objects that one severely injured itself by repeatedly striking at a fly pinned in the center of a ring of needles (Maier and Schneirla, 1964).

These examples are but a few of those available in the literature, but they demonstrate the wide range of stimuli to which organisms can respond selectively. True, all such genetically transmitted mechanisms impose a certain inflexibility on the creatures so endowed, but they make a net overall contribution to adaptation potential by abetting responses to certain energy shifts vital to the survival of the species. They are thus stimulus "emphasizers," "selectors," or "filterers" like those that may have preceded the more flexible and dynamically responsive apperception process.

References

Allen, R. D. Amoeboid movement. *Scientific American,* February 1962, 206: 112-120.

Baldus, K. Experimentelle Untersuchungen über die Entfernungslokalisation der Libellen *(Aeschna cyanea). Zeitschrift für Vergleichenden Physiologie,* 1926, 3: 475-505.

Bristowe, W. S. *The comity of spiders.* Vol. 2. London: Adlard, 1941.

Davis, C. M. Self selection of diet by newly weaned infants. *American Journal of Diseases of Children,* 1928, 36: 651-679.

Eibl-Eibesfeldt, I. Nahrungserwerb und Beuteschema der Erdkrote *(Bufo bufo L.). Behavior,* 1952, 4: 1-35.

Evans, D. R., & Browne, L. B. The regulation of taste thresholds for sugars in the blowfly. *American Midland Naturalist,* 1960, 64: 282-300.

Goodson, F. E., Hermann, M. G., & Morgan, G. A. Water consumption of the rat as a function of drive level. *Journal of Comparative and Physiological Psychology,* 1962, 55: 769-772.

Gregory, R. L. *Eye and brain: The psychology of seeing.* New York: McGraw-Hill, 1966.

Griffin, D. R. *Animal structure and function.* New York: Holt, Rinehart and Winston, 1962.

Hall, R. P. *Protozoa: The simplest of all animals.* New York: Holt, Rinehart and Winston, 1964.

Harriman, A. E. The effect of a preoperative preference for sugar over salt upon compensatory salt selection by adrenalectomized rats. *Journal of Nutrition,* 1955, 57: 271-276.

Hasler, A. D. Guideposts of migrating fishes. *Science,* 1960, 132: 785-792.

Holter, H. How things get into cells. *Scientific American,* September 1961, 205: 167-174.
Jennings, H. S. *Behavior of the lower organisms.* New York: Columbia University Press, 1906.
Keenleyside, M. H. A. Some aspects of the schooling behavior of fish. *Behavior,* 1955, 8: 183-248.
Loomis, W. F. Glutathione control of the specific feeding reaction of hydra. *Annals of the New York Academy of Science,* 1955, 62: 209-228.
Lyon, E. P. On the theory of geotropism in paremecium. *American Journal of Physiology,* 1905, 14: 421-432.
Maier, N. R. F., & Schneirla, T. C. *Principles of animal psychology.* New York: Dover, 1964.
Marler, P. Studies of fighting in chaffinches. 3. Proximity as a cause of aggression. *British Journal of Animal Behavior,* 1956, 4: 23-30.
McDermott, F. A. Observations on the light-emissions of American Lampyridae. *Canadian Entomologist,* 1917, 49: 53-61.
Pantin, C. F. A. Behavior patterns in lower invertebrates. *Symposium Society Experimental Biology,* 1950, 4: 175-195.
Pumphrey, R. J. Hearing in insects. *Biological Review,* 1940, 15: 107-132.
Ratner, S. C., & Denny, M. R. *Comparative psychology: Research in animal behavior.* Homewood, Ill.: Dorsey, 1964.
Richter, C. P. Total self regulatory functions in animals and human beings. *Harvey Lectures* (1942-1943), 1942, series 38, 63-103.
Roth, L. M. An experimental laboratory study of the sexual behavior of *Aedes aegypti. American Midland Naturalist,* 1948, 40: 265-352.
Russell, E. S. Perceptual and sensory signs in instinctive behavior. *Proceedings Linnean Society London* (Zool.), 1943, 154: 195-216.
Schneider, D. Elektrophysiologische Untersuchungen von Chemeund Mechanorezeptoren der Antenne des Seidenspinners *Bombyx mori L. Zeitschrift fur vergleichende Physiologie,* 1957, 40: 4-41.
Solomon, A. K. Pumps in the living cell. *Scientific American,* August 1962, 207: 100-108.
Stellar, E., & Hill, J. H. The rat's rate of drinking as a function of water deprivation. *Journal of Comparative and Physiological Psychology,* 1952, 45: 96-102.
Thorpe, W. H. The learning of song patterns by birds, with especial reference to the song of the chaffinch. *Fringilla coelebs. Ibis,* 1958, 100: 535-570.
Tinbergen, N., & Perdeck, A. C. On the stimulus situation releasing the begging response in the newly hatched herring gull chick *(Larus argentatus Pont). Behavior,* 1950, 3: 1-39.
Tugendhat, B. The normal feeding behavior of the three-spined stickleback *(Gasterosteus aculeatus L.). Behavior,* 1960, 15: 284-318.
Wald, G. Life and light. *Scientific American,* October 1959, 201: 92-100.
Wilson, E. O. Chemical communication among workers of the fire ant *Solenopsis saevissima* (Fr. Smith) 1-3. *Animal Behavior,* 1960, 10: 134-164.

3

Input

Let us look at our fingers: It has taken millions of generations of natural selection to produce these appendages in their present form. There is perhaps nothing remarkable in such a statement, but let us now extend it. Not only do we have fingers; we also are capable of experiencing pain, red, sweet, cold, and many other sensations. The capacity to receive such inputs must also result from millions of generations of environmental shaping. This assumption applies to all the experiential inputs that may be registered within an organism. It took countless testing and retestings of variant input systems before the sense organs and their characteristic inputs as we know them could be achieved.

The Problem of Sensation

History

For years the structuralists tried to classify the various components of experience. They mapped the skin's sensitivity to pressures and tried to determine the different dimensions of sound, sight, and smell, breaking these dimensions down into series of just noticeable differences. It seems strange now that they never asked the function of each component in the survival of the organism or how sensory attributes aid individual adaptation. Perhaps we can excuse this oversight, for the structuralist movement was dying even as Charles Darwin's theory rose to ascendance. But what about the functionalists? Their orientation was based on Darwin's theory, and William James had declared early and often that the mind could never have come into being had it not served adaptive functions. Why, then, did his followers not turn to the categories established by the structuralists and seek to evaluate their adaptive contributions? The foundation had already been laid: They believed that the mind is the subject matter of psychology and insisted on an evolutionary perspective. What happened? E. Boring has suggested that the explosion of behaviorism effectively fragmented functionalism, but the explanation does not go far enough. The real obstacle seems to have been the functionalists' preference for descriptive generalities. James became so committed to his stream of consciousness that he never escaped it; he described consciousness as one might describe a car: pointing out that it runs continuously on roads, stops and starts frequently, and belongs to somebody. Even from his description of thought itself, in which he achieved probably his greatest specificity, we gain little insight into the variables affecting the "stream" of thought or the particular role of thought in adaptive behavior.

John Dewey, J. R. Angell, and even E. B. Carr, who provided the most systematic expression of the movement's principles, also seem to have been limited to global terms. Carr proclaimed that mental activities are those processes responsible for "the acquisition, fixation, retention, organization, and evaluation of experiences, and their subsequent utilization in the guidance of conduct." There is little to quarrel with in this statement, but where do we go from here? It is one thing to plead that these processes are critical to understanding behavior; it is quite another to evaluate their specific contribution to behavior. We might have assumed, for instance, that Carr would have dwelt at length on the manner in which each sensory attribute contributes to more effective responses, but his consideration of this topic is skimpy at best. Carr thought that one of the basic criteria for evaluating an organism's relative evolution is its capacity to respond effectively to objects at greater and greater distances: Animals higher on the phylogenetic scale increasingly use "distance receptors" like those in the human eye and ear; there is corresponding reduction in the use of "contact receptors." But Carr has little more to say about the evolutionary significance of specific sensory mechanisms.

In this chapter we shall attempt to argue the adaptive contribution of sensory attributes to the total economy of the organism. But before we begin we must consider an issue of awesome complexity: the so-called "mind-body problem." Anyone who insists that components of experience function in behavior must grapple with it.

"Mind" Versus Body

What is sensation? How does physiological excitation or activation result in "psychological" sensation? The historical dualism between mind and body is at the core of the problem. The psychological attribute sensation has stimulated formulation of such traditional constructs as spirit, mind, consciousness, and soul. Yet its own precise nature is an unresolved question. Sensation has been ignored, evaded, and defined away by psychologists, but just when this tenacious ghost seems at least to have been laid, it revives with new ambiguities. The sources of its vitality are its primary representation of the external environment and its triggering of reactions within that environment.

Sensation is perhaps the most important evolutionary solution to the input problem in complex organisms. We assume that experience, or what has been commonly called "mind," evolved because it allowed organisms to adapt more easily to their environment. This assumption leads us to an even more basic question: Do components of experience have some function beyond the neural excitations in the brain from which they are derived or with which they are identified? We assume that these components are simply the manner in which neural excitations are manifested and that they have no function apart from their physical processes, as artificial light is the manifestation of electricity in a filament.

Those who have argued that "mind," or "consciousness," has a separate and unique function beyond the physical are in the curious position of insisting on the function of a process that exists, if at all, only in a kind of metaphysical limbo. If experience does have a function apart from physical changes, it must to that extent exist in a sphere apart from the physical. If so, where and how? We believe, on the other hand, that for every component of experience, regardless how subtle or fleeting, there is a still unknown physical process with which it may be identified.

Let us consider an input sequence. Light of a particular wave length strikes the retina. The consequent action of the receptors sends an impulse down the optic nerve to the occipital lobe of the brain. Suddenly this physiological-neurological process appears to be transformed, and the individual has the "psychological" experience of red. It is here that the dualism comes to focus. We shall assume that before the particular experience or sensation, there may be several transformations (as when at least three kinds of transmission—mechanical, fluid, and neural—precede the actual registration of a sound). Some physical process must conclude every input sequence, and sensation is in our view simply the experiential manifestation of that physical process.

The various components and qualities of experience are, however, almost infinite in number. Is there a different physical process for each of them? We believe so, but we do not know the types of fluctuations in process that account, for example, for the myriad tastes that man is capable of experiencing. Apparently the great variety of taste experience is derived from the simultaneous stimulation of the four basic kinds of taste receptors—those for sweet, sour, bitter, and salty—and receptors registering texture, temperature, and odor. We know even less of the total process initiated by such a complex of receptor action; what finally culminates in the unique taste of pumpkin pie, for example?

We have only begun to define the particular matrices of stimulation that result in given experiences, and we can therefore surmise only vaguely the processes specific to such experiences.

Must the culminating process occur in some particular part of the brain? Not necessarily. Future research may reveal that locus is a pertinent variable; but more likely it will reveal that the uniqueness of a given experience reflects activation of particular excitation matrices or frequencies or both.

Other views invariably require the existence of an impalpable, unextended (that is, not occupying space or time) "mindstuff." Man is described as an open or split system, and those areas in which the "mindstuff" works are considered beyond scientific investigation. But there is more than simple pragmatism to justify our own hypothesis. It is also the simplest hypothesis available, not incompatible with any knowledge that we have, consonant with the available facts—sketchy as they are—and amenable to further derivations. For science these advantages are quite enough, particularly when the unsatisfactory implications of the alternative positions are taken into consideration.

It might reasonably be concluded from this analysis that we are epiphenomenalists, that we consider experience a nonfunctional artifact of physiological changes. But our views are precisely the opposite. Even as light is a natural and functional outcome of various physical processes in the flashlight, so components of experience are natural and functional outcomes of physicochemical and electrical transitions. But why, if we accept the hypothesis that mind and body are one, do we assume experience to be functional at all? Why could not the organism function equally well with only the physical aspects of the natural processes? But can the function of the filament be considered apart from the light that it produces? The light and the filament cannot be separated because they are actually parts of only one process; it is the scientist's perspective that creates a dualism. (We add parenthetically that improvements in flashlights have been directed toward producing more effective light and that many a filament was tried and discarded along the way.)

Just as we can look at the flashlight from two points of view—processes manifest in the filament or light emitted—so we must examine the input process in terms of the physical changes accompanying it, as well as of the experience itself. At present, however, the components of experience are the only data available on such processes and must therefore serve as the basis for our inference of general principles. It is as if we were seeking to learn how flashlights work when data only on the light emitted were available. As knowledge and techniques expand, researchers will probably be able to pin down the particular processes that occasion various categories of experience, but the time is not yet. And even when this advance occurs there may still appear to be two processes, rather than one. When measuring instruments are used the process will be described in terms of "recording units," but in studies by the organism in which the process occurs it will still be described in terms of components of experience.

We thus assume that there is but one event, composed of the experience and the physical process. Our only knowledge of the total process is, however, that yielded directly by experience. When we use terms like "pain," "pleasure," and "red" (all of which have traditionally referred to categories of experience), we mean the total event and not only its subjective aspects. Why do we use such terms, fraught as they are with ambiguity? We must use them; they constitute most of the language available for discussing sensory processes. But we shall borrow heavily from both cybernetics and information theory when the concepts of these areas seem applicable.

According to the theory being developed here, then, sensation is the basic input of the most highly refined homeostatic mechanism that natural selection has so far evolved. Given protoplasm as the basic constituent of life, some input technique at least similar to sensation might have been predicted as a source of integration as organisms became more complex. Rather than being puzzled by the apparent duality of the process, we should study it from a practical and, if possible, experimental point of view. Even as we combine hydrogen and oxygen under certain conditions in order to study their transformation into water, we may, when our techniques become sufficiently refined, determine which physical processes are consistently paired with given "psychological" experiences. We are by no means presently prepared for such research, nor will we even place primary emphasis on such processes here. We wish simply to demonstrate that the physical, experienced event can be considered as a natural phenomenon and that sensation (the major ingredient of "mind," "spirit," "consciousness," and so on) may be reviewed as a kind of input that has evolved in a natural context. The primary issue of sensation here is how it assists the organism to adapt more easily to its environment.

The Functions of Sensation

What has been the function of sensation in abetting survival? Could an equally effective organism have evolved without this particular kind of input? It is easy to conceive of an entity that could respond differently to various energies without this attribute: As a matter of fact, every complex contemporary organism is a composite of many different types of input-output mechanisms. A casual examination of the human being, for instance, reveals several homeostatic systems that involve sensation only secondarily, if at all. The first, and probably the most primitive, are the processes intrinsic to cell functioning (see chapter 2, note 1) and underlying metabolism and growth. Other homeostatic devices include the various reflex-arc processes of the body and the regulatory activity of the nervous system. These mechanisms and many others very likely appeared individually in living organisms.

As evolution proceeded, however, several kinds of homeostatic systems apparently became integrated in a single organism. It is also probable that many types of nonsensory input appeared in the course of evolutionary trial and error, only to be discarded and replaced by more efficient systems. But as organisms became more and more complex, simple input devices were no longer sufficient; a method of representing the multitude of energy changes inside and outside the organism simultaneously became necessary for effective behavior.

It is quite probable that the initial emergence of sensation and its basic differentiations reflected the two kinds of survival needs imposed on every motile life element. First, as life processes, regardless of simplicity, require energy, primitive creatures must have been able to ingest material that could be used for energy. Such behavior required internal changes sufficient to predispose individuals to ingest such material when available energy reached a given level of depletion. In their most rudimentary form these changes were probably somewhat like shifts in the osmotic characteristics of contemporary cells, but they nevertheless represented the initial phase in development of the highly refined "need systems" of complex contemporary organisms. The amoeba represents such a rudimentary system. After ingesting large quantities of material, it remains quiescent for long periods. As time passes, however, it becomes increasingly active and increasingly prone to ingest further material. Even at this level, however, the organism is selective, for incorporation of carbon or glass into the plasmagel does not affect behavior, whereas assimilation of "digestive" materials markedly reduces reactions.

The first motile life elements must also have been able to respond differentially to energy changes arising from the external environment. Initially these responses would have been at best only diffuse reactions to the impacts of energy at particular levels, regardless of type. But, as evolution progressed, zones of particular sensitivity must have developed, allowing organisms to respond to ever more subtle changes. As a contemporary prototype of such crude initial differentiation, let us consider the flagellate protozoan *Euglena* (see chapter 2, note 5). On the anterior portion of this one-celled animal there is a small reddish spot. Sudden shifts in the intensity of light falling on that spot occasion abrupt changes in the animal's movement. We believe that all sense organs evolved from such rudimentary beginnings. Initially, differential response to varied types of energy was no doubt minimal, but, as organisms became more complex, the specialization of receptors that partly accounted for this complexity also allowed the organism to respond with greater precision to more subtle energy shifts. At approximately the same time, and perhaps contingent on such complexity, receptor systems allowing reaction to more subtle and varied changes within the structure of the organism emerged. This discussion leads us to the following postulate.

Postulate of sensation: Each type of sensory input represents energy changes (whether internal or external) that have had enduring importance in the maintenance of optimum equilibrium during the evolution of the species.

There are many different types of receptor systems in the body, each shaped by the workings of natural selection to be responsive to a particular kind of energy change. The input from such mechanisms may be divided into several relatively distinct categories, according to function.

Primary Disequilibrium (Drive) Input

As organisms became more complex those conditions that were hazardous—either critical internal imbalances or possible external damages—came to be represented by appropriate kinds of input, which have traditionally been called "primary needs." The remarkable aspect of such input is not that it is occasioned by hazard but that *as introduced* it constitutes in itself the disequilibrium required for action. Organisms react not to a hot iron but to pain, not to loss of body fluid but to thirst, not to hours of deprivation but to hunger. In all these instances the input itself constitutes the spur initiating and sustaining behavior so that the probability of regaining balance in that particular system is greater.

From a functional point of view this primary spur, or drive, can be divided into three classes: drive arising from such deficits as thirst, hunger, and the need for oxygen; that arising from pain, heat, cold, and so on; and that arising from surfeits like those leading to defecation, urination, and sexual intercourse.

There also seem to be at least three different means (what we shall call "transmitting mechanisms") of introducing information into the organism. First, there may be a specialized receptor (commonly called exteroceptor) responding to particular kinds of externally imposed energy change, as do rods and cones in the eye or nerve endings in the skin. Second, free nerve endings (either interoceptors or proprioceptors) in certain areas, such as body organs and muscles, may be activated by appropriate stimuli, as in the experience of internal pain and body position. Third—and by far the most difficult to understand—the blood itself may constitute the transmitting mechanism. Here we must assume a process in the brain that is differentially responsive to slight shifts in the chemical or liquid constitution of the blood, even as the receptors in the nose are differentially responsive to shifts in the chemical composition of the air.[1]

Regardless of the particular kind of transmitting mechanism used, the primary function of a fair proportion of the input is to represent disequilibrium. But disequilibration input may also serve as a cue. Increasing hunger is often the cue to return home for dinner. This example suggests a characteristic essential for differential responses to imbalances in various systems. The input representing each type of critical imbalance must be *qualitatively* different, which leads us to postulate a "doctrine of specific need qualities" reminiscent of Johannes Mueller's doctrine of specific nerve energies (1843). We may state it formally: Each of the various mechanisms that transmit information about critical imbalances in the body must also transmit qualitative distinctions among imbalances. Such specificity is of prime importance when learning (see Chapter 5) enters into adaptation. Were such drive states not distinguishable, the organism would be unable to orient itself appropriately to food and water sources, for example. There are also differences among drive inputs from the various transmitting mechanisms, which we may designate by the term *vividness*. Certain drives are simply more intolerable than others. In general, those that are more critical to the survival of the organism generate more vivid input: Pain is more intolerable than comparable levels of thirst and thirst more intolerable than hunger. "Vividness" represents such intermechanism differences but there is also a quantitative intramechanism range of difference that is even more important in behavior: that of intensity. When a transmitting mechanism can be isolated, we find a relationship between the degree of activation and the intensity of input: Pain varies from barely noticeable to extreme, and so do heat and cold. This dimension of intensity underlies the basic corollary of our theory and accounts for the relationship between degree of imbalance and rapidity of compensatory response (see Chapter 2).

Although many experiments have correlated activation of trauma receptors with concomitant shifts in experience (registered as pain, heat, or cold), few have described the relationship between activation mechanisms transmitting deficits or surfeits and corresponding changes in experience. This lack of research reflects partly the great difficulty of isolating such mechanisms and partly psychologists' emphasis on overt behavior. If, as we believe, such input provides the major spur to action, the problem of motivation cannot be adequately grasped without considering it. An effort should be made to isolate the particular mechanisms that account for various kinds of disequilibrium input, so that their activation can be correlated with changes in experience. Of course, psychologists have been exploring the relationships between both food and water deprivation and corresponding activity for many years. Although their data generally support the basic corollary of the present theory (the longer the period of deprivation, the more rapid will be the organism's equilibratory activity), to leave the essential mechanism of motivation—the experience of disequilibrium—out of the picture is unjustifiable in a science that seeks understanding of human beings. When an animal is deprived of food, for instance, the important factor determining its behavior is not the hours of deprivation but the qualitatively distinct disequilibrium input (hunger) that arises from processes activated by this deprivation and interacts dynamically within the total matrix of experience to determine action.

Primary drive input serves the major function of initiating and sustaining activity so that critical imbalances in the various body processes are more likely to be resolved. We have suggested that such input varies in quality, vividness, and intensity and that each of these dimensions is critical in adaptive behavior. Without differences in quality the organism could not respond appropriately to circumstances pertinent to a particular imbalance; without variations in vividness the latency of response would be the same for imbalances in vital systems as for those in systems less critical to immediate survival; and without fluctuations in intensity the organism would respond as rapidly to inconsequential imbalances as to those that are immediately critical to survival.

Another class of disequilibrium input occasions reductions, rather than increases in activity; homeostasis is abetted by inaction and quiescence. Although the relevant transmitting mechanisms have not yet been identified, the experiential derivatives have been long recognized: fatigue and nausea.

Fatigue occurs when a given muscle or muscle complex falls into physiological disequilibrium from overactivity; either oxygen and sugar are depleted or excessive waste products build up. Although the actual receptors occasioning such input are unknown, that the input is correlated with extensive muscular activity is beyond question. How does inaction permit a return to equilibrium? The blood provides both sugar and oxygen and removes waste products; as its flow is relatively constant, compensations occur automatically with time. The rate of movement toward equilibrium, according to the basic corollary of the theory, will describe a negatively accelerating curve. The adaptive function of fatigue thus seems obvious. Without such input a given muscle or muscle complex might be used to the point of tissue damage.

The input nausea also occasions quiescence, except for the specific response of vomiting when it is extreme. We may also assume that this input has an adaptive function, in that it occasions removal of noxious material from the organism or allows return to equilibrium in adjacent systems that have initiated the input reflexively.

Cue Function Input

Several receptor systems of the body introduce input that is at least in ordinary ranges, essentially neutral in terms of disequilibrium. Such components may, however, activate a secondary disequilibrium (see Chapter 5), thus serving as cues for avoiding or approaching situations crucial to the organism's welfare. When such input loses its neutrality it is said to have acquired "valence": positive when it occasions movement toward an energy source and negative when movement is away from imposed energy.

In human beings, and in most complex organisms, cue input includes the experiences of light, sound, taste, odor, and certain kinds of touch. Its major contribution to adaptation resides in its capacity to acquire disequilibratory significance through learning, which in turn allows much greater flexibility in behavior. Another contribution, perhaps almost as crucial, is to give moment-by-moment information about the organism's orientation. When an individual moves within its environment, much of the input from such receptors, though relatively neutral in terms of disequilibrium potential, provides a basis for continuing adjustments in position, direction, and momentum. It thus serves a monitoring function similar to that served (as will be discussed later) by the input from kinesthetic receptors.

Implicit in an evolutionary view is the notion that each sensory modality must occasion input qualitatively different from that of others. These variations in quality are essential, for differential responses to the energies imposed would be impossible otherwise. Indeed, if there were no discernible difference among the sensations resulting from stimulation of different receptors, a non-functional increase in complexity would result: If two receptors introduced precisely the same input, differential responses would be impossible, and the condition would inhibit, rather than abet, survival. The basis for Mueller's doctrine of specific nerve energies is thus easily justified from the point of view of adaptive functioning.

Cue input has another characteristic that makes a vital contribution to increased flexibility: Its apparent locus varies. Visual components appear to originate in the eyes and taste in the mouth; more important, tactile input appears to be localized on the skin. This characteristic is probably as critical for adaptive behavior as are the differences in quality previously mentioned. If it were absent, the organism would be unable to make precise responses to threats to particular parts of the body. When a person burns his right hand, he hurriedly withdraws that hand, rather than the left one; if a cockroach were to crawl up his leg, he would know precisely where it was. Although all sensory material has this characteristic, it varies in specificity from one transmitting mechanism to another. The input from skin receptors is unusually clearly localized, whereas that from visceral mechanisms is vaguer. Whether such variation in specificity reflects the type or dispersion of pertinent receptors or whether certain circumstances impose more diffuse stimulation is difficult to determine. The fact remains that specificity of locus is characteristic of all sensory input and makes an essential adaptive contribution.

A related problem, and one that has baffled thinkers on the subject for years, involves the following question: Although all sensory input is occasioned by processes within the central nervous system, how is it that the input *appears* to be located in the receptors or—as with visual and auditory input—at varying distances *from* the receptor? The words on this page appear to be located a number of inches from the reader, although the input components representing them are certainly within him.

Are we born with the capacity for externalizing stimuli and loci, or are they learned? One conclusion seems certain: We are born able to recognize the differences in quality between taste experience and visual experience. Whether ability to localize is innate, learned, or both, however, is still open to debate. But, even if future research reveals that learning is predominant, it will still be necessary to assume that the *capacity* for such arrangement of cues is innate. Furthermore, as pointed out by R. H. Lotze, differences in quality will undoubtedly be found to play an important part in the learning of specificity: without them, discrimination among the inputs from different loci would be impossible, and learning could not occur.

Not only does cue input vary in quality and apparent locus, it also differs in intensity. Generally speaking there is a direct relationship between the proximity of a cue and the amount of energy received; as distance increases, sound waves diminish, and light waves are diffused. That such changes can be represented by corresponding reductions in sensory input would have been predictable; there is usually a critical proximity between a given cue and the situation (whether hazardous or beneficial) that it signals.

Finally, the input from *all* transmitting mechanisms of the body varies markedly in its potential for discreteness. From a functional point of view this difference is exactly what we would expect. There is one condition that ordinarily occasions thirst (loss of fluid), hunger (lack of food), or pain (trauma), and there are therefore only two requirements that such input must fulfill: Each type must vary along the dimension of intensity, and each must be qualitatively different from other types. But there are literally thousands of environmental conditions pertinent to reduction of such disequilibrium; hence the multivariate character of cue input from the visual and auditory receptors. To register food deprivation all that is necessary is representation by input varying in intensity and different from input representing other conditions of disequilibrium. But the situations in which food can be found are so numerous that the receptors for vision, audition, olfaction and so on work together to represent them. If the resolving power of the vision receptors were limited as is that of the transmitting mechanisms for thirst, hunger, and pain, we would see only variations in shades of gray.

As we shall see in Chapter 5, relative discreteness is important in learning. A woman, asked if she remembered her pain during childbirth, replied that she did not. Nor can anyone remember a specific pain or for that matter a specific pleasure. There is simply nothing of sufficient discreteness in such input to mark it off as different from all the other similar inputs that have been experienced. A specific pain or pleasure may emphasize the input from the circumstance in which it occurs. We can easily recall that pain or pleasure was experienced in a situation but not the specific pain or the specific pleasure. Neither are we able to remember a specific fear, a specific hunger, or a specific thirst. Disequilibrium input varies only on one continuum and thus precludes the possibility of specific recall.

There is another category of cue input that provides information about the relative positions and movements of various body components. It is well known that the receptors activated by specific body parts are located in the muscles, tendons, and joints and are commonly subsumed under the label "kinesthetic sense." Every movement stimulates such receptors and sensory material is thus introduced. Although on most occasions such input is hardly discernible, it does provide a basis for monitoring the various activities in progress. This function is important in all overt behavior and particularly when new motor skills are being acquired. Then each movement activates receptors introducing sensory input that in turn provide feedback about the precision and progress of the behavior. When actions have become habitual, as in typing and walking, input becomes attenuated (that is, less of it is apperceived) and, as long as the behavior proceeds smoothly, relatively less important to the organism.

Sensory material from receptors in the semicircular canals of the ears serves much the same function, except that the position and relative movements of the *entire* body are involved. Still the input from such receptors, which incidentally results from reflexive activation by other receptor systems (there is no experience peculiar to the receptors in the semicircular canals), allows continuous monitoring of gross movement and position.

Such input also contributes to adaptive responses. Without it, continuing behavior would be erratic and disorganized, for moment-by-moment information essential to compensatory adjustments would be unobtainable. We may surmise that such techniques of compensatory feedback developed early in the evolutionary context. Some such mechanism must have emerged simultaneously with organ differentiation and gross body movement, in order to allow at least the minimum of integrated behavior necessary for survival.

So far, we have considered two different types of input: that representing primary disequilibrium and that serving as cues. It should be emphasized that the sensations constituting primary disequilibration are occasioned by changes in physical energy (depletion or imposition) that generally represent hazard. Cue sensation represents energy changes that do not, at least within ordinary ranges, threaten the organism. Both types of input are initially represented as components of disequilibrium. Sensations representing hazardous energy shifts are, however, much more persistent and powerful than are cue sensations, unless the latter have become associated with primary inputs.

Equilibrium (Pleasure) Input

Input reflecting equilibrium, considered superficially, poses certain problems for homeostatic theory. The postulate of process, it will be recalled, states that all activity is equilibratory. Yet there are certain instances in which the basic motivation for behavior seems to be a search for "pleasure," rather than escape from "displeasure," in which pleasure becomes a critical goal for an organism that is already in optimum equilibrium in all pertinent systems.

Pleasure is certainly a kind of sensory input, but the search for the relevant transmitting mechanism has been completely fruitless, at least until quite recently. It seems to be located at specific points, like the genitals during intercourse and the mouth during eating, but neither specific receptors nor particular free nerve endings are apparently responsible. The same stimulation that occasions pleasure when the organism is deprived may produce discomfort when it is sated. Pleasure apparently arises from the process of equilibration, as when the organism is eating or having orgasm, but there is no discernible pleasure input when pain is alleviated.

Recent findings by J. Olds (1960) have shed some light on both the general locus of such input and the manner in which it motivates the organism. When a microelectrode is implanted in certain regions of a rat's brain stem, behavior can be affected to remarkable degrees by small voltages of electrical current.

Olds shaped the rat's behavior moment by moment by introducing a short pulse of shock immediately after a particular movement. Furthermore, he found that rats will learn a multiple-unit maze and sometimes even cross an activated shock grid in order to stimulate themselves in the brain. This research suggests that there are particular areas of the brain that function as pleasure centers and that organisms will actively pursue pleasure for its own sake. Do these findings demonstrate that at least certain activities are *not* occasioned by disequilibrium, thus nullifying the postulate of process? Careful consideration of this problem suggests not. It is the loss or reduction of pleasure, not its presence, that activates the organism. A child may remember that he derived pleasure from eating an ice-cream cone; that it is only remembered pleasure, rather than pleasure presently experienced, may be sufficiently disequilibratory to initiate and sustain activity. Similarly, a certain amount of the disequilibrium that causes organisms to persevere in such activities as eating or masturbation may be occasioned by recognition that the pleasure just previously experienced has been reduced or is no longer present. The reader may complain at this point that we are assuming a disequilibrium that does not exist. What is the source of this hypothetical input, which is presumably introduced when pleasure is removed? If sexual intercourse were forcibly interrupted just before orgasm, powerful disequilibrium input in the guise of frustration or anger would result. The motivations introduced by pleasure are always experienced as either frustration or anger occasioned by its absence or interruption or as fear that certain conditions may end.

If pleasure is a type of input that does not serve primarily either as disequilibrium or cue, what is its basic function? Pleasure appears to have three interrelated functions, contributing to monitoring, discrimination, and emphasis.

The human being comprises a number of systems that may fall into disequilibrium; some can be returned to balance almost immediately (for example, by removal of a painful stimulus), whereas others require prolonged activity before an optimum condition can be regained (as in eating). Where the activity must be of some duration, pleasure provides continuous feedback on the progress of equilibration, and its cessation is a cue that balance has been regained. This monitoring function of pleasure, coupled with input occasioned by the loss of pleasure, helps to sustain equilibratory activity at reasonable levels. As monitoring is much more important for homeostatic systems that require prolonged activity, a more intense pleasure component could be predicted for their equilibration: Sexual behavior should be *more* pleasurable than defecation and eating *more* pleasurable than drinking.

Our discussion leads us again to a principle similar to Mueller's doctrine of specific nerve energies. In order for pleasure to function as a monitor, the input from equilibration of a given system must be distinguishable from that arising from equilibration in other systems. Otherwise the pleasure inputs from different systems would be confusing, and the monitoring mechanism would hinder, rather than abet, survival. Such specific qualities of specific pleasure are probably not as important for adaptive behavior as are specific nerve energies derived from the various sense modalities and from primary mechanisms transmitting deficit and surfeit; pleasure occurs when the appropriate activity is already in progress, but qualitative variations among the different transmitting mechanisms are required for differential responses to occur in the first place.

It appears that certain loci in the brain stem, as well as adjacent areas, are responsible for the different kinds of pleasure input and that the relative deficit within a given system affects the activation of these centers: For example, eating occasions pleasure in a hungry but not in a sated animal. Olds (1960) has dramatically confirmed this common-sense notion. He found an area in the brain of the rat that is peculiar to pleasure associated with satisfying hunger and a comparable one for sex; then he demonstrated that an animal will stimulate itself in the appropriate area *only* when the corresponding drive is present. The deficit is thus critical in determining whether or not stimulation of the brain will produce pleasure.

If several such pleasure centers do exist and if they are peculiarly responsive to various imbalances within the body, we may ultimately solve one of the most baffling problems of motivation: discovering how both animals and human infants select adequate diets in "cafeteria" situations. A rat maintained on a calcium-free diet for an extended period and then allowed to choose between one food with a low calcium content and another with a high calcium content will choose the latter. How does it make this discrimination? It may be that the deficit sensitizes an appropriate center in the brain so that the food with high calcium content will produce more pleasure than will the other; pleasure would then provide both the basis for discrimination and the motivation for choice. Olds and Peretz (1960) demonstrated that a castrated rat would not stimulate its sex-reward area unless the hormone androgen had been injected into its bloodstream. If the presence of a hormone can sensitize a sex center, it seems not unreasonable to assume that a lack of calcium may sensitize an appropriate hunger center.

This discussion suggests that pleasure may contribute to adaptive behavior in another way, extending the monitoring function already described to provide the basis for certain fundamental discriminations. It is true that the human being soon loses its ability spontaneously to select adequate food— but not until learning has overpowered the pleasure-discrimination mechanism (see Chapter 5).

Another adaptive function of pleasure is emphasis. In Chapter 5 we shall argue not only that learning is contingent on the introduction of sensory material but also that certain characteristics of such material are critical in the establishment of enduring memory residuals. Pleasure adds to the intensity and discreteness of other inputs, so that encoding can occur more readily: It emphasizes both the equilibratory activity and equilibrium itself. As previously suggested, this function is particularly important when prolonged activity is required for an optimal condition to be regained; it is thus more important in the so-called "consummatory activities" like eating, drinking, and copulation than in avoidance learning.

From the point of view of adaptation, pleasure thus fulfills several functions: It contributes directly to disequilibrium, it provides cues to allow monitoring of equilibratory behavior, it furnishes the basis for discrimination among specific hungers, and it furthers learning by emphasizing those aspects of behavior that are equilibratory.

Existentialists may complain that we have overlooked the fundamental contribution of pleasure to life. Without pleasure life would not be worth living, and an organism devoid of pleasure would end its life if it were capable of comprehending the significance and means of suicide. If joy is the purpose of existence, how can we place pain and hunger at the center of man's evolution and his present nature? It is true that man appreciates most those aspects of his life marked by pleasure. No utopia has been built around pain and hunger. But we are not concerned here with man's value judgments about either his present or his future life; we seek instead to discover the attributes that were vital in his evolution up to this point, that even now are crucial to his every act. We could exist without pleasure and joy and perhaps without pain and hunger— but not for long.

Secondary Disequilibrium (Drive) Input

Learning is involved in most, if not all, examples of secondary disequilibrium. Some cue or circumstance occasions changes within the organism; these changes in turn produce an input that initiates and sustains certain behavior. The relationship between the cue and the internal changes is learned. What input really activates behavior? Most of it has been considered under the heading "emotion," though some of it goes under the even more ambiguous label "feelings" and there is a third category that has no name in the literature.

Emotions. The shadings of emotional input are so subtle and so plentiful that in every language an entire lexicon of adjectives has had to be developed to represent them. All the categories are vague, but some—like envy, greed, awe, and suspicion—are so ephemeral that we must leave them to the novelist and the poet. There may be such distinct inputs, and they may be functional, but we shall not include them in this evaluation. Others, like fear, guilt, anger, and love are so basic that we cannot leave them without brief comment.

Fear is the most important, for it functions as the spur to avoidance behavior. Without this kind of experience the use of cues would be minimal. Organisms would have remained at the most rudimentary levels of response and behavior.

Guilt also makes a vital adaptive contribution, at least in those mammals that must cooperate in order to survive. It is the input that forces individuals to abide by rules that are (or were at one time) essential to the welfare of the group. Without guilt human society could not have developed, and the human being could not exist.

Anger or hostility or aggression is also a vital input. As many experiments on frustration have demonstrated, it spurs the organism to greater efforts to overcome obstacles or adversaries. And love (of many varieties) provides the impetus for people to remain together during pregnancy and infancy.

We have already discussed the general functioning of emotions (in Chapter 2). They endow previously neutral cues with disequilibrium significance and they speed responses. Their contribution to learning will be examined in Chapter 5 and to abnormal behavior in Chapter 8.

Feelings. "Feelings" are highly diffuse experiences, the origins and functions of which are difficult to pin down. Actually the psychological status of "feelings" has not changed appreciably since the structuralists first argued about their classification on one or several different dimensions. We shall not extend this argument. But we do suggest that "feelings" have a function not fulfilled by less amorphous input: providing information on the *general* welfare of the organism. This monitoring function, though not as discrete as that of pleasure or kinesthetic feedback, is still important. To feel "good" or "bad" is not without adjustment significance. The activity level of the individual is affected by such input. When it is reduced more rest is possible, and when it is increased more rapid general adjustments can be made.

Flare Input. Although the third category of experience also makes a vital contribution to behavior, we can find no record of it in the literature. Despite its universality in human beings, and perhaps in all mammals, it is difficult to describe, probably because its manifestations are so transitory. An example may help. Let us assume that a person's family has gone out for the day, leaving him alone in the house. He goes down to the basement, and suddenly he sees a man in the shadows. Within less than a second he will experience what we shall call "flare input." It appears to originate in the viscera, but it also seems to be derived from nerve endings that are generally distributed throughout the body. It can have profound effect on behavior, an effect central to certain abnormal states (see Chapter 8). Although psychologists have apparently overlooked or ignored this phenomenon, it is probably related to the psychogalvanic reflex (PGR). Both occur within less than a second after the stimulus has been applied. Furthermore, the PGR can be measured on any part of the body, suggesting that it too is a general response. From a behavioral point of view, the "startle response" may also exemplify such input; it too is a highly generalized reaction, suggesting the activation of widely dispersed nerve endings. Although flare input ordinarily subsides within a few seconds, its occurrence may become chronic in some circumstances (see Chapter 8).

Discussion. The previous analysis suggests that disequilibratory inputs are of two kinds, those representing physiological imbalances and those instigated by cues occasioning internal changes. Even if we were to stop here, we would have

drawn a fairly sophisticated picture of motivation describing the organism's behavior as sustained by drives that are in perpetual flux as imbalances are resolved
and new cues encountered. The process of adjustment is considered one of
continuing compensation in response to shifting inputs of promise or peril to
the organism.

But this picture, realistic as it seems, is oversimplified. It makes no allow-
ance for the organism to move without specific input and assumes that movement itself will cease as soon as the effects of such input have passed. But
organisms do not always move more slowly as drive declines; they do not "run
down" as soon as they reach equilibrium, as if they were toys with unwinding
springs. Rather, they continue, at least during the waking state, to move in the
environment and to react to it. They appear to be motivated by generalized
input that remains at a relatively high level, even after specific drives have been
alleviated.

What is that input? Is it synonymous with "feelings," as we have described
them? Or is there some new category of input still unclassified? One point
seems clear: Its diffuse nature complicates the problem of recognizing and investigating it. It is indeed so amorphous that it leaves almost no record in
memory, and its very generality lessens the possibility of specific definition.
This drive appears to be synonymous with general arousal, which intensifies responses to more specific inputs; alertness and curiosity may be included in it.
The sleepy student who takes benzedrine experiences a sudden upsurge of such
input; he is suffused with new enthusiasm and energy.

The higher an animal is on the phylogenetic scale, the greater the influence
of such generalized input seems. For most animals, at least those that are not
domesticated, hunger and fear are in perpetual process. But civilized man is
not often acutely hungry, almost never extremely thirsty, and seldom afraid of
physical danger. He is typically motivated by amorphous drives, by general inputs vaguely subsumed under such terms as "curiosity," "ambition," and
"adventure."

When behavior is initiated and sustained by such inputs the individual himself is hard put to comprehend the origin and direction of his motivations. He
will often explain his behavior by saying simply that "it is what I wanted to
do," implying that his own volition is somehow responsible for his acts. We
have previously suggested that much human behavior is volitional, motivated by
threats to the integrity of the autocept. But much other behavior is assumed
to be volitional when it actually is not. It results from input so diffuse, so
lacking in specific content, yet so persistent in its influence, that the individual
mistakenly attributes it to his own will.

The adaptive contribution of a generalized drive seems considerable. Not
only does it maintain the organism in a state of heightened vigilance, it also
brings the organism into contact with broader segments of the immediate environment and thus provides the opportunity for encoding salient features of that

environment. Such learning may then allow specific responses to particular dangers or deficits and provide much more facile resolution of disequilibrium.

Despite this description of a generalized drive input, we are not yet certain of its existence. The primary drives are so universal and the shadings of input that we call "emotion" are so diverse and persistent that the notion of a non-specific activator may be an inference from ignorance. Is there a "Big D?" Perhaps there is; the adaptive significance of such an input outlined in the previous discussion suggests its likelihood, but future research must give us the answer to this question.

Evolutionary Interdependence

The preceding discussion suggests that the various transmitting mechanisms of the body (whether specific receptors, free nerve endings, or fluids) permit the introduction of vital information. These mechanisms, because they are derived from evolution, have been shaped by the laws of natural selection and represent those conditions that have been critical in the gradual emergence of a particular species. The "reality" for any species must be limited to those energy dimensions to which differential responses were important during its evolution. When a given energy dimension was not pertinent to survival, no transmitting mechanism was evolved. When a given dimension was central to the survival and evolution of a species, that dimension is represented by highly refined transmitting mechanisms and consequent representation in sensation. Hence the relatively highly developed visual system of the vulture and the olfactory mechanism of the hound.

A slight extension of this point allows us to infer that surface receptors of the body that are nearer to highly vulnerable or functionally crucial organs will be more responsive to energy shifts signifying potential hazards. We would predict greater tactual sensitivity near the eyes or on the neck than on the thigh or back. Heavily armored body organs would have relatively few such receptors. It is not accidental that the human brain is largely insensitive to stimulation. Not only is it protected by the skull, but also circumstances sufficiently extreme to occasion trauma to the brain usually result in death. Receptors in the brain are thus not necessary; furthermore, stimulation (if such receptors did exist) would be nonfunctional, for the organism would typically be incapable of response by the time that it occured.

From this discussion we can derive two corollaries of sensation.

Those energy shifts that are most immediately hazardous will be represented by types of sensation that are correspondingly more intolerable (as pain is more vivid than is hunger).

Those energy shifts that are most crucial to the survival of a particular species will be represented by more highly refined receptors and consequent sensation mechanisms (as the hound has a more sensitive nose and the vulture a more sensitive eye).

Indeed, both corollaries, when considered in the evolutionary context, appear obvious; they are simply reflections of the correspondence that must necessarily exist between the organism and the agency that molded it.

Although both these corollaries pertain to the relative efficiency of different modalities, the same logic applies to a dimension of input from one particular receptor system. That is, each modality will be most sensitive to shifts in physical energy in those ranges that are most crucial for the organism's survival. An organism that feeds on a class of individuals whose vocal utterances occur primarily within a given range will, as a result of evolutionary symbiosis, develop an auditory sensitivity peculiar to the frequency and amplitude of these vibrations. And the receptors of the organisms preyed upon will be particularly sensitive to the energy changes that signify the approach of the predator.

The possible interrelationship between a particular receptor system and the survival circumstances of an organism has been dramatically demonstrated by recent experimental work on the eye of the frog at the Massachusetts Institute of Technology (Lettvin *et al.*, 1959). The investigators determined the response of the frog's eye to different optical stimulus patterns by inserting microelectrodes into the optic nerve and measuring the impulses sent toward the brain over individual nerve fibers. The frog's eye apparently responds to four different kinds of information. Of most interest to us is the neural response initiated by small objects moving jerkily across its visual field. The size of the objects that produced maximum response corresponded to the dimensions of flies and other appropriate insects when they are in striking distance of the frog's tongue! This finding suggests that the frog's eye is peculiarly responsive to the presence of insects in its environment and allows us to surmise that this "bug-perceiving" mechanism has evolved through the millions of generations during which frogs have depended upon catching insects for survival.

An evolutionary orientation also allows us to infer the particular segment of a given energy dimension to which an organism will be most sensitive. From an adaptation point of view, we would predict that any given receptor will be most sensitive at the lowest discernible intensities because it is more important for an organism to apprehend a given energy change initially than afterward. For example, as there is a direct relationship between the distance of a sound and its intensity, the ability to apprehend very low intensities would allow an organism much more time to avoid a predator or much greater ease in determining the presence of potential food. This observation leads to a further corollary.

The farther above the threshold a given stimulus is, the greater will be the increase in energy required to bring about a noticeable difference.

As a given receptor and its consequent sensory representation would not have developed at all had they not had survival value, this corollary should apply to all sense modalities; indeed, the hundreds of experiments performed by psychophysicists generally demonstrate that it does.

Within the almost limitless editions of living creatures there are many examples of the interdependence of process or structure that must emerge when two or more species play mutually important roles in the evolutionary environment. It need hardly be mentioned that evolutionary interdependence can never be considered apart from the general environment, which always serves as a more basic determinant of a given species' characteristics than does any particular ecological companion; regardless of the extent and duration of the effective relationship, the general environment will contribute a greater number of crucial adaptation circumstances than a single species could. In general, however, the degree to which an organism's sensory equipment is attuned to the energy changes peculiar to any other creature is in direct proportion to the extent and duration of the interdependence between their antecedents during evolution.

The different transmitting mechanisms of the body are thus primarily responsive to the narrow segments of the energy fluctuations relative to which differential response was of some adaptive value during a species' evolutionary history. The interrelationship among various dimensions and the resolving power of a receptor system are so well known and so universally taken for granted that it does not seem astonishing that the physical characteristics for sound are frequency, amplitude, and complexity and that each is faithfully represented by pitch, loudness, and timbre. Or that the physical characteristics of the electromagnetic continuum—again frequency, amplitude, and complexity—are represented by hue, brightness, and saturation. It seems astonishing only when we think about it for a bit.

Why are certain modalities limited to such narrow segments of energies that are omnipresent? Let us consider the electromagnetic continuum: On this dimension wave lengths vary from one-billionth of a millimeter (for the cosmic particle) to twenty-five miles (the radio broadcast band). Yet eyes—the most universal of all transmitting mechanisms—are responsive only to a very narrow band of wave lengths. What a waste of information! Why is there a response only to the range between 400 and 800 millimicrons? Why has nature fixed on this segment to the exclusion of the rest? Why do we not have X-ray eyes or orbs responsive to the total range? Two conditions seem to have limited eyes, whether those of newts or of Isaac Newton: the reflection potential of this segment and the injury potential of wave lengths not within it. The eye can provide information only to the extent that it responds to reflected energy, but wave lengths below violet do not reflect; they tend to penetrate. Those above the red tend to go around an object in their path. When we combine the reflection requirement with the notion that wave lengths below violet and above red are injurious to the eye, the limitation of response to the narrow band does not seem strange; rather, we recognize it as simply another example of the evolutionary imperative suggested by the postulate of inference.

Summary

From a functional point of view, sensory input may be divided into three basic categories. First, there is disequilibrium or drive, input, which may be either primary or secondary, depending upon whether it is induced by energy shifts occasioning unlearned physiological reactions or by previously neutral cues that have come, through learning, to activate secondary disequilibrium mechanisms. Although primary disequilibrium typically increases the activity of the organism, there are at least two notable exceptions (fatigue and nausea) that occasion quiescence. Secondary disequilibrium input permits deneutralization of cues and emergency activation of the organism. In its less extreme manifestations it also provides background input that monitors the general welfare of the organism.

The second class of sensations, which we call "cue input," though initially neutral, may develop the capacity, through learning, to activate secondary disequilibrium mechanisms. When such valence becomes established, the organism can avoid and approach situations pertinent to its welfare. This input also has a monitoring function: It provides information allowing moment-by-moment compensatory adjustments in direction, momentum, orientation, and position.

Finally, equilibrium input (pleasure) provides emphasis to facilitate encoding, allows monitoring of equilibration activity, and by its absence or reduction may induce disequilibrium input (as when pleasure is remembered, rather than actually experienced) that initiates and sustains movement toward cues.

As a complex organism is comprised of many interacting process systems that continuously fluctuate in response to an ever-changing environment, information about both internal and external changes must be made available for effective differential responses. Sensation, it is conjectured, is the most highly developed evolutionary solution to this input problem.

Notes

[1] Many kinds of behavior are activated by the presence or absence of particular substances in the bloodstream. Hunger has perhaps most often been the object of research. As early as 1916 A. J. Carlson hypothesized that hunger might be correlated with the rise and fall of blood sugar. His hypothesis was bolstered by the finding that insulin injections, which lower blood sugar, also increase hunger. But W. W. Scott and his colleagues (1938) found little or no correlation between normal blood-sugar levels and the hunger drive. According to glucostatic theory (Mayer, 1955), it is the level of a particular type of sugar—glucose—rather than blood sugar per se that determines the experience of hunger. J. Anliker and J. Mayer (1957) found a correlation between the intensity of hunger and the level of glycogen in the liver. Further support for this theory comes from a finding that the only metabolic energy source that can freely cross the blood-brain barrier and be used by the brain cells to form adenosine triphosphate (ATP) is glucose (Wenger, Jones, and Jones, 1956). The brain area that apparently functions as the hunger center is the lateral hypothalamus. The level of glucose brought to these areas via the bloodstream may very well be responsible for the experiences of hunger and satiation (B. A. Cross, 1964).

A. Frossberg and S. Larson (1954) have reported that fasting increases the amounts of glucose and phosphorus taken from the blood into the lateral hypothalamus. It seems clear that blood content of some kind is responsible for hunger and eating behavior. Wenger and his colleagues (1956) have reported that injecting the blood of a starved animal into the circulatory system of a well-fed one intensifies stomach contractions in the latter. Reversing the experiment inhibits the contractions.

It has been ascertained (Morgan, 1965) that in conditions of thirst the amount of water in the blood tends to remain constant at the expense of the tissues, including the brain. But C. T. Morgan also found that it is probably the change in osmotic pressure of the blood, rather than the amount of water as such, that is significant in thirst. An increase of the sodium and chloride concentrations (Adolph, Barker, and Hay, 1954) in the blood appears to activate the posterior portion of the pituitary gland to secrete antidiuretic hormone (ADH), which prevents diuresis, until the water-intake balance is restored (Arnold, 1960). Thirst thus appears to result from changes in the osmotic pressure of the blood, which in turn lead to secretion of ADH until water is consumed. Changes in the osmotic pressure of the blood following dehydration stimulate cells of the hypothalamus, where ADH is also secreted, thus suggesting that the cells secreting ADH may also function as osmoreceptors (Morgan, 1965).

The blood also seems to be an important agent in emotional reactions, E. E. Levitt (1965) has summarized studies suggesting that anxiety and fear responses result from increases of adrenaline in the blood stream and that anger responses result from increases of noradrenaline. Sexual behavior is also influenced by the presence of hormones in the bloodstream. In the female estrogen and progesterone are responsible (in most species); in the male androgen is responsible.

An interesting sidetrack to this discussion can be found in a report by R. B. Heath (1954). When an extract (taraxein) from the blood of psychotics was injected into the circulatory system of normal individuals, the latter became abstracted and slow, lost touch with the environment, and reported themselves unable to "think." Specific contents of the blood thus may affect more of our experience and consequent behavior than we have any notion of at this time.

2R. C. Bolles (1967) has adopted the term "Big D" for a possible third kind of drive, apart from those derived from physiological imbalances and those instigated by cues. Such a general drive component could manifest itself in at least two different ways: the mechanism could either accentuate the effects of drives already present or could actually introduce new components.

What is the evidence on this question? Many behavioral studies have suggested that an animal can be completely sated in all pertinent systems in a totally familiar situation yet still indulge in activity at a relatively high level. Doesn't this conclusion indicate the presence of a generalized drive? Unfortunately, questions can always be raised: Is the organism really completely devoid of ordinary drive input? Is it without any hunger, thirst, fear, sexual desire, and so on? Is the situation really completely familiar?

Bolles and J. de Lorge (1962), for instance, demonstrated that rats continued to explore a familiar maze 95 percent of the time during a ten-minute period even when sated. But the possible presence of other kinds of input was not entirely ruled out. B. A. Campbell and B. O. Sheffield (1953) found that sated rats in a homogeneous auditory and visual environment demonstrated less activity than they did during a "stimulation period." But they still demonstrated a fairly high level of activity. What instigated this activity? It could have been instigated by some Big D mechanism.

Even though every effort is made to control specific drive conditions, there is still a baseline of activity (unless the animal is asleep). Does this fact indicate the presence of a generalized drive, or does it suggest that there is always some "leakage" of specific input?

After examining a large number of studies on this topic, Bolles (1967) has concluded: "Generalized drive has turned out to be a puny fellow compared with the Big D we had expected to find: he cannot carry much explanatory weight." Although the quantities of contradictory data reveiwed by Bolles could push him toward that conclusion, we cannot accept it. When all sources of specific drive have been removed, a baseline of activity can still be found. And this activity is fundamental to survival: Without it the organism would cease to respond once specific drive inputs had been removed. And in a environment where unknown dangers lurk, such relaxation would have ensured the extermination of the species.

A respectable store of data has been accumulated (see Chapter 8, note 4) to suggest that a minimum of stimulation (at least during the waking state) is required for optimal adjustment in most, if not all, mammals. When the organism is deprived of all stimuli, it seems actively to seek them. Is such a need for stimulation related to or part of the "Big D?" It might account for exploratory activity, play, grooming, and the like, which have often been discussed as indicators of a generalized drive. We even seem to have a name for this condition: "boredom."

Work on the reticular activating center is perhaps even more pertinent. Many studies (for example Olds and Peretz, 1960; French, 1957) have suggested that the RAS actively contributes, probably through its effects on other brain centers, to the level of consciousness and generally alerts the organism to rapid response to any and all stimuli. N. H. Hyden and P. W. Lange (1965) have found shifts in enzyme activity in the RAS during sleep and wakefulness. During sleep enzyme activity was found to be high in the neurons and low in the neuroglia; during waking the reverse was observed. No rhythmic changes of this nature were found in the other brain structures. S. E. Glickman (1960) and Olds and Peretz (1960) found that the RAS is even more particular in its functions: Areas whose stimulation are rewarding were found directly adjacent to areas whose stimulation produces escape behavior. As the complicated task of unraveling the various functions of the RAS continues, more and more data suggest that this center contributes to the orientation reaction, exploratory responses, and heightened arousal (Batini, 1959). Is it the source of "Big D?" Is "Big D" derived from a generalized firing of neurons within the RAS or from some still undiscovered effect that it may have on other areas?

[3]We can see at a casual glance that each species has evolved in a particular manner to suit its own environmental niche. But aside from the obvious structural developments (giraffes' long necks, which permit them to eat the top leaves of trees) there are many examples of small yet significant deviations from the typical evolution of sense organs, though less obvious, they are just as important for survival.

Vision is probably the sense that varies most. Eye sensitivity is extremely important to nocturnal animals, and large eyes in these species is thus a logical development. It is seen in extreme form in deep-sea fish and nocturnal birds, whose eyes occupy major portions of their total head areas. Other night adaptations are the dilated pupil and the large spherical lens positioned far from the cornea, so that the image appears small but is as bright as possible (Duke-Elder, 1958). The eye of the nocturnal insect is also specially adapted to the dark: The pigment sheaths are not complete, and the lenses of adjacent ommatidia perform together to produce single images (in contrast to the multiple images seen by diurnal insects) (Waterman, 1961). Other organisms can adapt their photoreceptors to the degree of light; the cones and rods in the mammal eye and the changing properties of some insects' single receptors are examples (Dethier, 1953). The horse's eye is oval and slanted in the head with pupil and nonelastic lens situated near one end; this structure makes possible the simultaneous focusing of near and far objects and gives a wide panorama. The horse can thus eat and watch for predators at the same time (Ratner and Denny, 1964). The bee can distinguish ultraviolet light, which enables it to identify particular flowers (Ratner and Denny, 1964).

There are also variations in hearing mechanisms. Birds lack the pinna (outer ear) probably because it would impede flight speed. Instead they have a covering of feathers, which hinders hearing but cuts down noise. In the bat, however, the pinna has become extremely large, for hearing has apparently made an enduring contribution to the species' survival (Pumphrey, 1961). Owls have developed an uncanny ability to locate prey by sound; their wide heads maximize binaural time differences (Payne, 1962). Sound travels much more rapidly in water than in air, whereas light scatters in water permitting vision only for short distances: hence the development of echo location by the porpoise (Kellogg, 1961).

H. W. Lissman (1951) has described an interesting development among the Mormyiridae and Gymnotidae, fish families inhabiting the muddy rivers of Africa and South America, where vision would be useless and hearing relatively ineffective. Survival thus became contingent on development of some sensory technique that would be appropriate to the surroundings. Both kinds of fish send weak electrical impulses from the tails to locate objects in the water. Any object more or less conductive than water and at least one millimeter in diameter can be detected (Lissman, 1963).

The nose has also been acutely developed when essential. Many hunted animals are extremely sensitive to the smells of predators. Mollusks have developed the ability to smell starfish and to escape (Passano, 1957).

Another variation of sensation, though difficult to categorize, is the sensitivity of the legs of many common butterflies to chemical substances, particularly sugar, which aids them in detecting food (Ratner and Denny, 1964).

[4]In the history of human warfare, the development of weapons and defense systems has engendered a reciprocal spiral, for the invention of a new technique for killing is always followed by a counterdefense stratagem. When different species have been involved in mutual or interdependent evolution an analogous pattern has occurred. The hawk and the owl both have ears that are remarkably effective in the locating of sound sources, whereas small birds, their traditional prey, have evolved the capacity for emitting warning notes above the optimal frequency for phase-difference cues but below that required for effective binaural intensity differences (Marler, 1955). The bat has developed both an effective sonar and the agility sufficient to prey on certain species of moth; the moth in turn has evolved not only sensitivity to the bat's sound probes but also remarkable capacity for aerobatics designed to avoid the predator (Roeder, 1963). Small creatures like field mice have developed acute hearing for the

detection of predators, whereas the owls that prey on them have evolved soft fringes on the edges of their wing feathers, which dampen the noise of flight (Thorpe and Griffin, 1962). As might be expected, owls that feed on fish, for which silence is relatively unimportant, have no such fringes. The sensory system of the pike is peculiarly responsive to small moving objects in the water, whereas the minnow, its traditional prey, has evolved the strategy of movement cessation and slow sinking when it encounters water in which the predator has just been swimming (Goz, 1941). Even more dramatic examples of the pattern of ploy and counterploy that marks interdependent evolution are techniques of defensive mimicry by which an organism evolves certain similarities with the predator, like the "eyes" on the wings of some species of moths and butterflies (see note 5) or the capacity to emit the odor of a noxious species (Brower and Brower, 1960).

These examples are only a few of the possible strategies. One species develops an exceptional eye, and another evolves camouflage techniques to puzzle it; one becomes hypersensitive to movement, and another becomes capable of disengaging its tail, which remains wriggling to confound the predator while its erstwhile owner flees. And so the eternal struggle and interdependent evolution of predator and prey go on, with each new offensive technique countered by another of more or less effectiveness. Curiously, it is the relative imperfection in both arenas that allows continuation of both species, for when interdependent specialization proceeds past a certain point neither can survive alone.

5 There are many examples in which the evolution of one species has been partly or entirely dependent upon that of another. An example of total mutual dependence is that between the termite and certain species of protozoans that live in their stomachs (Farb, 1959). This relationship developed because termites cannot digest cellulose, whereas protozoans can; but protozoans cannot bite into wood fibers to obtain it. The entire colony of termites is fed by mutual regurgitation, and with the food go the protozoans. Most termites harbor between one and three species of protozoans, but in each race of termites the specific protozoans are the same. There is one protozoan that exists only in two termite species, a Californian and an African species, and nowhere else in the world. In every instance neither the termite nor the protozoan can survive without the other (Farb, 1959).

Cuckoos never raise their own young; they deposit their eggs in unrelated birds' nests. As these other birds will either abandon nests with strange eggs in them or push the intruders out, evolution of "egg mimicry" has developed in the cuckoo, so that its egg will look exactly like the other eggs in the nest. The astonishing aspect of this adaptation is that in different areas cuckoos have entirely different types of eggs, depending upon the eggs of the other species (Baker, 1942).

Butterflies and moths like *Caligo* and *Precis* have developed wings that, when spread, mimic three-dimensional owl eyes, thus effectively frightening away predators (Blest, 1957). The Noctriidae, Geometridae, and Arctriidae families of night-flying moths, which are prey for bats, have developed receptors capable of "hearing" bats' ultrasonic cries from more than 100 feet, enabling them to take evasive action (Roeder, 1965).

Interdependent evolution also exists in higher animals and plants. The *Orphrys* orchid mimics the appearances and odors of certain female species of bees and wasps, so that it will be pollinated by male insects attempting to copulate with it (Stebbins and Ferlan, 1956).

Birds that have consistently served as prey for hawks are able to respond to a particular experimental stimulus (a short neck) by taking evasive action. This stimulus, when moved backward, looks as if it has the long neck of a goose and thus does not evoke the escape response. Domesticated birds do not exhibit the typical response, thus demonstrating fairly rapid adaptation (Manning, 1967).

The Amphiprion (fish) and Stoichactis (sea anemone) also exhibit mutual dependence. The fish gains protection from the anemone while dropping food to it. But the nematocysts in the anemone's tentacles are dangerous, so the fish must first go through a period of acclimatization by building up mucus on its skin to raise the threshold of discharge (Davenport and Norris, 1958). This response reflects a relatively recent interdependence because of the necessity for acclimatization.

References

Adolph, E. F., Barker, J. P., & Hay, P. A. Multiple factors in thirst. *American Journal of Physiology,* 1954, 178: 538-562.

Anliker, J., & Mayer, J. The regulation of food intake: Some experiments relating behavioral, metabolic, and morphologic aspects. In *Symposium on nutrition and behavior.* New York: National Vitamin Foundation, 1957.

Arnold, M. *Emotion and personality.* Vol. 2. *Neurological and physiological aspects.* New York: Columbia University Press, 1960.

Baker, E. C. S. *Cuckoo problems.* London: Witherby, 1942.

Batini, C., *et al.* Effects of complete pontine transecticns on sleep-wakefulness rhythm: the midpontine pretrigeminal preparation. *Archives Italiennes de Biologie,* 1959, 97: 1-12.

Blest, A. D. The function of the eyespot patterns in the Lepidoptera. *Behavior,* 1957, 11: 209-256.

Bolles, R. C. *Theory of motivation.* New York: Harper & Row, 1967.

Bolles, R. C., & de Lorge, J. Exploration in a Dashiell maze as a function of prior deprivation, current deprivation and sex. *Canadian Journal of Psychology,* 1962, 16: 221-227.

Boring, E. *A history of experimental Psychology.* New York: Appleton-Century Crofts, 1950.

Brower, L. P., & Brower, J. van Z. Experimental studies of mimicry: Reaction of toads to bumble bees and their Asilid-fly mimics. *Proceedings of the 11th International Congress of Entomology,* 1960, 3: 258.

Campbell, B. A., & Sheffield, F. D. Relation of random activity to food deprivation. *Journal of Comparative and Physiological Psychology,* 1953, 46: 320-322.

Carlson, A. J. *The control of hunger in health and disease.* Chicago: University of Chicago Press, 1916.

Cross, B. A. The hypothalamus in mammalian homeostasis. *Symposium of the Society for Experimental Biology and Medicine,* 1964, 18, 157-194.

Davenport, D., & Norris, K. S. Observations on the symbiosis of the sea anemone Stoichactis and the pomacentrid fish, Amphiprion Percula. *Biological Bulletin,* 1958, 115: 397-410.

Dethier, V. G. Vision. In K. D. Roeder (ed.), *Insect physiology.* New York: Wiley, 1953.

Duke-Elder, S. *System of ophthalmology:* Vol. 1. *The eye in evolution.*
London: Kimpton, 1958.

Farb, P. *Living earth.* New York: Pyramid, 1959.

French, J. D. The reticular formation. *Scientific American,* 1957, 196(5):
54-60.

Frossberg, A., and Larsson, S. On the hypothalamic organization of the nervous mechanism regulating food intake. 2. Studies of isotope distribution
and chemical composition in the hypothalamic region of hungry and fed rats.
Acta Physiologica Scandinavica (Supple. 115), 1954, 32: 41-63.

Glickman, S. E. Reinforcing properties of arousal. *Journal of Comparative
and Physiological Psychology,* 1960, 53: 68.

Goz, H. Über den Art- und Individualgeruch bei Fischen. *Zeitschriftfur
verglelchende Physiologie,* 1941, 29: 1-45.

Heath, R. G. (ed.). *Studies in schizophrenia.* Cambridge: Harvard University
Press, 1954.

Hyden, N. H., & Lange, P. W. Rhythmic enzyme changes in neurons and glia
during sleep. *Science,* 1965, 149: 654-656.

Kellogg, W. N. *Porpoises and sonar.* Chicago: University of Chicago Press, 1961.

Lettvin, J. U., *et al.* What the frog's eye tells the frog's brain. *Proceedings of
the Institute of Radio Engineers,* 1959, 47: 1940-1951.

Levitt, E. E. *The psychology of anxiety.* New York: McGraw-Hill, 1965.

Lissmann, H. W. Continuous electrical signals from the tail of a fish, *Gym-
narchus niloticus. Nature* (London), 1951, 167: 201-202.

Lissmann, H. W. Electric location by fishes. *Scientific American,* 1963, 208:
50-59.

Manning, A. *An introduction to animal behavior.* Reading, Mass.: Addison
Wesley, 1967.

Marler, P. Characteristics of some animal calls. *Nature,* 1955, 176: 6-8.

Mayer, J. Regulation of energy intake and the body weight: The glucostatic
theory and the lipostatic hypothesis. *Annual of the New York Academy of
Sciences,* 1955, 63: 15-43.

Morgan, C. T. *Physiological psychology.* New York: McGraw-Hill, 1965.

Mueller, Johannes. *Handbuch der Physiologie des Menschen,* II, Book V.
Philadelphia: Lea and Blanchard, 1843.

Olds, J. Differentiation of reward systems in the brain by self-stimulation
techniques. In Ramey and O'Doherty (eds.), *Electrical studies and the unanesthetized brain.* New York: Harper & Row, 1960.

Olds, J., & Peretz, B. A motivational analysis of the reticular activating system.
Electroencephalography and Clinical Neurophysiology, 1960, 12: 445.

Passano, L. M. Prey-predator recognition in the lower invertebrates. In B. T.
Scheer (ed.), *Recent advances in invertebrate physiology.* Eugene, Oregon:
University of Oregon, 1957.

Payne, R. S. How the barn owl locates prey by hearing. *The Living Bird,*
1962, 1: 151-159.

Pumphrey, R. J. Sensory organs: Hearing. In A. J. Marshall (ed.), *Biology
and comparative physiology of birds.* Vol. 2. New York: Academic Press,
1961.

Ratner, S. C., & Denny, M. R. *Comparative psychology: Research in animal
behavior.* Homewood, Ill.: Dorsey, 1964.

Roeder, K. D. *Nerve cells and insect behavior.* Cambridge: Harvard University
Press, 1963.

Roeder, K. D. Moths and ultrasound. *Scientific American,* April 1965, Vol. 212, pp. 94-102.

Scott, W. W., Scott, C. C., & Luckhardt, A. B. Observations in the blood sugar level, before, during and after hunger periods in humans. *American Journal of Physiology,* 1938, 123: 243-247.

Stebbins, G. L., & Ferlan, L. Population variability, hybridization, and introgression in some species of Orphrys. *Evolution,* 1956, 10: 32-56.

Thorpe, W. H., & Griffin, D. R. The lack of ultrasonic components in the flight noise of owls compared with other birds. *Ibis,* 1962, 104: 256-257.

Waterman, T. H. Light sensitivity and vision. In T. H. Waterman (ed.), *The physiology of the crustacea.* Vol. 2. New York: Academic Press, 1961.

Wenger, M. A., Jones, F. N., & Jones, M. H. *Physiological psychology.* New York: Holt, Rinehart and Winston, 1956.

4

Primary Encoding

In Chapter 3 we defended the view that the various transmitting mechanisms, both central and peripheral, evolved as essential devices for information gathering and that sensation in all its dimensions is the evolutionary solution to the problem of input in complex organisms. Inside and on the surface of the human body there are literally thousands of specialized nerve endings: some scattered widely, some clustered at particular loci, but all reacting to particular kinds and intensities of energy change and capable of instigating functionally pertinent experience.

It is now necessary to posit a central area into which all these inputs are being continuously fed. Such an *integration matrix* is necessitated by the simple fact that accumulation of information without integration would be nonadaptive. The human being (and probably all mammals) is bombarded, at least while awake, by hundreds of inputs from energy changes that are taking place inside him and around him. An overt response to each of these components as it occurred would be impossible, because of structural limitations; it would also lead to completely unorganized behavior. An organism that responded to each of the myriad sensory inputs being introduced could not survive even in its elementary form, let alone make the long journey to our present stage of evolution.

The integration matrix, then, is a construct reflecting conditions that must have existed in the evolutionary context. As human beings are products of evolution and are certainly complex organisms, they may have such matrices. What has been called the "field of consciousness" or in Wilhelm Von Wundt's term *Blickfeld* is, in our view, the sensory aspect of this matrix,[1] but it involves more than sensory input alone. It includes all of the sensory *and* memory material that is potentially available for focalization (see Chapter 6). The term "central area" implies a site in the brain where the various integration processes actually occur; but it seems more realistic to think in terms of central functions, rather than of location as such.

Input fusion and structuring are particularly amorphous topics to discuss partly because of certain traditional ambiguities. Historically, the process of input organization has been subsumed under the term "perception," and part of the difficulty arises from the absence of clear-cut distinctions among sensation, perception, and attention. We shall try to reduce this ambiguity—or at least to provide a more compatible context for our own discussion. Sensation as described in Chapter 3 included *all* the raw experiential input from the various transmitting mechanisms of the body. Perception, on the other hand, refers to the particular unity, form, and organization (input fusion and structuring) that such raw sensory components come to assume *automatically* because of either learning or innate processes. "Attention" (the term "apperception" seems preferable, as we shall see later) refers to the process by which inputs (sensory or memory) come briefly into focus.

A study of sensation, then, must deal with raw experiential input per se; an analysis of perception must concentrate on the manner in which such sensory materials are fused and structured; an evaluation of apperception must focus on the variables that affect the rapid shifting from one component to the next. This last problem constitutes the paramount task of psychology, according to our view, and will be discussed in Chapter 6. Let us now consider, however, the specific issue of input fusion and structuring that has classically been subsumed under the label "perception."

A simple example will clarify the problem. An adult human being perceives a three-dimensional world populated by such phenomena as trees, chairs, and houses, which are always changing in shape, size, brightness, and proximity. This world and the entities that populate it appear to have remarkable constancy and simplicity, despite such continuous fluctuation. A particular phenomenon is perceived as "the same," even though "it" rarely, if ever, activates receptors in precisely the same manner on different occasions. We may hypothesize, as did William James (1890), that the experience of the newborn baby consists of an undifferentiated panorama of input from various transmitting mechanisms. Bits of input follow one another in chaotic disarray, a "booming, buzzing confusion." Yet in a remarkably short time the perception of phenomena within three-dimensional space begins and assumes an orderly progression.

Certain basic questions emerge from this brief consideration. What are the relative influences of "heredity process" and "experiential input" in the development of this three-dimensional space populated with entities? How are discrete sensory inputs synthesized as whole experiences? How do we perceive movement? From what source does our notion of time come?

Heredity versus Environment

As such problems are traditional in psychology and yet remain largely unresolved, a brief historical review may prove helpful in clarifying them and in setting the stage for our own treatment. First, we should note two obvious positions on the genesis of perceptual fusion and structuring: called the "nativist" and the "empiricist" positions. The most extreme nativist would insist that such organizations result entirely from inborn processes; the most extreme empiricist would insist that all such patterning is derived from characteristics of experiential input. For obvious reasons there have been few defenders of either extreme position. Even the most radical empiricist must admit (though some have failed to do so publicly) the existence of an innate process that arranges experiential cues in prescribed ways, and the most zealous nativist must concede that the innate structuring properties of the organism must have some experiential input on which to work before their existence can be demonstrated. The issue remains very much alive, with one group insisting that innate processes are most important and the other replying that the structure of perception is determined by the organism's "transactions" with its environment.

History

The early empiricists, and Aristotle as well, held the view that the "mind" is a tabula rasa and that knowledge is derived solely from experience. Curiously, the first hint that experience can be affected by inherent factors came from the empiricist James Mill (1829). Although he thought that each sensory component is in some fashion still represented in the whole, he spoke of amalgamation of such elements into a composite *different* from its elements. He applied the term "fusion" to this amalgamation. It is true that he was interested in such relatively simple examples of composites as "noise" and "hue," which result when different sound- or light-wave frequencies are presented simultaneously, but he did contribute the suggestion that the fused elements produce entirely unique experiential wholes. Even among the ranks of the empiricists an inherent process was implicitly assumed, for how else could they explain such amalgamation?

Mill's concept of fusion was the direct antecedent of his son John Stuart Mill's *mental chemistry* and Wundt's *creative synthesis.* It was no longer assumed that the parts are still contained within the whole, though the principle remained the same: Sensory components when presented simultaneously can result in a composite different from its parts. In the concepts of fusion, mental chemistry, and creative synthesis we find the first hints of experimental phenomenology: the view that the ways in which sensory inputs are combined into wholes different from their parts can be determined empirically. Neither

John Stuart Mill nor Wundt paid more than lip service to this approach, however; Mill was content with philosophical commentary, and Wundt was more interested in discovering the elements of experience than in studying what happened when they are combined. With the advent of behaviorism the emphasis shifted away from experience altogether. It seems ironic that in behavioral terminology (like "stimulus complex" or "stimulus manifold") Mill's notion of combinations of elements is unmistakably embodied.

Experimental phenomenology has been the province mainly of Gestalt and neo-Gestalt psychologists. C. von Ehrenfels' *form qualities* are certainly wholes derived from combination of elements, but not until M. Wertheimer did we have clear demonstrations of phenomena that were determined by the manner in which sensory components are presented. Even the Gestalt psychologists, however, neglected the problem of how perception of phenomena emerges from raw experiential input. It is true that they have heavily emphasized the innate organizing principles of perception—in particular *pregnanz,* as exemplified in operation of subsidiary principles like "figure-ground reversal," "closure," and so on—but these principles are related primarily to general structuring of the perceptual field, rather than to perception of phenomena per se. Indeed it seems that in Gestalt psychology phenomena are considered as simple givens derived from innate ways of knowing. When Gestaltists discuss the brain field, which generates the form that perception assumes, they take for granted the presence of phenomena *within* this field. We may thus assume that a tiger standing on a bland terrain will stand out as "figure," but the Gestaltists offer no explanation of the circumstances that produce perception of the phenomenon "tiger"; they simply affirm that inherent factors are responsible.

Gestalt principles could have been tested experimentally for their relative applicability to both the development and consequent perception of phenomena, but this work has never been done. The antipathy toward historical variables common to most Gestalt psychologists and their fixation on the *experimentum crucis,* that is, phenomena immediately demonstrated by experiencing, have both undoubtedly contributed to the relative sterility of their thinking in this respect.

Similar criticisms can be addressed to the transactionalists. They too have been primarily interested in the general structure of perception, though they have tried to consider it as a product of the organism's interactions with its environment. G. Berkeley was the first transactionalist; in *New Theory of Vision* (1709) he stated the notion that has been basic to the movement, from R. H. Lotze (1852) and H. L. F. V. Helmholtz (1924) to modern adherents: that the structure of perception is derived from cues given in experience. Most transactionalists assume an innate capacity for cue arrangement, but they all insist that perceptual organization has its genesis in experience and develops gradually as the child grows older. The general orientation of the transactionalists might lead us to expect intensive investigation of the variables accounting for the emergence of phenomena from experiential input, but such work has not yet materialized. They have traditionally been more interested in sensory cues related to localization of sound, perception of three-dimensional space, and the constancies.

Although human beings undeniably perceive spatial and temporal contexts populated with phenomena, there are remarkably few data on the genesis of phenomena and only a few more on the development of the perceptual context. The nativists insist that phenomena are directly experienced through the effects of innate process on experiential input, without intervening learning. The empiricists, on the other hand, insist that perception of phenomena is derived from experienced cues and is thus a function of the organism's prolonged interaction with its environment. As for experimental evidence, the antagonists are at a stalemate.

To what extent are fusion and structuring direct manifestations of inherited processes? Today there is an environmental bias in views of the genesis of perceptual organization: Such organization is assumed to originate in the manner in which cues are experienced, rather than being already fully operative when sensory input is imposed. Although we are largely in agreement with this bias, at least as far as human beings are concerned, the alternative position cannot simply be dismissed.

Relative Adaptive Contributions

What kind of perceptual organization would allow an organism the greatest adaptative facility? The nativist interpretation would win by definition, if time involved in adaptation were the criterion. But would such a gain in time impose inflexibility sufficient to outweigh the adaptation advantages obtained? All intrinsic characteristics—reflexes, instincts, and possibly perceptual organization—contribute to rapid and efficient reactions in appropriate circumstances, but they inevitably exact their price in reduced flexibility. If the nativist view of perceptual organization is correct, even the youngest organism can profit, but it must then bear the burden of inflexibility for life. Is the initial advantage worth the price? In many species it probably is. Relatively simple organisms restricted to narrow environmental niches and already bound by inherited behavior mechanisms might gain more from intrinsic perceptual organization appropriate to their particular survival problems than they would lose. They are already so "stimulus bound" that a little more inflexibility would not matter much.

There is another point, difficult to formulate, which may be pertinent here. Innate mechanisms seem to come in "constellations." An inherent "technique" reduces general flexibility, thus increasing the probability that other inflexible mechanisms will also be integrated into a process repertory. If the evolutionary solution to a particular survival problem has been development of an instinctive pattern, it is very likely that other inherited mechanisms will also be found. Conversely, the more solutions to specific survival problems can be learned, the greater is the probability that flexibility will prevail in other areas. Integration requirements alone may thus determine whether or not organisms guided mainly by inherited behavior mechanisms will also be bound by intrinsic and inflexible perceptual organization.

In certain organisms one specific and vitally important survival requirement may tip the balance in favor of innate process: The young of many species must begin to move through space immediately after they are born. Intrinsic perceptual organization thus contributes more to adaptation facility than it subtracts. Many mammals are probably born with the ability to see depth and to respond appropriately to objects at varying distances from them, but human beings and other anthropoids probably are not. Because the young are cared for by their parents during the more vulnerable stages of their life, the survival value of this attribute is not high enough to justify the corresponding inflexibility. Furthermore, at least in human infants motor facility is so rudimentary during the first few weeks of life that such organization would not be functional anyway. Our notion of process "constellations" should not be forgotten. The almost universal human use of learning in other areas of adaptation may require flexibility in perceptual organization as well. We thus accept a generally— but not entirely—empiricist interpretation of perceptual organization in the human being.

Not even the most avid empiricist can deny, however, that certain innate factors profoundly affect the integration matrix of the human being. The most obvious kind of influence is that experience comes to us already divided into separate and distinct modes. As thinkers like John Locke, Charles Bell, and Johannes Mueller have pointed out, and as we have discussed in Chapter 3, each transmitting mechanism introduces input with its own characteristic quality and sometimes a degree of vividness peculiar to itself. Both the quality and the relative vividness of sensory material are doubtless functions of the organism's structure. No matter how often a person has seen red or been thirsty, hungry, in pain, or nauseated, the characteristic nature of the input remains unchanged.

Furthermore, as the different organ systems that constitute the human body reflect the various conditions that shaped the organism during its evolutionary journey, it seems not unreasonable to infer that at least some of the ways in which sensory input is organized may also represent such circumstances. Our receptors have come to reflect particular types and intensities of energy shift; why should not innate organization of perception directly reflect long-term consistencies in the environment during evolution?

We *are* suggesting that the axioms of Euclidian geometry may be innately represented. In the struggle for survival a straight line has always been the shortest distance between predator and prey, between the hunted and a tree, and this bit of basic information may be intrinsically represented in our species—

as may the other geometrical axioms as well. We are not avid supporters of René Descartes, Immanuel Kant, and Ewald Hering, but we do believe that an organism shaped by natural selection probably reflects in both its internal processes and its external appearance certain enduring consistencies of its survival context.

In all candor, we have never been impressed by the empiricists' refutation of the nativists' arguments. Helmholtz is not convincing in his discussion of geometrical axioms, in which he posits another kind of world, perhaps *inside* a sphere, where the Euclidian axioms would not hold; in such a context the shortest distance between two points would *not* be a straight line, parallel lines *would* meet, and so on. He seems to have forgotten that *we* live on the outside of a sphere, where the same logic should apply. More important, he failed to take evolution into account. Even if we hypothesize a galaxy of non-Euclidian worlds we cannot assume that a creature similar to a human being would evolve in any of them. The organisms that would develop in such strange contexts would also be strange and might manifest within their innate process systems the non-Euclidian character of their worlds; when pursued they might run in curves or indulge in spiral flight. Helmholtz's other argument, that the geometrical axioms must be derived from experience because experience is required to demonstrate them, is even more disappointing. That a principle requires experience for its demonstration tells us nothing about its genesis. We might as well argue that spiders learn to spin their webs because researchers observe the spinning process with their eyes!

Regardless of how we explain the geometrical axioms or try to relate them to perception, one conclusion seems evident: Inherent factors must underlie *all* fusion and structuring. Whether we believe that perceptual organization is present at birth or must await certain cues, the nativist conclusion holds. The real issue, then, is whether learning is required for perceptual organization to take place or whether such organization automatically occurs with the first input. Let us assume for the moment what is probably true, that the capacity to organize experienced cues is inborn but that it depends for its actualization upon certain characteristics of sensory input. The question now becomes: Which characteristics of input are most important in the emergence of the perception of phenomena within the confines of three-dimensional space?

The Emergence of Phenomena

To begin our discussion of this question, let us reconsider certain characteristics of the survival context. A realistic position is implicit in an evolutionary orientation; that is, we presume the existence of organisms and an environment external to them. Two further inferences about the external environment are possible. First, it consists of many relatively distinct units that vary in their distances from one another. Second, such units are in a process of constant change. Some of them, rocks and trees, for example, shift only in reaction to contact with other features of the environment, whereas others, like organisms and machines, react in this way and are also capable of locomotion. The external environment of any given organism thus consists of fluctuating entities located at varying distances from one another. It is in such a context that species have evolved.

Let us schematize those features of the external environment that are crucial to survival as fluctuating blobs located at varying distances from one another. We might predict that the capacity to perceive phenomena within three-dimensional space would emerge in complex organisms, but which characteristics of input would be most critical in the emergence of such perception? There seem to be two, though one is more basic than the other.

"Edgeness"

We believe that the fundamental sensory characteristic is "edgeness." Things have edges, which are represented in sensory input as continuous linearity. No particular form is required, but the input must be qualitatively distinct from other input within the integration matrix. When such unique input occurs, a "blob" emerges in perception. There can be little doubt that the perception of edges is totally the result of innate processes: The visual receptor system reveals an intrinsic responsiveness to variations in brightness and color. As edges, at least in the visual modality, are always manifest in terms of brightness or color differences between thing and other thing, the ability to recognize them must be present in the first visual exposures of the child, assuming the receptors have matured sufficiently to be responsive. "Edgeness," according to our view, is then the most fundamental attribute of the perception of things. It arises from shifts in reflection characteristics between thing and other thing. As the receptor responds automatically to light-wave frequency and amplitude variations, perception of "edgeness" is affected little by learning.[3]

Although there is always danger in such extrapolation, some recent work with animals has emphasized the fundamental role of "edgeness" in the visual transmitting mechanism. J. U. Lettvin and his associates (1959) discovered two types of receptors for "edgeness" in the frog's eye: sustained-contrast detectors for stationary contours and moving-edge detectors. In an even more striking piece of research, D. H. Hubel and T. N. Wiesel (1962) succeeded in isolating in the cat cortical neurons that fire only when the retina is stimulated by edges at specific angles. That is, groups of retinal receptors must be stimulated along specific straight lines in order to excite *particular* neurons in the visual cortex.

It seems very likely that the resolving mechanism for edges became more central as organisms became more complex. But, regardless of the manner in which this characteristic is fed into the system, it still remains fundamental to all perception of things. That it depends upon gradients of the stimulation of receptors—whatever the specific nature or distribution of these receptors—seems beyond doubt. Without edges to stimulate receptors differentially the field of vision itself would be undifferentiated; a bland, amorphous continuity. It is true that edges need not be sharp, but there must be some shift in activation of receptors, however gradual, or the field will remain unpopulated. In this discussion we have dealt primarily with vision, but the same logic holds for all other transmitting mechanisms. Sounds also have edges, as do tastes and tactual input; in every instance the characteristics that define the edges are shifts in receptor activation.

Movement

Another characteristic of the environment is almost as basic as is "edgeness," and it undoubtedly plays a crucial role in both the perception of things and the emergence of perception of three-dimensional space. We refer to movement, both actual and relative. As an organism moves, other items in its environment appear to shift in relation to one another; if a particular item in the environment changes position it always does so against a more static background.

The newborn baby not only sees edges; it also sees edges that are constantly shifting and coalescing, overlapping, changing in shape, changing in size, and changing in distinctness. And in every instance such change is produced by variations in reflection characteristics, which occasion differential responses in the receptors. As the experience of movement is derived from shifts in "edgeness," its perception is as likely to be intrinsically founded as is the perception of the edge itself. We refer again to Lettvin's remarkable study and to the "bug perceiving" mechanism discussed in Chapter 3. Lettvin and his colleagues demonstrated that movement provides such a basic form of information for frogs that it is represented by specific receptors in the eye: The eye, rather than the brain, is the critical "resolving organ" for this information. Does the human eye also have receptors specific to movement? Probably not. The input underlying our perception of movement is derived from differential stimulation of generalized receptors in the eye, but actual resolution is very likely accomplished by some central mechanism. We may still ask, however, why human beings see *continuous* movement, a bird flying, for example. As an item moves across the visual field *different* receptors are activated; why then do we not see movement as series of little jumps?

Wertheimer's experiments on apparent movement have probably answered this question and perhaps contributed much more. Let us review his findings. We recall that, when horizontal and vertical lights flashed alternately approximately twenty times a second, the subject saw the light "moving" from one position to the other. When the frequency of alternation was increased to approximately forty flashes a second the subject saw each light as stationary and without flicker. It appears that Wertheimer actually measured the duration of the neural reverberation occasioned by each light stimulus; that movement "emerged" when the interval during which each light shone exceeded the period required to dissipate the reverberations of the previous stimulus. Increasing the frequency demonstrated the same principle, except that then the reverberatory "overlap" occurred relative to each individual light. Although there may be a gap between the units of energy imposed, there is thus no gap in the sensory input introduced. Each such reverberation must last approximately one-twentieth of a second, and when any imposed energy exceeds this frequency the gap in the sensory input disappears. We believe that the same principle that accounts for the lower absolute threshold for pitch also accounts for the apparent movement demonstrated by Wertheimer. In the former instance the continuous tone, rather than the separate stimulus, is heard when reverberation from the last unit of energy overlaps with the reaction to the present one. If the same frequency is involved in each succeeding unit, a constant unvarying tone is heard, but if the frequency shifts the tone "moves" up or down the scale. In both the perception of tones and the perception of apparent movement, continuing experience is derived from discrete inputs occurring sufficiently close together to occasion reverberatory overlap.

Indeed, this principle can be extended to explain the perception of all movement. Usually when any object is changing its position relative to the background, the shift in light energy imposed occurs so rapidly that there is reverberatory overlap between the object as "just seen" and the object as "now seen"; just as we perceive successive "stills" in film as moving pictures. Shifting edges and reverberatory overlap between the edge as just seen and the edge as now seen account for movement. The innate factors that make such perception possible are the differential activation of receptors, reverberation of the transmitting mechanism once it has been activated, and an unknown process that translates overlapping inputs into perceived movement.

This interpretation raises another problem, which every organism must resolve if it is to survive: how to differentiate between changes in receptors produced by the organism's own movements and those occasioned by the movement of other entities in the environment. There is a shift in the reflection characteristics of objects impinging on the retina whether the individual moves his eyes, his head, or his entire body—or simply observes something else changing its position. Yet somehow the organism automatically subtracts the effects of its own movements and makes fair judgments of the motion of things external to it. Obviously this ability is critical to adaptation. An organism that could not distinguish between the retinal changes produced by its own movements and those produced by other motion within its environment would have little chance of surviving.

What cues occasion such subtraction? Certainly they must include some characteristic of the visual input that is present when the organism moves but is not present or is altered when something in the environment moves. Careful analysis suggests that a critical cue may be movement parallax. When an organism moves forward, all other items in its environment appear to shift backward in corresponding and consistent progression, but when something in the environment moves this consistent progression is missing completely.

But what happens when *both* the organism and items in the environment are moving simultaneously? The organism can still subtract the effects of its own movement and make fair judgments of the velocity of external movement. How? Once again, movement parallax or a subsidiary cue implicit in movement parallax seems primarily responsible: From the vantage point of the observer there is a consistent increase in the velocity of items as a function of decreasing distance. We can check this notion: If we shake our heads we note that items nearer to us "move" more rapidly than do those farther away. When any item fails to shift with a velocity consonant with that of the other items at the same distance, that item itself is automatically perceived as moving; it stands out as does an erratic goose in a migratory formation.

But what happens if the head is held still and the eyes alone are moved? Different retinal points are stimulated, but there is no movement parallax to serve as a cue that one aspect of the organism, rather than something in the environment, is moving—yet the whole environment does not appear to move. To complicate the problem even further, it is easy to demonstrate that we see items in ordinary motion through an arc before our eyes while we are simultaneously moving our eyes back and forth. There obviously must be cues other than movement parallax that permit subtraction of the effects of eye movement in such situations. What are they? Perhaps they are derived from the movement of the eyes per se and from the lack of input normally derived from the movement of head or body. Every organism with a movable eye has certainly had sufficient experience in following moving objects with its eyes to develop kinesthetic cues important in such an essential subtraction.[4]

The issue is very likely more complex than we have indicated. Many cues may combine, as in depth perception, to provide the basis for effective and expedient solution to movement problems. No problem is more critical for survival, and it is most likely that any process that important would involve several complementary and even overlapping indicators. Fortunately, the problem is open to research; it should be fairly easy to devise a context in which the background, various intervening stimuli, the subject's eyes, and his head can all be systematically manipulated to determine the contribution of different cues to the perception of different kinds of movement.

We believe that both actual and relative movement underlie the emergence of the figure-ground effect in visual perception and that learning plays an important part in its manifestation. When, as a function of learning, the two basic determinants of perception of things—"edgeness" and movement—are supplemented by such traditional cues as convergence, parallax, accommodation, and perspective, perception of phenomena in three-dimensional space occurs.

"Something" Perception

That items in the environment have reflection characteristics different from those of their context has been responsible for the emergence of the most basic constancy: the constancy of unity. The edge of any thing goes completely *around* it, and this characteristic is universal. The basic information that items exist as unities becomes integrated and is unconsciously imposed on everything that we see. The Gestalt psychologists have long interpreted the phenomenon of closure as the result of an innate organizing principle. There may be such a principle, but it is not necessarily innate. More probably it is derived from the automatic—and irresistible—tendency to perceive items as wholes, though this tendency emerges from countless experiences of items with reflection characteristics that distinguish them as units from the surrounding field.

We may assume that this automatic "coercion" of sensory input is manifest early in the child's life, so that from then on he perceives "blobs" within a three-dimensional context. Almost immediately, and probably concomitantly with this process, "something" perception emerges. The fundamental circumstance underlying this emergence is probably the recurrence of similar sensory inputs.

It has been noted by a number of observers, beginning with G. M. Stratton, that the process underlying perceptual organization is so malleable that it can be altered by relatively short experience with inverting lenses.[5] It therefore seems reasonable to assume that this process has already had certain basic effects, which have become relatively stable by the time that the child is two or three months old. He is probably already capable of perceiving "blobs" within a three-dimensional context, even before "something" perception begins. But, as similar "blobs" of sensory input recur again and again, "something" perception does emerge. The "blob" that initially represented the child's mother becomes a "something." All items in the child's environment gradually emerge from their nebulous state into the familiarity of "something."

Although each "blob" of input is constantly changing in size, shape, and brightness, the child soon comes to perceive all items in his environment with comparative accuracy. Once again the automatic and irresistible character of the perceptual process is demonstrated. Regardless of the fact that the retinal image of a particular item is in constant flux, the child automatically perceives it as the same item. We may surmise that the "warping effect" of the organizing process is in the direction of the most common characteristics of a given item. The child learns to perceive the window as rectangular, simply because when he directly faces the window the image *is* rectangular. Without doubt he sees it more often as a trapezoid, but only one rectangle is possible, whereas an almost limitless number of trapezoids is possible. The one single form that is imposed more often than any other is therefore the one that becomes predominant.

The warping effect of the perceptual process also occasions coercion toward the most common size and brightness of a given item. A piece of coal appears

black, regardless of how much light is reflected from it—as long as it retains
its "something" status. But if sufficient cues for recognition are removed it
will revert to a "blob," and brightness constancy will break down. To reverse
the logic, constancy will not emerge until a given item has been presented sufficiently often to become familiar, and coercion always operates in the direction
of the most frequent size, shape, or brightness of the stimulus. The particular
context within which a given item occurs is also important in determining perception. For example, another human being in a relatively unfamiliar context
may be used as the scale for size and distance of other items in the environment.

Summary

The type of learning that helps to account for perceptual organization is far
different from that ordinarily considered in traditional discussions of the topic.
Perceptual learning, which we call "primary encoding," is, as Helmholtz has
suggested, unconscious and irresistible. Once such structuring has occurred it
remains relatively fixed and is automatically manifest whenever input is presented. Such learning is basic to the figure-ground effect and to the organizing
principles that the Gestalt psychologists believe to be innate. Primary encoding
thus determines the form that sensory input will assume whenever it is introduced again.

We therefore postulate that human beings, and probably most mammals, are
structured so that the organization of sensory cues depends upon the manner
in which they are presented. The primary encoding process that occasions such
organization is innate, but sensory material must be presented in certain prescribed ways before it will be structured. "Edgeness" is considered the basic
attribute underlying perception of "things," whereas movement, both relative
and absolute, is probably essential to development of perception of three dimensions. Perception of "something" probably results from recurrent presentation
of similar inputs and emerges after more primitive structuring has taken place.
Constancies in perception result from recurrent presentation of similar components. Warping of the primary encoding process while the context is held constant tends toward the characteristic that has been presented most often.

We consider the primary encoding process to have two fundamental equilibratory characteristics: active coercion of sensory input so that it assumes
organization and subsequent retention of this organization. That is, there is a
drive toward phenomenological emergence, and there is another drive toward
phenomenological integrity.

Primary encoding thus involves three interdependent, though functionally
distinguishable, outcomes. First is the emergence of spatial context, based on
the intrinsic capacity of receptor systems to respond to edges and movement
and abetted by cues arising (at least in vision) from convergence, parallax, accommodation, and the like. Second is emergence of phenomena occasioned by
the simultaneous introduction of inputs from the same and different modalities.

Finally, constancies develop from the recurrence of phenomena under many different conditions of brightness, distance, and perspective. When these three principles operate simultaneously, the perceptual world of the human being is relatively complete and has achieved its maximum level of functioning. This discussion leads us to the following postulate of perception.

Fusion and structuring simplify function by integrating certain enduring consistencies of the environment in a framework that determines the unity, continuity, and context of ordinary sensory input.

Time

The simple fact that it is impossible to maintain a steady state in any organism that is in perpetual interaction with an ever-changing environment means that rhythm is intrinsic to life. There is constant alternation between overbalancing and surges of compensatory activity. There are rhythms in every aspect of life: in the homeostatic activities of the cell, in the heart beating, in food ingestion, in elimination of waste, in the estrus cycle of the female rat, and the menstrual cycle of the human female. Almost every life process involves cyclical action. Every organism is comparable to Ptolomy's universe, in which a vast swarm of cyclical mechanisms constitutes an interlocking system of wheels within wheels, each turning at its own tempo.

Rhythm also marks the fluctuations of energy in the natural environment. The earth turns, and night becomes day; it tilts, and winter turns to summer. The moon waxes and wanes, and the tides rise and fall. These and hundreds of other independent and derivative cycles characterize the environment—and probably always did. Organisms came into being in a context full of such rhythms, and it is small wonder that a fundamental synchrony exists between biological and environmental cycles. Not only do organisms represent the environment morphologically; they also reflect it in their cyclical behavior. The daily cycle of color shift in the fiddler crab continues even in perpetual darkness (Brown, 1958). The mussel placed in still water perseveres in its tidal rhythm of water propulsion (Rao, 1954). The palolo worm, true to its lunar impulses, breeds once a year, usually on a single particular day (Clark and Hess, 1943). There are many examples of "biological clocks" that reflect internal homeostatic rhythms or recurrent changes in the environment; each of them determines the tempo of some critical activity. These rhythms are important not only because they demonstrate the close cyclical harmony between environmental change and organic response but also because they suggest solutions to the "problem of time" in human beings.

What is time? In an organism's daily and other rhythms a biological clock appears to be in operation; the dimension of time seems to have become internalized. Surely time must exist as an objective phenomenon? We do not think so. The *pace* of change within the organism or within the environment may be learned or represented genetically, but time need not therefore exist as an objective dimension. Motion, change, process, or whatever we call it characterizes both the environment and the individual, but time we believe exists only for the latter. It is a subjective experience arising from perceptions of change in the environment and in the self. Although the notion of time is derived from, and can have meaning only in relation to, motion, it is not identical with motion, any more than the experience of red is identical with a wave length of 680 millimicrons.

The human being's conception of time is much less discrete and definitive than is his experience of color. It is a learned conceptual structure built up in much the same way as are those for the various constancies: Perceived cues derived from the pace at which our experience fluctuates become fused in a subjective framework for other experiences. Time, like size constancy, exists only in the experience of the observer. In size constancy our most common experience with an object becomes the representation that is cast upon it regardless of the size of the retinal image. In "time constancy" the same thing seems to happen. An average of experienced tempos becomes the representation and is the reference used each time the individual thinks about time in the abstract or makes a judgment of how much time is passing.

In simple creatures the cadence of events important for survival may be internalized, and then time frequently becomes synonymous with a rhythm of responses triggered and sustained by some cyclical stimulus. A rat placed on a fixed-interval schedule encodes in its own body or behavior the rhythm of the schedule. In the human being the cadence of all input, punctuated and emphasized by certain more critical transitions, is also encoded, to provide a subjective summary of the flow of experience. Lower organisms are capable of internalizing (through either learning or heredity) certain critical cadences. And human beings can also internalize the pace of experiential change. They can both perceive motion and encode its tempo, remembering the way things were and comparing it with the way things are now. Human beings are not only aware of succession but have also come to apprehend its pace and to represent the total process in the word "time." As the rhythms of human physiology and the effective environment are very similar, the phenomenon of "time constancy" must be quite similar in all human beings.

If this view of time is correct, each person's "concept of time passing" should be vulnerable to distortion through changes in the ordinary cadence of events. If familiar transitions (either internal or external) are speeded up, subjective time appears to move more slowly; and the reverse. But the subject must not *notice* that there has been a shift in the pace of the transitions, for then he may simply recognize that this or that process has changed its cadence, rather than perceiving a shift in the pace of *time*. When visceral changes are speeded up by means of drugs or fever or when a subject watches a film of familiar activities in faster motion (but not enough for him to notice), he will feel that time is passing more slowly, and each minute, as measured by the clock, should increase in subjective length.[6]

The Emergence and Function of the Autocept

It has been noted that the last organism on earth that we would expect to "discover" water would be a fish. Similarly, what we call the "autocept" has so far eluded explanatory endeavors. We believe, however, that the self emerges as a perceived phenomenon, according to the same principles (see Chapter 2) as those for the emergence of a house or a triangle.

Let us consider the human baby. Even before birth the processes underlying learning and memory are operative. It is also likely that a fair amount of recurrent sensory input is introduced during embryonic life. The beating of the mother's heart and the action of the fetus' own viscera are repetitive and consistent; according to the principles previously discussed, this input becomes fused and provides the basic core of the self.[7] Even while an embryo the individual touches parts of its own body and may indulge in sucking behavior; recurrent input from these activities becomes incorporated.

After brith the number and variety of consistent experiences are dramatically increased. Input from eating, elimination, and breathing is added to the basic core that we have mentioned and to the rhythms of hunger and thirst. When the exteroceptors have matured sufficiently, certain of the recurrent sights, sounds, and touches of the child's immediate environment become integrated. A given autocept is thus at its core a composite of the experiences most frequent and most consistent during the individual's early life: pain, hunger, pleasure, cold, mother's face, and so on. It is a complex of interdependent and overlapping memory representations that have been fused into phenomenological unity. This unity continues to expand and develop as other inputs become incorporated. More and more recurrent experiences are slowly fused into the autocept as the individual matures. Always the beating of the heart and other visceral changes impose continuity, and consistent dual experiences result when the child touches different parts of his body.

Indeed it is this last kind of input that establishes the boundaries of the self. There are no edges, as with trees or houses, but dual stimulation provides an "edge" of sorts. When a child touches something other than his own body, the dual input is absent. As he grows older and has more experience of the difference between "single source" and "dual source" inputs, the boundary between self and nonself becomes clearer.

In Chapter 2 we suggested that the autocept has several adaptive functions. It is a simplifying mechanism that effectively integrates the most proximal and recurrent experiences. As the individual experiences himself as a unity, a threat comes to affect not isolated aspects but the entire self, thus facilitating integrated

behavior. Perpetual feedback from the actions of the viscera and certain enduring memory residuals provide a basis for identity and allow continuity of the
organism through time. For instance, the memory residual of one's mother's
face is a lasting encode, remaining relatively unchanged. Apperception of this
encode and other basic memories provides a fundamental bridge across the gaps
of sleep and the perpetual fluctuations of other inputs. But the most important
function of the autocept—and one that we shall examine at length in later chapters—is to furnish an effective "need" system, which serves to direct and maintain the organism's behavior.

Volitional Behavior

"Volitional behavior" has been a persistently troublesome issue in the development of a theory of the human being. Such activity seems to be directed
by some agency independent of—or even opposed to—basic requirements of the
organism. For example, the human being apparently can disregard other imperative needs and spend his time thinking about an inconsequential subject.
"I" may, if "I" choose, spend the next five minutes thinking about sedimentary
rocks, a topic that interests "me" not at all. This ability "willfully" to direct
behavior, to choose among alternatives, to suppress certain materials and to
emphasize others, as well as the feeling of freedom concomitant with such activity, has been the source of great satisfaction to those who believe in "freedom
of the will" and a challenge to those who conceive of human behavior as lawful in all respects. Any comprehensive theory of human beings must deal with
this problem; a failure to do so is a fundamental failure, for "volitional activity"
is a basic characteristic of man's nature.

It is our position that so-called "volitional behavior" results when something
threatens the integrity of that intricately fused composite the autocept. It is
thus directly dependent upon the extent of fusion that has occurred. This
point is clearly demonstrated in the child's inability to sustain concentration on
a topic for any length of time—unless, of course, the activity is directly related
to one or more of the obvious need systems. As age advances and more recurrent inputs are integrated into the autocept, the ability to concentrate on the
uninteresting becomes fairly refined until, by the time the child reaches college,
many teachers and textbook writers can capitalize on this attribute with varying
degrees of effectiveness.

As we mentioned in Chapter 3, much behavior is assumed by the individual
to be volitional when actually it is not. Certain activities have become so habitual that no specific input appears to instigate them. Others may be motivated
by generalized drives (see Chapter 3, note 2), which are so diffuse that the inputs characterizing them are difficult to isolate. In both such kinds of activity
the individual tends mistakenly to attribute his behavior to the autocept. The
inputs characterizing the autocept (those arising from visceral activities and
basic memories) are immediate and perpetual, whereas those that directly

motivate the behavior are amorphous and indefinite. If a person indulging in some habit or playing a particular game were asked why he was doing that particular thing, he would probably answer, "because 'I' wanted to"—thus mistakenly attributing to the autocept behavior instigated by inputs from other sources.

The attribute that ensures the individual's identity; that constitutes the "I," or the "ego," and that sustains volitional activity is learned. Not only is there an intrinsic drive for emergence of the autocept, but there is also a powerful drive to retain a particular organization of a given self system. As we shall see in Chapters 6-8, the autocept has significance as a motivational system and "volitional behavior" has some meaning.

The Adaptive Function of Primary Encoding

How, then, does primary encoding assist the adaptation of the organism? How would the human being be less adaptable if this attribute were absent? Why did such a representational system develop in complex organisms?

The perceptual world of the human being is a *better* than adequate representation of the physical world, at least from the point of view of adaptation. It is "better" because it both summarizes the critical relationships and consistencies of that world and excludes characteristics of no survival significance. We recall that the eye is sensitive only to a narrow segment of the electromagnetic continuum—in which the reflection potential is at a maximum (see Chapter 3). It is this evolutionary choice that has made perception of edges and movement possible. If our eyes were sensitive only to infrared, for instance, lines, cracks, and edges could not be seen. The eye became responsive to edges because critical survival circumstances consisted of items with boundaries; the process underlying perception of movement (whether peripheral or central) emerged because the edged things in our survival context actually *did* shift in position. Items in our environment are located at varying distances from one another and their relative distances were—and still remain—critical to survival (both to finding food and to avoiding predators). The never-ending process of natural selection has ensured that this critical information on moving edges at varying distances will be represented and that the capacity to perceive three-dimensional space (whether it is peripheral, that is, within the rods and cones or some other receptor, or in the brain itself) would evolve. But it was not enough that our progenitors were responsive to other items in a three-dimensional context. As the reflection characteristics of other creatures varied greatly according to distance, light, and perspective, the adaptive necessity for summarization had an impact on process, and perceptual constancies developed. We do not have to respond to a thousand perspectives but to only one item, which retains its identity and unity, regardless of the momentary shifts in shape, size, and brightness.

But the constant process of natural selection has refined our perceptual system even further. As each item that moved in the survival context offered multiple signals of its presence, different receptor systems developed: We can both hear and see the tiger and perhaps smell it if it comes close enough. Along with multiple receptors came the ultimate and perhaps most functional type of summary: the fusion of inputs *across* modalities. Could it have been predicted? Any given entity in the physical environment is represented by simultaneous energy characteristics. The entity exists as a unity, even though its presence may activate various receptor systems. A process that ensures unity for such simultaneous inputs emerged: Whether we taste, smell, feel, or see an apple, it is still recognized as an apple. Although any particular entity may be apprehended in various ways, it is still that entity, and the organism need respond only to its unity within a physical environment in order to find—or to avoid being—food: the ultimate functional simplification.

That items in the environment consist of moving "blobs" defined by boundaries ensured that an eye responsive to varying reflection characteristics would come into being. But such an eye has itself been responsible for a counterdevelopment in some animals through evolutionary time: Many species have camouflage techniques to protect themselves from being preyed upon. Sometimes cessation of movement is vital. At others the edges of the individuals are either broken up or melt into the environment (see Chapter 3, note 3): The chameleon remains unnoticed on the twig and the rabbit undetected in the bush.[8]

Summary

Although we admit to an empirical bias toward notions of the emergence of fusion and structuring, we must assume the inborn capacity for such organization. The innate process underlying such patterning has at least two vitally important equilibratory characteristics: It encourages fusion and structuring, and it maintains the integrity once they are present. We thus assume that human beings are structured in such a way that, once certain experiential cues have been introduced, the process will mold this input so that it automatically assumes the unity and (separateness) characteristic of our experience. We may quibble about the relative influence of nature and nurture and argue about the postulation of a "coercing" brain field, but that process does coerce input to assume unity and organization there can be little doubt. On this point we believe the Gestalt psychologists are completely correct. Furthermore, there can be little doubt that the process occasioning coercion is innate and manifests itself in much the same manner in creatures of like structure. Even as we assume that our sensory input is alike to the extent that we are structured alike, we can assume that similar organization of such input will occur to the same extent.

In each of us there is thus an innate drive toward the emergence of perceived phenomena and also a drive toward integrity of perceived phenomena. When particular sensory inputs have once been fused into a phenomenon, there is a tendency to perceive that complex as a unity thereafter. A tree is perceived as a tree, though the totality is actually composed of many bits of input; it is almost impossible to perceive it otherwise. If we doubt that there is a drive toward organizational integrity, we need only participate in a simple mirror-drawing experiment to recognize the difficulty implicit in trying to counter existing perceptual structures. Many students who have tried mirror drawing (see note 5) can vouch for another characteristic of the process underlying perceptual organization: its remarkable plasticity. After drawing stars for two hours while observing progress in a mirror, a remarkable number of students will write their signatures as mirror images.

The learning that occasions the emergence of perception of phenomena within three-dimensional space and accounts for the development of the autocept is called *primary encoding,* to distinguish it from secondary encoding, which we shall deal with in the next chapter; it is considered primary because it provides encodes of both the fundamental unit and the context relative to which more traditional learning occurs.

From an evolutionary point of view such primary encoding could have been predicted. If a physical environment exists and embodies certain enduring consistencies, a process representing such characteristics would have great adaptive utility and would be expected to arise in the course of natural selection. By manifesting the universal consistencies in the physical environment, primary encoding reduces the complexity of ordinary learning, which can then be concentrated on the more variable contingencies encountered during the individual's life span. In one sense primary encoding may be conceptualized as species learning, for all members of a given species are structured so that essentially the same perceptual organization will emerge. In human beings, for instance, though we may not know which particular experiences will be encoded, we may predict that they will assume unity and structure as imposed by the universally represented primary encoding process.

Primary encoding may also be viewed as a simplification mechanism. By representing the universal consistencies in the organism's environment, it effectively distinguishes such consistencies from the more variable contingencies to which the individual must adapt. Writers like Helmholtz have noted that the unity and organization occasioned by primary encoding are both unconscious and irresistible—characteristics that fit neatly into our theory. We can assume that such learning represents universal consistencies that need not be altered once encoded but may serve as a functional backdrop for the kaleidoscope of ordinary experience.

Notes

[1]Immediately the question of relationship or overlap between "consciousness" as it is usually used and "apperception" and "integration matrix" arises. Is consciousness limited to what is apperceived, or is it identical with what exists in the integration matrix? Our solution to this vexing problem is somewhat

arbitrary. "Apperception" refers here to the process of focalizing on certain materials within the integration matrix; by definition, then, it is more restricted in its application than is "integration matrix," which includes all material from *both* memory and sensation available for focalization. "Consciousness" has typically been restricted to *the sensory* material available for focalization; our "integration matrix" thus encompasses both the *Blickfeld* and the "preconscious" as defined by Sigmund Freud.

2There is a growing body of evidence suggesting that at least some forms of perception are present at birth and do not have to be derived from experience; there is also increasing evidence that much genetically derived behavior is dependent upon experience for improved performance.

R. L. Fantz (1957; 1958) has demonstrated that chicks hatched in the dark and without experience of food or water pecked significantly more frequently at a form shaped like a grain than at any other object, flat or solid. M. I. Kurke (1955) has found that lack of visual experience does not greatly hamper the chick's depth perception, but the further development of such discrimination is enhanced by integration of experiential cues. R. Fishman and R. B. Tallarico (1961) have discovered that chicks hatched in the dark can discriminate depth at the age of three hours. E. H. Hess (1956) placed a hood containing a distorting prism above the heads of chicks reared in the dark and found that their innate sense of spatial location was not adaptable, even when survival depended upon it.

R. D. Walk and E. J. Gibson (1961) found that rats reared in the dark showed the same preference for the shallow side of a visual cliff as did rats reared in the light. S. M. Nealey and B. J. Edwards (1960) had similar findings. Further experiments by Walk and Gibson (1961) led them to believe that motion parallax (nearer objects move more rapidly than farther ones from the point of view of a moving subject) is an innate cue for depth but that use of textural density as a cue must be learned by these animals. K. S. Lashley and J. T. Russell (1934) found that rats reared in the dark were just as accurate in judging jumping distances as were rats reared in the light. They concluded that visual perception of distance and differential application of energy in jumping to compensate for distance are not learned but result from some innately organized neural mechanism.

A. H. Riesen (1947) discovered that chimpanzees reared in darkness have poor figure recognition, though color recognition is immediate. Fantz (1961) had similar results with monkeys. L. W. Gellerman (1933) reported that chimpanzees and two-year-old children can recognize a triangle that has been rotated 120 degrees but only after their heads have also been rotated. As adults recognize the form immediately, without moving their heads, we may conclude that recognition of form inversion must be learned. R. Held and A. Hein reached similar conclusions (1968) working with kittens; they found that voluntary movement with concurrent visual feedback is necessary for development of visually guided behavior.

In determining the extent of innate perceptual ability in human beings, the problems are greater, for the experimenter cannot decide arbitrarily at what time an infant is to see. Furthermore, any response dependent upon motor coordination must await physical maturation, at which time the possibility of learning threatens contamination. M. von Senden's study (1932) of congenitally blind adults who gained sight through removal of cataracts comes closest to revealing just how far visual perception depends upon experience. He concluded that these subjects had an immediate impression of relative depth but were unable to estimate absolute distance; they would try to reach out for something yards away or would overreach something close by. Their discrimination of solidity was also poor, but their figure-ground segregation was good, and they learned color immediately. Although they could already distinguish squares, circles, and triangles tactually, visual discrimination of these forms took many months. D. O. Hebb (1949) has concluded from this and other studies that the perception of a square or a circle is learned slowly and depends originally on multiple visual fixes.

Despite the obstacles, there have been many studies of perception in infant subjects, though the dividing line between innate ability and learned behavior is often difficult to draw. Wertheimer (1961) studied the psychomotor coordination of auditory and visual space in one human infant, born by means of natural childbirth, before she was ten minutes old. He found that auditory localization and a coordinate primitive spatial localization were present. F. Stirnimann (1944) found that glancing at moving objects was well developed in day-old neonates. W. P. Chase (1937) found that infants 15 to 17 days old were able to discriminate color by following colored ovals moving against different colored backgrounds. D. Trincker and I. Trincker (1955) demonstrated that under light adaptation neonates' color sensitivity was equal to that of adults but that under dark adaptation, it was not achieved until the age of one month. W. R. Baller and D. C. Charles (1968) found no absolute evidence of color discrimination in the first two weeks of life.

B. C. Ling (1942) demonstrated the convergence of the eyes near the beginning of the second month. Fantz (1961a) followed up by investigating infant discrimination between a sphere and a disk of equal diameter under eight conditions. He found differential responses to textured objects under direct lighting but under none of the other conditions. Infants less than three months old did not differentiate in binocular tests, but in monocular tests they did. Fantz concluded that the use of both eyes interferes with vision in the early months, whereas binocular vision improves visual performance later. Gibson and Walk (1960) found that ability to perceive depth in the visual cliff is probably present from birth. B. L. White and Held (1966), working with institutionalized children, found that visually directed reaching (and thus depth perception) speeded up after supplementary experience. These studies imply that a primitive form of depth perception may be innate but that experience is necessary to develop it.

Fantz (1966) found that the complexity and patterning of the human face can be selectively attended to from birth and that the particular arrangement of features can be perceived by at least the third month. C. Buhler's study (1930) implies that differential responses to the human face (as distinct from the rest of the environment) are learned. This conclusion has been supported by A. Gesell and F. L. Ilg (1949).

Fantz, J. H. Ordy, and M. S. Udelf (1968) have shown that even in the early weeks of life, infants have considerable pattern vision, which improves over the first six months—suggesting that there is some unlearned organization in the infant's perception. Fantz (1966) has further observed that from birth visual attention to pattern is much greater than to color and brightness alone. In another study (1961b) he demonstrated the existence of form perception in infants between one and fifteen weeks old. J. S. Watson (1968) concluded that perception of object orientation is well developed by the fourteenth week.

All these studies suggest that the inflexibility of innate visual perception decreases as we go up the phylogenetic scale, that human infants are born with primitive visual perception, and that visual behavior can be most efficient only after some learning.

3Certain contemporary interpretations of perceptual organization are remarkably similar to this one. Gibson's texture theory (1950), for instance, assumes that the receptors of the eye respond differently to varying reflection characteristics of the object. He particularly emphasizes texture but also believes that there are changes or breaks in the gradients of textures corresponding to corners, edges, and steps. As S. H. Bartley has stated the position (1958), edges are formed by "abruptions" in gradients and corners by vortexes from which gradients extend. Such features constitute the irreducibles from which innate perception of depth is derived. Although essentially we agree that it is the differential responses of the visual mechanism to reflection characteristics of the physical world that constitute the foundation of perceptual organization, we do not think that texture has much to do with depth perception. It is certainly true, as Gibson has suggested, that the closest portion of a surface appears to have a coarser texture than do more distant segments, but this characteristic does not seem an important cue in depth perception for two reasons: First, texture gradients are not usually even discernible until the entire surface is close to the observer, and, second, the assumption that the organism, even before experience, sees "coarser" as closer and "finer" as farther away is unacceptable.

H. Helson's adaptation-level theory (1948) is essentially identical to our own view of how the constancies develop. He believes that from our many experiences of brightness, shapes, and sizes a residual representing an "average" of all such inputs emerges and that perceptual "judgments" are relative to this average.

4Irving Rock (1966) has given a much more detailed account of this problem. He has observed that the retinal displacement occasioned by the organism's own movements is discounted, so that the world appears stationary (position constancy). He has also noted that G. M. Stratton (see note 5) and others who wore reversing lenses at first saw the environment as moving when they turned their heads; it took some time before this "swinging of the scene" ceased. Rock has suggested that the world appeared to move because head movements evoked memory traces of the speed or direction of image displacement (of stationary objects) different from those of the current image. This explanation is compatible with our position that certain cues from experience, which are consistently different for head movement, eye movement, and environment, are subject to primary encoding as a basis for differentiation. But, although we believe that movement parallax and kinesthesis provide the basic input for such discriminations, Rock thinks that the essential information is based on a central record of intended (or commanded) movements or is perhaps derived from induced movement of the self, as when the individual is carried along in some mode of transportation.

Recently two studies (both of which Rock has evaluated at length), by R. L. Posen (1966) and H. Wallach and J. H. Kravitz (1965), were designed to study the effects of altering the amounts of image displacement caused by head movement. Both studies used a technique that allowed systematic alteration in the speed of image shift as the head moved. When there was a discrepancy between the movement of the image and that normally experienced when the head moved, the target seemed to be in motion, though it was actually stationary; it was necessary to move it in order to make it appear static. Both studies, as well as that of Stratton, suggest that there is rapid adaptation to the effects of the misleading cues—and that the cues to position constancy are derived at least partly from movement parallax when the head or body changes position.

5Once perceptual fusion and structuring have occurred what variables can alter them? The experimental evidence suggests that only learning or conflict among previously integrated cues can do it. Stratton's classic experiment with the inversion of the retinal image, which has been replicated many times (see Munn, 1955), is well known. Although there is some disagreement about the extent of perceptual inversion, most studies indicate that after only three to five days the individual wearing the lenses automatically begins to see his topsy-turvy world more naturally. Our own findings (confirmed many times in our laboratory, during demonstrations with introductory students) that subjects will automatically write the mirror image of their signatures after only two hours of mirror drawing, furnish further evidence on the importance of learning in perceptual organization and on the remarkable flexibility of this process. A study by R. Schafer and G. Murphy (1943) demonstrated that, when cues are almost balanced, a relatively short training period may be sufficient to establish a perceptual predisposition. They used drawings in which two faces in figure-ground rivalry were presented to different groups of children. After establishing an approximate 50-50 reversibility ratio, they selectively rewarded and punished the children when the faces were separately presented. The faces were then recombined and presented tachistoscopically for very short intervals. Under these conditions the children tended to perceive the rewarded but not the punished face.

The many demonstrations by L. B. Ames and his colleagues (see Cantril, 1950; Ittelson and Cantril, 1954; and E. P. Kilpatrick, 1953) show clearly what can happen when previously integrated cues are in conflict: Rotating trapezoids appear to oscillate, familiar objects appear distorted in size and shape, marbles seem to roll uphill, and totally scrambled patterns of stimuli appear meaningful and familiar. Perhaps the most dramatic demonstration is provided when objects without cue distortion are presented simultaneously with rotating trapezoids: Cubes appear to fly through space, and cardboard tubes seem to bend and even to break through the trapezoids to which they are attached. These demonstrations suggest that the individual's perceptual world is the contribution of a remarkable complex of cues operating in combination and that the familiar furniture of our world can be dissolved into a series of question marks when these cues are placed in conflict.

6Empirical data on time are sketchy, to say the least. P. A. Sorokin and R. K. Merton (1937), E. E. Evans-Pritchard (1940), and K. Lovell (1966) have described primitive societies in which names of social phenomena have been used as time expressions (as "in a rice-cooking" for "in a short while"). They often have words for this year, last year, and next year but none actually equivalent to "time." The year is arranged in the order of important events like harvest or planting time. Time is only a series of events. Children perceive it in the same way.

Until the child is about age five, time and space are undifferentiated. L. B. Ames (1946) discovered that the use of words relating to time far precedes the actual comprehension of what they mean. Words describing the present are often found in children 24 months old, for the future in those 30 months old, for the past in those 36 months old. Words for duration, rather than order, rarely appear before 36 months. S. R. A. Court (1920) did a study of one bright child and reported that his thinking was dominated by the present until he was two years old, whereas his conception of the past reached back no

longer than a few days. Between the ages of two and five years temporal concepts gradually developed, and concepts of the past and future expanded.

E. C. Oakden and M. Stuart (1922) concluded that development of the child's
knowledge of temporal concepts and relations is slow but begins well before he
goes to school, that he first learns the meanings of words in ordinary use, that
he relates periods of time to personal experiences, that understanding chronol-
ogy and historical epochs is an extremely difficult step for him, and that temporal details are far less important in his thought than are matters of space.

D. Springer (1952) found this sequence of comprehension in four-to six-year-
olds: development of general concepts; understanding sequences of events;
learning to tell time by hours, half-hours, and quarter-hours; learning to set the
clock hands, and finally learning to explain why a clock has two hands.

N. D. Bradley (1948) has suggested that in the first six years time is related
to personal activities; by eight years understanding of time words used in the
calendar has increased. L. M. Terman (1916) discovered that a child is eight or
nine before he clearly comprehends time periods and has sufficient interest in
them to keep close track of the date. M. Stuart (1925) found that children
reach the age of nine before time perspective becomes accurate beyond the span
of a generation; seventy-five percent of the eight-year-olds in his study were not
sure whether or not their grandmothers had been alive in 1492.

Jean Piaget and B. Inhelder (1969) believe that the idea of time is derived
from the notions of speed and distance. Lovell and his colleagues (1962) showed
that the child up to at least age six thinks of "faster" and "slower" as changes
in relative positions, rather than as distances moved per unit of time. Piaget
(1946) also found that accurate perception of simultaneity comes before understanding of the equality of synchronous intervals. He further demonstrated that
young children judge age by size; not until events can be ordered and happen-
ings coordinated with intervals can age be understood as independent of visual
perception.

A few collateral studies include reports on the relative instability of human
time perception. Illness and high body temperature can make time seem much
longer (Cohen, 1964). Lower socioeconomic groups have shorter time-compre-
hension spans (LeShan, 1952). Delinquents also have poor perceptions of duration (Siegman, 1961). One of the more frequent symptoms of mental distur-
bance is distorted perception of time (Goldstone and Goldfarb, 1966); M.
Levine and his colleagues (1959) have demonstrated that the ability to perceive
time accurately is related to intelligence.

[7]Organization of the autocept apparently begins during fetal development with
one of the most important and empirically demonstrable inputs: the mother's
heartbeat. D. Morris (1967) has pointed out that 83 percent of right-handed
mothers and 78 percent of left-handed mothers prefer to hold their infants in
the left arm, close to the heart, because the babies are quieter there. He has
reported a study conducted in a hospital nursery where a heart beat recording
was played. Sixty percent of the infants cried at some time while the recording was off, whereas only thirty-eight percent cried when the recording was on.
Another study of older infants used various recordings in the babies' bedrooms
at home. The control group slept in silent rooms. One experimental group
slept in rooms with lullabies playing, a second with a metronome set at a normal heart rate of seventy-two beats a minute, and a third with the recorded
sound of an actual heartbeat at seventy-two beats a second. The infants in
the final group fell asleep in half the time that it took those in the other three
groups.

[8]Mimicry, perhaps more clearly than any other feature in nature, demonstrates the manner in which seemingly unimportant variables can influence the course of evolution. Any chance modification that aids in the struggle for survival, even to a minute degree, may be incorporated; in time these increments are fused to represent a functional attribute. All camouflage techniques are examples of mimicry that assist in evading discovery: The zebra's stripes help it to hide from the leopard, and the leopard's spots help it to catch the zebra. Camouflage is most dramatic in the chameleon, which can change its color at any moment, in order to mimic the terrain and reduce its chances of being caught. The classic study of industrial melanism in the moth by H. B. D. Kettlewell (see Chapter 1, note 5) is not only the clearest confirmation of Charles Darwin's theory, it also focuses on a remarkable example of mimicry evolving through the process of natural selection. Throughout the animal kingdom mimicry augments the survival chances of certain species by increasing the probability of critical mistakes by other organisms. This observation holds whether the camouflage reduces a soldier's chances of being observed or increases the chances for reproduction among orchids (see Chapter 3, note 4).

That mimicry is not limited to animals has been amply demonstrated by the English botanist John Measures.

W. J. Burchell (1822) was the first to mention the phenomenon of mimicry in literature. He wrote, "On picking up from the stony ground what was supposed a curiously shaped pebble, it proved to be a plant . . . [which in] colour and appearance bore the closest resemblance to the stones among which it was growing." The plant mentioned is known today as *Lithops turbiniformis.* These plants vary in appearance, depending upon the types of rocks among which they are found; those growing in limestone and quartz areas are gray or pale in color, whereas those that grow in sandstone or red-clay areas are brown or yellow (Marloth, 1929). Other plants belonging to the genus *Pheiospilos* look almost exactly like pieces of granite. When they are not in flower, it takes a keen eye to distinguish them from the stony areas in which they are found. "During the dry season the leaves look just like lumps of stone" (Marloth, 1904).

Titanopsis calcarea offers an almost perfect example of mimicry. This plant, as the name suggests, lives in predominantly limestone areas and is almost indistinguishable from the lime tufa in the crevices of which it grows. But it is *Anacampseros papyracae* that offers the most remarkable example of deception. The entire plant is covered with white scales so that it looks just like bird droppings, which are in perpetual abundance around it. It is therefore rejected by animals that would otherwise eat it.

How can this mimicry among plants be explained? In the same way that any camouflage technique is explained. Those members of the species that were slightly more similar to their surroundings had a little better chance of survival, and thus through countless generations they took on the appearance of rocks, or feces, or some other material in their immediate environment. All the plants mentioned are succulent (Jacobsen, 1960), and their general attractiveness as food for birds and mammals has determined the process by which this camouflage technique emerged.

References

Ames, L. B. The development of the sense of time in the young child. *Journal of Genetic Psychology,* 1946, 68: 97-125.

Baller, W. R., & Charles, D. C. *The psychology of human growth and development.* New York: Holt, Rinehart and Winston, 1968.

Bartley, S. H. *Principles of perception.* New York: Harper & Row, 1958.

Berkeley, G. *An essay toward a new theory of vision.* London: J. M. Dent and Sons, 1709.

Bradley, N. D. The growth of the knowledge of time in children of school age. *British Journal of Psychology,* 1948, 38: 67-78.

Brown, F. A., Jr. Living clocks. *Science,* 1958, 130: 1535-1544.

Buhler, C. *The first year of life.* New York: Day, 1930.

Burchell, W. J. *Travels in the interior of South Africa,* Vol. 1. London: Longmans, 1822. P. 310.

Cantril, H. *The "why" of man's experience.* New York: Macmillan, 1950.

Chase, W. P. Color vision in infants. *Journal of Experimental Psychology,* 1937, 20: 203-222.

Clark, L. B., & Hess, W. N. Swarming of the Atlantic palolo worm, *Leodice fucata* (Ehlers). *Papers from Tortugas Laboratory,* 1943, 33: 21-70. (Carnegie Institute of Washington, Publ. 524).

Cohen, J. Psychological time. *Scientific American,* November 1964, 211: 116-122.

Court, S. R. A. Numbers, time and space in the first five years of a child's life. *Pedagogic seminary,* 1920, 27: 71-89.

Ehrenfels, Christian von. Ueber Gestaltqualitäten, *Psychologische Forschung,* 1890, 14: 249-292.

Evans-Pritchard, E. E. *The Nuer.* New York: Oxford University Press, 1940.

Fantz, R. L. Form preferences in newly hatched chicks. *Journal of Comparative and Physiological Psychology,* 1957, 50: 422-430.

———. Depth discrimination in dark-hatched chicks. *Perception and Motor Skills,* 1958, 8: 47-50.

———. A method for studying depth perception in infants under six months of age. *Psychological Record,* 1961a, 11: 27-32.

———. The origin of form perception. *Scientific American,* May 1961, 204: 66-72.

———. Pattern discrimination and selective attention as determinants of perceptual development from birth. In A. H. Kidd and J. L. Rivoire (eds.), *Perceptual development in children.* New York: International Universities Press, 1966.

Fantz, R. L., Ordy, J. H., & Udelf, M. S. Maturation of pattern vision in infants during the first six months. In N. S. Endler, L. R. Boulter, and H. Osser (eds.), *Contemporary issues in developmental psychology.* New York: Holt, Rinehart, and Winston, 1968.

Fishman, R., and Tallarico, R. B. Studies of visual depth perception. 2. Avoidance reaction as an indicator response in chicks. *Perception and Motor Skills,* 1961, 12: 251-257.

Gellerman, L. W. Form discrimination in chimpanzees and two-year-old children. 1. Form (triangularity) *per se. Journal of Genetic Psychology,* 1933, 7: 427-454.

Gesell, A., & Ilg, F. L. *Child development: The infant and child in the culture of today.* New York: Harper, & Row, 1949.

Gibson, E. J., & Walk, R. D. The visual cliff. *Scientific American,* 1960, 202: 64-71.

Gibson, J. J. *The perception of the visual world.* Cambridge: Riverside, 1950.

Goldstone, S., & Goldfarb, J. L. The perception of time by children. In A. H. Kidd and J. L. Rivoire (eds.), *Perceptual development in children*. New York: International Universities Press, 1966.

Hebb, D. O. *The organization of behavior*. New York: Wiley, 1949.

Held, R., & Hein, A. Movement-produced stimulation in the development of visually guided behavior. In N. S. Endler, L. R. Boulter, and H. Osser (eds.), *Contemporary issues in developmental psychology*. New York: Holt, Rinehart and Winston, 1968.

Helmholtz, H. von. *Physiological optics* (translated by J. P. C. Southall). New York: Optical Society of America, 1924.

Helson, H. Adaptation-level as a basis for a quantitative theory of frames of reference. *Psychological Review*, 1948, 55: 297-313.

Hess, E. H. Space perception in the chick. *Scientific American*, 1956, 195: 71-80.

Hubel, D. H., & Wiesel, T. N. Receptive fields, binocular interaction and functional architecture in the cat's visual cortex. *Journal of Physiology*, 1962, 160: 106-154.

Ittelson, W. H., & Cantril, H. *Perception: A transactional approach*. New York: Doubleday, 1954.

Jacobsen, H. *A handbook of succulent plants*. Vol. 3. London: Blandford, 1960.

James, W. *Principles of Psychology*. New York: Holt, 1890.

Kettlewell, H. B. D. Darwin's missing evidence. *Scientific American*. 1959, 200: 48-53.

Kilpatrick, F. P. *Human behavior from the transactional point of view*. Hanover, N. H.: Institute for Associated Research, 1952.

Kurke, M. I. The role of motor experience in the visual discrimination of depth in the chick. *Journal of Genetic Psychology*, 1955, 86: 191-196.

Lashley, K. S., & Russell, J. T. The mechanism of vision: A preliminary test of innate organization. *Journal of Genetic Psychology*, 1934, 45: 136-144.

LeShan, L. L. Time orientation and social class. *Journal of Abnormal and Social Psychology*, 1952, 47: 589-592.

Lettvin, J. U., Maturans, H. C., McCulloch, W. S., & Pitts, W. H. What the frog's eye tells the frog's brain. *Proceedings of the Institute of Radio Engineers*, 1959, 47: 1940-1951.

Levine, M., Spivack, G., Fuschillo, J., & Travernier, A. Intelligence and measures of inhibition and time sense. *Journal of Clinical Psychology*, 1959, 15: 224-226.

Ling, B. C. A genetic study of sustained visual fixation and associated behavior in the human infant from birth to six months. *Journal of Genetic Psychology*, 1942, 61: 227-277.

Lotze, R. H. *Medicinische Psychologie*. Leipzig: Weidmann Press, 1852.

Lovell, K. The development of scientific concepts. In A. H. Kidd and J. L. Rivoire (eds.), *Perceptual development in children*. New York: International Universities Press, 1966.

Lovell, K., Kellett, V. L., & Moorhouse, E. The growth of the concept of speed: A comparative study. *Journal of Child Psychology and Psychiatry*, 1962, 3: 101-110.

Marloth, R. Mimicry among plants. *Translations of the South African Philatelist (Philosophical) Society*, 1904, 15: 97-102.

———. Stone-shaped plants. *South African Journal of Natural History*, 1929, 6: 273-280.

Mill, James. *Analysis of the phenomena of the human mind.* London: Baldwin and Cradock, 1829.

Mill, J. S. *System of logic ratiocinative and inductive.* New York: Harper and Brothers, 1848.

Morris, D. *The naked ape.* New York: McGraw-Hill, 1967.

Munn, N. L. *The evolution and growth of human behavior.* Boston: Houghton Mifflin, 1955.

Nealey, S. M., & Edwards, B. J. Depth perception in rats without pattern vision experience. *Journal of Comparative and Physiological Psychology,* 1960, 53: 468-469.

Oakden, E. C., & Stuart, M. The development of the knowledge of time in children. *British Journal of Psychology,* 1922, 12: 209-236.

Piaget, J. *Le développement de la notion de temps chez l'enfant.* Paris: Presses Universitaires, 1946.

Piaget, Jean & Inhelder, Barbel. *The psychology of the child.* New York: Basic Books, 1969.

Posen, R. L. Perceptual adaptation to contingent visual-field movement: An experimental investigation of position constancy. Unpublished doctoral dissertation, Yeshiva University, 1966.

Rao, K. P. Tidal rhythmicity of rate of water propulsion in mytilus, and its modifiability by transplantation. *Biological Bulletin,* 1954, 106: 353-359.

Riesen, A. H. The development of visual perception in man and chimpanzee. *Science,* 1947, 106: 107-108.

Rock, I. *The nature of perceptual adaptation.* New York: Basic Books, 1966.

Schafer, R., & Murphy, G. The role of autims in visual figureground relationship. *Journal of Experimental Psychology,* 1943, 32: 335-343.

Senden, M. von. *Raum und Gestaltauffassung bei operienten Blindgeborenen vor und nach der Operation.* Leipzig: Barth, 1932.

Siegman, A. W. The relationship between future time perspective, time estimation and impulse control in a group of young offenders and in a control group. *Journal of Consulting Psychology,* 1961, 25: 470-475.

Sorokin, P. A., & Merton, R. K. Social time. *American Journal of Sociology,* 1937, 42: 615-629.

Springer, D. Development in young children of an understanding of time and the clock. *Journal of Genetic Psychology,* 1952, 80: 83-96.

Stratton, G. M. Vision without inversion of the retinal image. *Psychological Review,* 1897, 4: 341-360, 463-481.

Stirnimann, F. Über das Farbempfinden Neugeborener. *Annales Paediatrici,* 1944, 163: 1-25.

Stuart, M. *The psychology of time.* London: Routledge, 1925.

Terman, L. M. *The measurement of intelligence.* Boston: Houghton Mifflin, 1916.

Trincker, D., & Trincker, I. Die ontogenetische Entwicklung des Helligkeits und Farbenekens bein Menschen. 1. Die Entwicklung des Helligkeitssehens. *Albrecht v Graefes Archiv fur Opthalmogie,* 1955, 156: 519-534.

Walk, R. D., & Gibson, E. J. A comparative and analytical study of visual depth perception. *Psychological Monographs,* 1961, 75: (Whole, No. 519), 15.

Wallach, H., & Kravitz, J. H. The measurement of the constancy of visual direction and of its adaptation. *Psychonomic Science,* 1965, 2: 217-218.

Watson, J. S. Perception of object orientation in infants. In N. S. Endler, L. R. Boulter, & H. Osser (eds.), *Contemporary Issues in Developmental Psychology.* New York: Holt, Rinehart and Winston, 1968.

Wertheimer, M. Psychomotor coordination of auditory and visual space at brith. *Science,* 1961, 134: 1692.

White, B. L., & Held, R. Plasticity of sensorimotor development in the human infant. In J. F. Rosenblith & W. Allinsmith (eds.), *The causes of behavior: Readings in child development and educational psychology.* Boston: Allyn and Bacon, 1966.

Wundt, Wilhelm von. *Beiträge zur Theorie der Sinneswahrnehmung,* Leipzig: Winter, 1862.

5

Secondary Encoding

The topic of learning can be examined on at least three levels. First, we may look at the environmental circumstances that encourage it. Theorists and researchers following this approach have focused on demonstrable relationships between environmental alterations and behavior changes of particular kinds. The basic principle of learning has been formulated by such investigators generally as "contiguity," "need reduction," or both. We shall call this approach *circumstance alteration.*

The second approach centers on physiological changes assumed to occur as results of circumstance alteration. Its adherents seek to isolate the actual change that apparently takes place within the organism on the theory that when a rat has learned a maze and can demonstrate its learning behaviorally, some change must have taken place. These investigators have used such hypothetical concepts as "trace," "neural bonds," "synaptic knobs," and "engrams" to suggest how memory material is physiologically represented. We call this approach *physiological alteration.*

We shall devote our own investigation to the third, experiential approach. Although experience is derived from still unknown physical operations (Chapter 3), it nevertheless constitutes a legitimate source of explanation. Furthermore, to make inferences from experience does not conflict with the other two approaches. Both environmental alterations correlated with particular behavior changes and the precise physiological location of the processes underlying such relationships must be studied exhaustively if we are to understand learning fully, but these approaches alone can lead to only partial understanding.

We shall begin our discussion of secondary encoding with a clarification of its overlap with primary encoding.

As the primary encoding processes appear early in the individual's life, the input that must be used from then on consists not of discrete sensory elements but of fused unities (phenomena) in three-dimensional space. The basic operations of primary encoding have been largely accomplished by the time that the child is two or three years old. The plasticity of this process should, however, be kept in mind: Although the visual field may achieve relative stability at an early age, its organization and structure can be altered by dramatically changed circumstances (see Chapter 4, note 4). Furthermore, learning of skills (development of motocepts) may continue throughout the individual's entire life, and the autocept, though its nucleus may have emerged early, doubtless continues to alter in organization at least until adulthood.

The particular "structure" that the integration matrix has assumed (as a function of primary encoding) is intimately related to the kind of learning that results in memory residuals. Once particular components have become fused so that both structure and phenomena emerge automatically, the input used in developing memory residuals will follow the same structure and unity. Before the city child has ever seen a cow his integration matrix has already been organized so that the first cow that he sees will be perceived as a unitary phenomenon in three-dimensional space. As he encounters more and more cows, a fused memory residual for the concept "cow" will come into being. This fused concept, then, develops not only because many similar cows have been experienced, but also because the integration matrix has already been structured to occasion apperception of phenomena per se.

Primary encoding thus profoundly affects the nature of the subsequent learning that occurs. Although the structure and fusion of the integration matrix may shift under dramatically different circumstances, secondary encoding must nevertheless deal with the type of unit and organization already imposed on input by primary encoding.

Development of Input Residuals

Because sensation constitutes a major portion of the initial input to the integration matrix (see Chapter 3), it seems likely that the material encoded will be largely derived from this source. Consideration of the characteristics of such input and the mechanism by which it is brought into focus should therefore allow important inferences about the nature of the encoding process itself.

Let us examine two principles that have commonly been considered basic to learning. Contiguity has been the most widely used "cement" for elements proposed by adherents of all persuasions from English associationists to stimulus-response theorists. Despite its general application, we believe that it is not a principle of learning per se but simply a statement of the spatial-temporal conditions that must exist before components can be associated. Actual learning depends upon certain characteristics of input that facilitate establishment of residuals within the memory process. The contiguity of two chalk marks on a blackboard may affect their relationship, but the process by which they were put there is quite different. Their presence reflects the characteristics of the chalk, the pressure with which it was applied, and the nature of the board. Similarly, the contiguity of two input components may be crucial in establishing an association between them, but the process that occasions their encoding is different altogether.

Another common principle is "need reduction" (whose many variants range from general "satisfaction" to more specific "drive stimulus reduction"). Indeed, in contemporary learning theory this principle carries such weight that it is sometimes put forth as *the* factor that accounts for all learning. Our view is different. Although we agree that previously neutral cues associated with the equilibration process may become deneutralized, nevertheless the reduction of need seems simply to imply certain conditions that facilitate encoding.

Let us consider how need reduction contributes to learning. First, we shall anticipate the argument of Chapter 6 assuming that drive input dominates in apperception as a function of its intensity, when other factors are constant. If an animal has been deprived of food for a long period, "apperceptual flooding" will occur: The input "hunger" will tend to jam out other input. But when an activity like eating reduces the intensity of hunger, other input, perhaps that derived from eating and from the general context, may be brought into focus. The reduction of hunger itself adds a quality to the continuous input process. Furthermore, the pleasure that typically, though not always, accompanies equilibration highlights both activity and circumstance.

Need reduction thus abets encoding by constituting a shift in the input process and by alleviating the apperceptual dominance of disequilibrium input, so that other components may be brought into focus. Pleasure underscores these other components, so that encoding can occur more readily.

This discussion implies an intimate relationship between apperception and encoding (the establishment of a replica of input in memory). We may thus state the first postualte of learning.

Any input component that is apperceived will be encoded.

We emphasize that without apperception there can be no learning. If material competing for apperception is sufficiently pervasive, a component that might be brought into focus under other circumstances will not be apperceived and will consequently not be encoded.

If the reader doubts that encoding is a direct and necessary outcome of apperception, he can try a few simple experiments. He can glance at an object, then close his eyes and try to remember what he saw. It is likely that he will remember. Or a friend can cut a deck of cards and show him one card for only a moment. Again he is likely to remember it. Although we might postulate subtle needs that could be said to be reduced by such behavior, such an explanation would be dubious. It is simpler to accept the obvious explanation: Apperception alone is sufficient to occasion an encode.

It would be informative to examine the type of encode that occurs first in the newborn child. Early encodes are probably almost exact duplicates of the input, so that when a child recalls a previous experience he will recall a fairly valid representation of the input. But as learning proceeds and fusion (as described in Chapter 4) of recurrent input occurs, the precise pictorial characteristics of the encode tend to be dissipated. After the learning of language they will be further dissipated, so that, in thinking, the individual may use the encode of the written or spoken word, rather than the pictorial residual of its referent. The encode usually becomes less directly representative of the input as the individual grows older, and for some people, at least, large segments of experience become fused in "blobs" that have little if any direct similarity to input. The capacity for abstract thought is, to some extent at least, a function of the degree of fusion of similar recurrent inputs; individuals capable of such "internal locomotion" tend to use little pictorial representation.

It is not by accident that the capacity for eidetic imagery is greatest in children and in individuals who have not been educated. Furthermore, we may surmise that the encodes of animals remain relatively undiluted by symbolic representations and by the more highly refined fusion mechanisms postulated for human beings.

We do not mean to imply that loss of the pictorial characteristics of encodes is always a progressive phenomenon[1] or that such loss is equally generalized throughout the memory of an individual. We may, however, hypothesize that the less novel a particular input happens to be, the greater will be the loss of precise pictorial recall; when we meet another person we have much more difficulty remembering the specifics of his features than recalling the wart on his nose. All human beings have features that are essentially similar, and aspects of the new person that are common to the recurrent input from countless meetings with other people tend to become fused in a generalized representation. The wart, on the other hand, does not fit; it stands out and may be recalled with remarkable pictorial clarity.

This somewhat whimsical example suggests that a fused encode may provide a basis not only for generalization but also for discrimination. The fused encode is a composite summary of a series of similar inputs; as such it provides the basis for similar reactions when similar input is imposed again. But it also represents a norm from which even slight deviations may stand out, thus providing the basis for discrimination.

Does this postulate also apply to prior encodes? If we apperceive the encode of a mother's face will our apperception strengthen that encode? Or if we apperceive a particular encode in a dream will the apperception strengthen the encode? In both instances the answer is yes. The postulate applies to *any* apperception, whether the input is derived from sensory receptors or from prior encodes and whether the person is asleep or awake. This discussion emphasizes a condition that is so basic to the encoding process that we may state it as a corollary.

The repetition of apperceived input will strengthen the encode.

Although repetition has generally fallen into disrepute as a principle of learning, this low status seems completely unjustified. Certainly the repetition of a stimulus or an activity provides no assurance that learning will result, for the mere presentation of a circumstance may or may not occasion apperception. But if apperception does take place repetition of input will strengthen the encode, other factors being equal. Clark L. Hull (1943) was essentailly correct in stating that strength of habit is a function of the number of reinforced trials, but he was correct for the wrong reason. It is not "drive-stimulus reduction" that strengthens the encode but the high priority for apperception that the equilibratory circumstance provides. Our corollary can thus be altered slightly:

If other factors are held constant, the more often a given input is apperceived, the more durable the resulting encode will be.

Two groups of subjects can learn the same list of nonsense syllables until they reach the same facility, but "overlearning" by either group will establish the encode series even more firmly. If practice makes perfect, extra practice will ensure that perfection lasts longer.[2]

This discussion suggests that one of the most important kinds of learning depends upon neither contiguity nor need reduction. Apperception of an input is the only requirement. This conclusion immediately suggests that much of the material that human beings learn is based on observation of other individuals performing different kinds of activities, with resulting encodes that permit the observers to imitate them. Recently the author demonstrated to a one-year-old child how to place rings on an upturned stick. When given the stick and rings the child performed the same activity, though before the demonstration she had never been exposed to such a problem. Later two upturned sticks were used, and red rings were placed on one whereas green rings went on the other; again the child imitated without difficulty. This kind of learning requires only that the child apperceive the various steps in the demonstration in order to imitate the behavior.

We believe, then, that learning through observation is far more crucial than is that demonstrated by rats or pigeons, on varying reinforcement schedules. The human being does not have to make a motor response in order to learn; as long as apperception takes place observation alone is quite sufficient. We agree that certain motor skills are necessary before such *observation learning* can be tested, but let us not confuse learning with the skills required for its demonstration.

Is the sudden elevation of observation learning to a position of such eminence original or remarkable? Hardly. Developmental and educational psychologists have been emphasizing this approach for years, and both high school and college teachers have long understood the value of demonstration experiments in instruction. At this writing one Skinnerian psychologist is diligently "magazine training" a group of rats in order to *demonstrate* to introductory psychology classes that the fundamental principle of learning is reinforcement! The only unusual feature of observation learning is that it has been so neglected by theorists and experimenters.[3]   On the rare occasion when it has been considered, it has been called "imitation learning," but this term is inappropriate. Through imitation the individual simply demonstrates that learning has occurred; the occasion for learning in the first place is apperception, or simple observation.

Apperception is thus necessary to occasion the initial encode, and repetition is required to establish it firmly. Three other variables—discreteness, intensity, and duration—not only affect the development of the encode but also influence the continuing process of apperception (see Chapter 6). Once again we are bedeviled by the intrinsic dilemma (see Chapter 1). Not only is more intense input more likely to be apperceived, but it will also produce a more durable encode if it is apperceived. The same is true of the variables of discreteness and duration. How do we resolve this organizational dilemma? There is only one solution, and it is far from perfect. When we discuss the influences of variables on the development of encodes we assume that apperception is taking place; in experiments designed to evaluate this influence we must be careful to hold apperception constant. For example, if we want to determine whether a bright, clearly drawn triangle produces a better image on film than does a dim, fuzzily drawn triangle, we must hold the shutter setting, the size of the lens opening, and the position of the camera constant. Similarly, in our discussion of the input characteristics that affect durability of the encode, we must assume that apperception not only occurs but is constant. In our search for the particular variables that affect durability, we shall once again adopt an evolutionary perspective, as represented in the second postulate of learning.

Those characteristics of sensory input that have had greater survival significance in the emergence of the species will produce more enduring memory residuals in the individual.

This postulate in turn leads us to consideration of discreteness, intensity, and duration, for which we offer one corollary:

If all other factors are held constant, the more intense, discrete, or enduring of two apperceived inputs will occasion the more lasting encode.

This corollary is not difficult to test. Let us assume two groups of subjects of equal ability. Both groups are given the task of learning a list of nonsense syllables. As a test of intensity one group is presented with the syllables dimly exposed, the other with the syllables brightly exposed. As a test of duration, all factors are held constant except the presentation time of each syllable. Discreteness is more difficult to test, but if all other factors are held constant syllables that are clearly separated from their background will occasion more durable encodes than will those that are not.

The importance of discreteness as a variable can perhaps best be understood if we consider what happens when inputs from different modalities overlap.

If the input from one receptor system overlaps the input from another system, a more durable encode will result.

A group of subjects given the task of learning a list of twenty nonsense syllables, one of which is presented with a tone, will learn that syllable more rapidly and remember it longer. The same prediction could be made for a syllable presented simultaneously with shock, but with extreme shock the pain would tend to block out the syllable, and less learning would occur. Indeed any overlap of modalities, regardless of the type of secondary input, results in a more durable encode unless the input is so pervasive that it displaces primary material. Of course, if apperception is a single-channel system—as we shall argue in Chapter 6—even nonpervasive auditory input may block visual input (or the reverse) when overlap is perfect and duration too short to allow apperceptual shift between the two components.

Overlap is only one of many ways to test discreteness. Any change in the input that sets a particular item off from those around it will occasion a more durable encode. For instance, the critical syllable is learned more rapidly when it is printed in a different color or in larger type than are the others on the list. The conditions that affect both apperception and encoding appear to be so intertwined that decades of experimentation with apparatus of remarkable precision will be required to assess how far a single given variable contributes to both processes. Let us take duration, for example. We assume that an input that remains longer in apperception than does another will occasion the more durable encode. But apperception is an intermittent periodic process; perhaps the more durable encode will result simply from occurrence of more apperceptions.

The variable of discreteness poses a slightly different problem. The more discrete the input (the more it stands out from the mass of other inputs in the integration matrix), the more likely it is to be apperceived. But it will not occasion a durable encode if it stands out only a little from the context in which it appears. There must be some characteristic of the input that sets it off from the others, or it will be fused with the encode of all similar inputs and be lost to specific recall: To the extent that it is discrete it is because it has some character that allows it to be encoded separately, rather than fused with the conglomerate.

With the apperceptive channel "fully open" there are only four variables that affect encoding: the number of times input is imposed, its intensity, its discreteness, and its duration. Other variables that affect establishment of encodes are secondary, influencing only the process of apperception (see Chapter 6) on which all such learning is contingent.

We have suggested that one fundamental type of learning, at least in complex mammals, consists of the automatic development of replicas of apperceived input within memory. We must now examine a kind of learning that is perhaps more crucial to adaptation and that very likely emerged earlier in the process of evolution. We noted previously that a cue must not only be encoded; at least in certain instances it must also occasion sufficient disequilibrium to initiate and sustain response.

Cue Deneutralization

In Chapter 2 we argued that organisms limited to inherited behavior mechanisms for adjustment to their environment would have greatly restricted survival potential. Facile adaptation requires development of attributes that allow the organism to change its responses according to the particular circumstances of its own existence. The capacity for *cue deneutralization* has made possible this major leap in adaptation facility.

Cue deneutralization has two major aspects. First, previously neutral cues must leave residuals in the organism, and, second, the cues must either represent or elicit sufficient disequilibrium to initiate and sustain action.

Let us consider the problem in the light of our evolutionary model. As we mentioned in Chapter 1, the survival of an organism depends upon conditions of minimal variation throughout its various process systems. We also suggested that deviations from such conditions may occur through the imposition of energy from some external source or depletion of the energy essential for life processes. This reasoning leads us to the third postulate of learning.

Any previously neutral cue which occurs consistently prior to the imposition of a critical circumstance will develop the capacity to differentially affect behavior.

If such learning is to be adaptive, any cue that occurs consistently before the appearance of a hazard or usable energy source must affect the behavior of the organism differentially. It must occasion movement either away from potentially harmful energy or toward energy source material. Although both approach and avoidance learning contribute to the maintenance of the organism's equilibrium, the circumstances that occasion each type are remarkably dissimilar.

Development of Negative Valence

A cue is neutral if it does not predictably affect behavior. When an organism consistently and repeatedly moves away from a previously neutral cue, that cue has acquired negative valence. Previously we defended the view that apperception alone is sufficient for an input to become encoded, but in avoidance the additional factor of motivation must be considered. What is the source of the drive input that engenders such behavior? The primary drive activates the organism to escape behavior, but it does not even operate when the circumstance is avoided. The child who avoids the stove is certainly not activated by the primary system: He does not even come in contact with the stove.

We conclude that all avoidance behavior must necessarily involve secondary activation. As we pointed out in Chapters 2 and 3, it seems most reasonable to assume that the disequilibratory input that initiates and sustains avoidance is derived from visceral action or generalized firing of neurons. A series of events is thus involved in every example of avoidance behavior. The cue must first be apperceived, this apperception must automatically produce visceral changes, the visceral changes must activate receptors, and the receptors must introduce disequilibratory input into the integration matrix. Before an organism can avoid, it must first learn to fear the cue, for fear is the drive input that engenders avoidance behavior.

In contrast, escape behavior is relatively simple and probably appeared much earlier in the course of evolution. All that is required is imposition of a noxious stimulus: Pain, cold, or fear triggers action and continues to do so until the organism removes itself from the noxious situation. No learning at all is required for such an equilibratory response; random activity instigated by the sheer presence of the primary input is sufficient to produce it.

We might question this conclusion on grounds that the organism typically does not immediately *stop* moving away from the critical situation just because the traumatic stimulus is no longer activating its receptors. Is there thus a kind of learning in escape behavior? Not necessarily. It is in this context that we see the adaptive function of the pain (current of injury) that continues to be introduced after trauma has been inflicted. If tissue has been damaged, the primary drive input (pain) continues even after the organism is no longer in contact with the critical circumstance. Of course, the general activation produced by visceral and other body reactions may keep the animal moving away from the stimulus for some time after all pain has dissipated.

Avoidance learning thus requires that the cue not only be encoded but that it activate a secondary system. We shall try to describe the characteristics of such input and the modes of presentation that influence development of negative valence.

Potentially harmful energy changes typically occur very suddenly. When we consider the "survival matrix" within which organisms have evolved and the fact that life is a continual process of eating and being eaten, the suddenness is clear. Every organism has evolved and still resides in a context of perpetual hazards from falls, blows, bites, and so on. It is easy to see how tissue damage can be represented by the most vivid sensation in the input repertory: pain. Not only do the energy shifts that produce tissue damage occur rapidly, but also the effects of such damage on survival are profound. The sensation of pain is a vital disequilibratory input and forms the basis for our discussion of the learning of avoidance responses.

The typical suddenness of the onset of pain and its gradual dissipation (because of the current of injury) have important implications for the development of negative valence. We might suggest, with Clark L. Hull, that lessening of pain, as well as its onset, is necessary for establishment of negative valence, but analysis within an evolutionary frame of reference tends to disprove this interpretation. If encoding is abetted to the extent that the input is discrete and emphatic, the onset of pain, rather than its termination, seems to be the crucial circumstance: Not only is the shift from input to no input much more sharply discrete at onset, but also pain is often most intense at the beginning. Furthermore, if the termination or lessening of pain were the essential circumstances, the period between introduction of the cue and the conditions required for it to produce fear would often be extended (because of current of injury). And, as the organism would theoretically move as rapidly as possible away from the critical situation, many extraneous components would be imposed during this gap to complicate discrimination of the crucial cue.

The crux of the argument against the importance of "termination or diminution" in avoidance learning lies in both its lack of parsimony, and its implication that a less functional mechanism would have greater survival value. Why assume that organisms were saddled with this remarkable limitation on flexibility, particularly when the simpler version appears more functional?

Do cues at the beginning or during input from depletion (as in hunger or thirst) acquire negative valence? If so, the fact is extremely difficult to demonstrate.[4] As such disequilibrium is minimal at first and increases only slowly, there is simply no discrete or emphatic shift in input that can occasion an encode. Furthermore, the deprived organism typically moves a great deal, and any changes that may occur will be associated with such a wide variety of input from the different sense modalities that specific learning is unlikely and would be nonfunctional if it did occur.

Escape behavior, then, may be initiated and sustained by input (like pain, heat, or cold) from the primary system, but *avoidance behavior* depends upon drive input from some other source. All avoidance behavior thus involves situations in which cues activate visceral or neural responses introducing secondary disequilibratory input into the integration matrix. The processes traditionally subsumed under the term "emotion" thus bring about the secondary disequilibrium essential for avoidance behavior. We are now in a position to state the corollary pertinent to such learning.

Negative valence will tend to adhere to any previously neutral cue that occurs just before the beginning of primary drive input, if both components are apperceived.

Several factors affect the strength of the avoidance properties that may develop: intensity of pain, frequency with which it is associated with the cue, temporal interval between the cue and the onset of pain, and probably many others. The influence of these variables on the learning of fear has already been investigated at great length, but more research is necessary to determine their precise effects and the influence of interaction among them.

We still have the problem of determining why the organism moves away from the cue. The answer seems simple. As the organism moves away from the cue the physical intensity of the energy from it lessens: The visual image becomes smaller, and odors and sounds are diminished. Each movement away from the cue thus reduces the disequilibrium occasioned by it. Previous learning does, of course, play a critical role in such avoidance: The primary encoding essential to the perception of distance must already have occurred and learning that "distance means relative safety" must already have taken place.

Development of Positive Valence.

What are the conditions under which previously neutral cues take on approach properties? From an evolutionary point of view any input that repeatedly occurs before an equilibratory circumstance should acquire the capacity to initiate and sustain activity toward that circumstance. Learning that accounts for development of positive valence should occur not when imbalance is increasing but when it is diminishing. The increase in input from depletion and elimination transmitting mechanisms is typically gradual, whereas its reduction in an appropriate situation is generally quite rapid. Not only is the equilibratory process (like eating, drinking, or defecation) more discrete because of its rapidity; it also receives secondary emphasis from the pleasure concomitant with it. And so encoding is abetted. The empirical evidence supporting this logic, at least as applied to hunger and thirst, now seems overwhelming. It is so well known that we shall not summarize it here (for an excellent review of this material, see Wike, 1966).

But what about the development of positive properties for cues associated with reduction of input like pain or heat? Do the cues present when pain is reduced also acquire positive valence? Theoretically, yes, but the fact is difficult to demonstrate because the negative valence assumed to accompany the *onset* of pain would typically override any positive effects derived from its termination. Although the experimental evidence on this point is still contradictory,[5] more precise designs and controls will probably demonstrate that cues contiguous with reduction of aversive drives do acquire approach properties. The following corollary may be stated:

Positive valence will tend to adhere to any previously neutral cue that occurs just before a reduction in primary drive input, if both input components are apperceived.

We assume that the previously neutral cue must *precede* reduction in the primary drive because the function of any adaptive cue is to initiate and sustain movement *toward* a situation of balance. Cues that come after equilibrium has been achieved would have a detrimental effect, for they would influence behavior inappropriately. Backward conditioning is completely nonfunctional, for the event to be approached or avoided would already have been imposed on the organism before the cue was even presented. The major function of learning cues is to allow the organism to respond before the advent of the critical situation. Backward conditioning would thus undermine the very condition that made cues functional in adaptation.[6]

We might suppose that simultaneous presentation of the cue and the critical characteristic of drive input (either onset or termination, depending upon whether the cue is to develop approach or avoidance properties) would provide optimal conditions for learning positive valence. But much evidence suggests that it does not. Not only must the cue occur before the critical portion of the drive input; sufficient time must also elapse between the two if a response is to occur. It takes time for the organism to react, and without such a reaction the cue cannot affect behavior relative to the critical circumstance. Numerous studies have indicated that the optimal time interval is approximately one-half second, though the cue may precede the critical component of primary drive input by as much as ten seconds and still acquire motivating properties.

The Motivating Properties of Positive Cues. Why does a positive cue serve as an activator at all? The organism is already activated by the primary drive, which moves with it as it changes position in the environment. The answer is as simple as it is compelling. Unless the cue produces a motivational increment beyond what existed in the organism before presentation, the organism will *not* move *toward* it but will persist in random activity. Can we not assume that the positive cue simply has a steering or orienting function, rather than the power to increase motivation? This approach begs the question, for a shift in the direction of any system requires an energy increment to bring it about.[7]

What is the source of input constituting extra motivation? Let us assume that a rat has learned to move toward a flashing light that signals the presence of food. What motivates this movement? We believe that the light directly occasions the apperception of food encodes which produce automatic changes like salivation, which in turn serve as the input of motivational increment. If we are correct, then two kinds of learning are involved in the association of positive properties with a cue. The cue must not only be encoded; it must also be able to activate the organism. In our example we have used flashing light as the previously neutral stimulus. It is likely that the sight and smell of most foods were initially neutral and only gradually came to elicit the preparatory responses initiating incremental motivation after association with the process of eating.

Under certain conditions motivation occasioned by cues may activate behavior even when primary drive input is minimal: An organism that is only slightly hungry may nevertheless move toward an appropriate cue. The sheer presence of the cue apparently increases drive input sufficiently to direct activity. At least three factors probably enter into such motivation: The cue tends to focus the small hunger input, to bring about apperception of related encodes which automatically activate preparatory responses, and to arouse anticipation of pleasure as a component of frustration.

We must still deal with another fundamental problem: Why does the organism move toward a cue when disequilibrium increases as it comes closer to the cue. Does this behavior not contradict the postulate of process, which asserts that all activity tends toward equilibrium? Let us consider an example that should clear up these apparent inconsistencies.

Our subject is a young man experiencing only slight sexual hunger. Suddenly he is placed in an appropriate situation with a desirable and receptive young woman, and after several intervening steps he has sexual intercourse with her. We assume that a particular series of events has occurred.

First, he has apperceived the young woman, which has brought pertinent encodes directly into focus. They have automatically activated his preparatory responses, thus introducing more "sexually toned" input into the integration matrix. Once this input has been apperceived it functions as an increment of drive. And here is the crux of the problem. Why does the young man not move away rather than toward the girl? With every move toward her his preparatory responses became more dramatic and the consequent disequilibrium greater. According to the postulate of process, each movement is *immediately* equilibratory, which is true even in this apparently paradoxical example. For each time that the young man moves toward the girl, the disequilibrium is briefly reduced, but the movement itself introduces new and more potent stimuli that increase net motivation. The young man moves step by step from frying pan into fire. Each movement in itself is equilibratory, but its result is greater activation.

The same logic applies to an animal's movement toward a food source. As the rat in our earlier example draws closer to the flashing light, each movement, though temporarily equilibratory causes more drive input. The cues previously associated with food become more predominant in apperception, occasioning more intense reverberations from accelerating preparatory responses. Furthermore, as drive increases, apperception is flooded with related input and associated encodes; there is a consequent jamming of components extraneous to hunger. The organism thus moves toward the cue as a moth moves toward a flame. The following corollary of positive cue motivation may be stated.

Any cue that occasions apperception of encodes that in turn produce visceral changes ordinarily present during equilibratory activity has the power to intensify motivation beyond that produced by primary drive input.

The conclusions to be drawn from this discussion are obvious, even from our own common experience. Human beings and probably other mammals do not even need externally imposed cues for increases in motivation to take place;

apperception of appropriate encodes may be quite sufficient. A slightly hungry person who thinks about a sizzling steak becomes more hungry, and almost any man under ninety can lie in a room and become sexually aroused simply by thinking about an appropriate partner.

But what is the nature of the motivational increment from the cue? It is likely related to changes occasioned by the apperception of encodes. Can the apperception of pertinent encodes actually occasion an increase in the primary drive, or are the repercussions of apperception different from those of the primary drive? Does thinking about food or a sexual partner actually increase appetite, or do changes brought about by such thoughts simply produce other motivational inputs additional to the primary drive? The answer to this question probably hinges on the source of the primary input. If the primary drive is initiated and sustained solely by shifts in chemical composition of the blood, it seems unlikely that a cue could increase it further. But, if the primary drive is at least partly the product of visceral changes, then an increase occasioned by the cue might activate more of the same receptors that contributed to the primary input. Apperception of the cue may actually increase hunger, whether for a sexual partner or a steak.

Regardless of which of these possibilities turns out to be correct, there is another source of motivation that typically operates when a positive cue is presented. The fact that pleasure is only being anticipated rather than actually experienced (see Chapter 3) adds an element of frustration. If we observe a six-month-old child, we can see him become suddenly alert at the sounds preliminary to his dinner. The longer he waits and the more sounds emanate from the kitchen, the more excited he becomes until, if the wait is prolonged, he bursts into frenzied crying.

In fact, whenever the disequilibratory input signifying deficit or surfeit is apperceived, an element of frustration enters the motivational complex: There is always a delay between apperception of drive input and satisfaction of the drive through consummatory or elimination behavior. In classical terminology the temporal gap between anticipation and realization constitutes a "barrier" between the organism and the satisfaction of its need, which defines the term "frustration" as it is commonly used. What input constitutes this additional motivation? Very likely it is that ordinarily apperceived as anger.

Experimental evidence demonstrating positive motivation produced by cues is considerable. The fact that Pavlov's dog would salivate to a metronome suggests that the conditioned stimulus had acquired the capacity to initiate visceral changes accentuating hunger or providing input additional to hunger. Many priming studies demonstrating that organisms will run faster when given bits of food or water just before the test trials strongly suggest that motivation is increased by incentives. The goal gradient almost universally observed in animals as they move toward equilibrium is further evidence of such motivational increment.

Appetites and Appetite Hierarchies. In the context of this discussion of motivating properties of positive cues the term "appetite" has special significance. Even if we accept the notion that an organism is born with a tendency to move toward certain specific stimuli, we must still assume that learning plays a major role in determining which particular circumstance is appropriate to each kind of disequilibratory input. Appetites develop through experience with quite specific functional objects and situations: Any number of different kinds of food can occasion reduction in human hunger, but the individual typically samples only a small number of the total population of such food items. When a particular food is eaten frequently, its encode becomes more firmly established and tends to be apperceived whenever hunger arises. If an individual were given nothing but rice to eat, that encode would be the only one available for food and would intrude into apperception whenever he became hungry. The input from preparatory responses and from frustration would add to motivation, and the individual would move toward cues signifying the presence of rice.

Particular appetites appropriate to all the various disequilibratory inputs are assumed to have developed in like fashion. The more often a drive input, regardless of its source, is associated with a specific object or circumstance, the greater will be the tendency for the encode of that object or circumstance to enter apperception when the given disequilibrium is introduced. No doubt, as various cafeteria studies have suggested, some organisms are born with at least rudimentary body wisdom, so that certain objects, activities, and circumstances appear intrinsically more appropriate than do others from the beginning. But it is relative quantities of experience with different kinds of equilibrators whether foods, sexual partners, or some other that establishes the ultimate appetite hierarchy of each individual.

Effects of Drive Shift on Positive Cues. We might conclude that certain approach properties of cues that arise from their role in primary drive reduction are manifested only when one particular disequilibratory state occurs in the organism, that a given cue like a bell that has been associated with hunger reduction will occasion approach behavior only when the organism is hungry.[8] From a functional point of view this conclusion seems logical, for generalized drive would orient the organism inappropriately: The organism might, for example, move toward food when thirsty or toward water when hungry. Although we believe that drive generalization does not occur, there are certain circumstances in which it may *appear* to occur.

It is possible that a cue for hunger reduction can positively influence a thirsty animal if it raises the hunger input until it predominates over that of thirst. Such an eventuality would more likely occur when the organism was only slightly less hungry than thirsty before exposure to the cue. A more dramatic example would be one in which a fairly hungry organism was aroused sexually by appropriate visual and tactual cues. As the sex drive increased the hunger would be effectively jammed. A researcher who assumed that the resulting copulation was caused by the hunger drive would obviously be mistaken.

Another example of shifts in drive dominance resulting from cues—and one about which some knowledge of the conflicting physiological systems involved is available—is that of a sexually aroused animal suddenly exposed to a cue signifying extreme danger. Fortunately, the input (fear) from visceral changes controlled by the sympathetic nervous system dominates the input (sexual drive) controlled by the parasympathetic nervous system. It is no accident that sexual excitation is the only automatic activation under the control of the parasympathetic system; it can thus easily be blocked by action of the sympathetic system. A sexually involved animal is doubly in danger, because of its rather vulnerable position during intercourse and because of flooding that may block cues critical to survival.

The following corollary can be stated:

The positive properties of a cue can be demonstrated only when the organism is apperceiving the disequilibratory input previously reduced in the presence of that cue.

This corollary explains the inconsistent results of researchers trying to demonstrate that cues accompanying the termination or reduction of an aversive drive will acquire positive properties. First, such cues may not have been apperceived by the organism, for the investigator typically has not used a discriminative stimulus paradigm. Second, and more important, neither the primary nor the secondary disequilibratory input has been present during the test. If a flashing light were used to signal the imminent termination of shock and if the animals thus trained were tested during either shock or fear, the corollary indicates that positive results would be obtained. That is, the animal would move toward the flashing light.

Discussion

This analysis suggests several differences between deneutralization of positive and negative cues. In approach learning the previously neutral cue acquires positive properties through association with reduction of disequilibrium and depends upon the presence of this particular input for its demonstration. In avoidance learning, on the other hand, the cue acquires negative valence through association with the onset of primary drive and depends upon input from a secondary activation system to affect behavior.

Examples will perhaps clarify both situations. A bell that has been associated with eating will acquire approach properties, but can affect behavior only when the organism is hungry. A bell that has been associated with the onset of pain will occasion avoidance behavior *whenever* it is sounded.

Although *both* positive and negative cues activate secondary systems, the functions of such input are quite different. Input from the secondary system provides the entire motivation for avoidance behavior but only a component of the motivation for approach responses, most of which comes from the primary system.

These differences seem quite logical from the point of view of adaptation. For the bell to have positive valence when the organism was *not* hungry would be detrimental to survival; it might move toward the cue when it was thirsty or in pain. But it is vital to the survival of the organism that the bell always produce avoidance behavior, for it is a cue to general danger.

The findings of Pavlovian conditioning experiments generally support the conclusions in this section, but they also pose other problems. Most theorists who have evaluated the Pavlovian paradigm have assumed that there is a simple transfer of properties from the unconditioned stimulus to the conditioned stimulus. Indeed, such a transfer does seem to occur, but it is simply an ostensible feature of the organism's reactions, not the process itself. In our view the organism never literally responds to the conditioned stimulus as such. Let us assume that we have associated a bell with the presentation of meat powder, so that after a number of such pairings the dog will salivate to the encode for meat powder whenever the bell is sounded; the salivation is elicited by this memory residual, not by the bell per se.

All cue learning, whether avoidance or approach, involves interposition of the encode between the cue and the response, and it is this encode that occasions automatic visceral changes introducing increment motivation.

The data from preconditioning and higher-order conditioning experiments fit easily into this interpretation. It will be recalled from our discussion of encode learning that the apperception of input is all that is required for encoding to take place. All preconditioning studies involve contiguous presentation of two neutral stimuli before conditioning training. If both these inputs are apperceived, both will occasion the establishment of encodes; if they are apperceived in close succession, a relationship between them should develop. Either one of them will then occasion the conditioned response when the other has been used as a conditioned stimulus.

In training for higher-order conditioning the sequence is changed, but the logic remains the same. Let us assume that a bell is already a highly effective conditioned stimulus. We pair it with a buzzer until the subject salivates to the buzzer alone. Although higher-order conditioning is very difficult to demonstrate, let us assume that in this instance it has taken place. If the bell and the buzzer are both apperceived, both will be encoded. When they are presented in close proximity an association between them should be established. Under these conditions the introduction of the buzzer will occasion apperception of the bell encode, which will be followed by apperception of the encode for meat powder.

The results obtained in both preconditioning and higher-order conditioning experiments thus result from association between at least two previously neutral stimuli. If one of these stimuli is deneutralized, whether after or before association training, the other will occasion the conditioned response. But in neither instance does the subject respond directly to the previously neutral cue. Regardless of the length of the association chain, the response is to the encode for meat powder.

Establishment of Associations

As we have explained in the previous sections, two different types of learning are assumed to occur in complex organisms: that involving establishment of encodes and that accounting for deneutralization of cues. A third kind of learning, the development of associations, also has fundamental importance. We may begin our examination of it simply by stating the conditions assumed to underlie it.

The strength of the association between two encodes is a direct function of the number of contiguous presentations of the two apperceived inputs.

Contiguity is thus the crucial circumstance for association learning, and repetition is a basic requirement for strengthening the association. It should be emphasized that there must be a time lapse between presentation of two components; otherwise, fusion will occur.

What is the optimum interval for development of associations between encodes? This question raises another problem. If the input components are widely separated, other inputs may intervene and interfere with the crucial association. Contiguity is thus important primarily because it tends to lessen the probablilty that extraneous encodes will disrupt the association. We recall the first postulate of learning: Any input component that is apperceived will be encoded. Therefore the more numerous the extraneous inputs between any two others, the greater the probability of interference will be. The last statement, with slight modifications, may be taken as a corollary of forgetting.

The weakening of an association results from the number of apperceived extraneous components intervening between the related encodes.

The circumstances occasioning the development of an association between any two encodes also account for serial learning. Accordingly, any number of inputs presented sequentially will tend to become associated to the extent that the series is repeated and extraneous inputs do not intervene; the same conditions that affect the learning of a maze by a rat also account for the encoding of a list of nonsense syllables or the refinement of a motor skill by a human being. In any such instance a series of inputs (whether specific bits or fused phenomena) becomes interrelated purely through contiguity and repeated presentation.

Many variables can, of course, affect the development of such encode chains, though apperception is always a requirement. They include the number of components in the series, their relative isolation from one another, the intensity of the similarity of prior encodes, and the similarity among the various components of the series. The effects of most of these variables on serial learning have been thoroughly examined by many investigators, from Ebbinghaus to B. J. Underwood, yet they continue to offer a vital approach to the study of human learning.

Summary

The principle assumed to be both necessary and sufficient for encoding is apperception of input, whether the latter is derived from one of the various transmitting mechanisms or from memory. Once apperception occurs, however, many other variables can affect both the speed of the encoding processes and the durability of the encode. "Forgetting," or "extinction," is assumed to result primarily from interference and is demonstrable when incompatible material distorts an existing encode or disrupts an established association. Three different types of learning are postulated: learning that accounts for establishment of encodes, learning that determines valence, and learning that produces associations.

Repeated references to apperception in the development of our theory indicate that the process of focusing on input is critical. In Chapter 6 we shall examine this process and assess its contribution to the behavior of complex organisms. It may be noted here, however, that apperception will emerge as the single most important principle in our theory, for it is the mechanism by which the particular input, whether sensory or recalled, temporarily most crucial for the equilibrium of the organism is brought into focus so that it can determine action. The term "attention" has long been used to represent what some investigators have also called "the selective nature of conciousness," but we reject it because it has typically been limited to the "selection" of sensory components only. We prefer the term "apperception," implying both sensory and memory input. From this point on, the term "focalization," rather than "selection," will be used, because the latter implies that "something or somebody" is doing the selecting. We believe that input is brought into focus according to laws of interaction among multiple components from both sensation and memory and that apperception must be considered a passive recipient, rather than an active selecting mechanism.

Notes

[1]Contrary to popular opinion, eidetic imagery is most pronounced in the early adolescent, rather than in the small child, though it is extremely common in both. According to G. W. Allport (1928), it is a kind of clear visual memory that inhibits creative thinking because the encodes cannot easily be separated and reassembled in new patterns. B. Berelson and G. A. Steiner (1964) have estimated that fewer than 10 percent of adults still retain the capacity, whereas H. Klüver (1926) quoted studies in which it was found in 99 percent and 88

percent of twelve- to fourteen-year-olds respectively. Klüver also found eidetic imagery more common in females than in males.

There is a characteristic that seems to belong to a number of apparently disparate events: the hallucinations occasioned by psychosis and drugs, the imprinting that can be demonstrated in many birds, the eidetic imagery common in children, and the hoarding behavior of rats that have been starved during infancy. In all these examples it seems that a particular chemical characteristic of the blood predisposes the organism to powerful and vivid imagery that remains as an enduring memory residual affecting behavior. When the circumstances are appropriate the organism appears not only to be motivated by the apperception of such vivid encodes but also to seek or to flee from their sensory duplicates. During certain maturational phases (like immediately after hatching in birds, soon after birth in rats, and during early adolescence in children) the chemical character of the blood produces imprinting whether of Konrad Lorenz, a food pellet, or the Beatles. When the drive appropriate to the imprinted object is being apperceived, the individual tends to be motivated toward replicas of the encode, at least when they are available: The ducks follow Lorenz, the rats hoard pellets, and the adolescent (it is not by accident that the capacity for eidetic imagery is greatest in pubescent children) goes to hear the Beatles. In psychosis when the relevant drive (guilt, anxiety, or hostility) is present the individual hallucinates the image and reacts to any situation even remotely similar to it. This common thread, the tendency for acute images to occur during certain critical periods of development and the further tendency for them to be apperceived and to influence behavior, is present in all these diverse phenomena.

[2]H. Ebbinghaus (1913) was the first to find that overlearning produces more durable encodes. W. C. F. Krueger (1929), using lists of monosyllabic nouns, found that overlearning significantly aided retention, but that increased overlearning produced a negatively accelerating curve. L. Postman (1962) repeated Krueger's experiment under better-controlled conditions and achieved the same results. B. J. Underwood (1954), using both nonsense syllables and paired-associate lists, found that overlearning significantly increased recall. L. S. Reid (1953) discovered that increased overlearning led rats to learn a reversal-discrimination task in significantly fewer trials than did rats with only small amounts of overlearning and rats with no overlearning. These results were confirmed by E. J. Capaldi and H. W. Stevenson (1957) and by B. H. Pubols, Jr., (1956), in a position-reversal experiment. J. S. Bruner and his colleagues (1958), also using rats, found this overlearning effect in a task consisting of a four-choice, serial-position problem, but B. B. Boycott and J. Z. Young (1958), J. M. Warren (1960), and Warren and his colleagues (1960) found that overlearning did not aid reversal learning in octopuses, chickens, and fish.

[3]Learning by observation or imitation has been demonstrated by many researchers. N. E. Miller and J. Dollard (1941) trained rats either to follow or not to follow a leader in a T maze. C. L. Darby and A. J. Riopelle (1959) found that monkeys can learn by imitation, and B. Dawson and B. M. Foss (1965) found that birds can learn to lift the lid from a container to obtain food after watching other birds. A. Bandura and A. C. Huston (1961) found that children tended to imitate certain aspects of an experimenter's behavior, even aspects irrelevant to the experiment. Bandura (1962) and Bandura and R. H. Walters (1963) have demonstrated the imitation of social and aggressive behavior of grade-school children. Bandura, D. Ross, and S. A. Ross (1963) and D. J. Hicks (1965) found that exposure to films of aggression led children to imitate the

forms of aggression seen, especially when the models in the films were adult males. Hicks (1965) has demonstrated in a retest that the aggression shown by the adult male model may still be imitated six months later.

More recently, in a series of ingenious experiments pioneered by M. H. Marx and repeatedly confirmed by M. E. Rosenbaum, observation alone has been found to be either equal or superior to performance with immediate knowledge of results. A communication from Marx (1971) outlines some of the basic findings and problems of this research.

Subjects who merely "observe" (that is, watch other subjects responding in a learning situation) were reported by W. A. Hillix and Marx (1960) to have acquired S-R connections more rapidly than had subjects who "performed" (engaged in trial and error with immediate knowledge of results). This superiority, which suggests greater efficacy in acquisition of a purely cognitive function, was attributed to either the observer's greater opportunity for rehearsal or greater interference from errors in the performer. It has since been repeatedly confirmed by Rosenbaum in an extensive series of experiments (see Rosenbaum and Arenson, 1968, for a summary of this work). But all these experiments used a task in which a chain or series of switches had to be learned; more recent research with discrete S-R units has generally failed to confirm observer superiority. In one such experiment (Marx and K. Marx, 1970), for example, no difference between observer and performer was found, though a reliable increment in the frequency of subjects showing greater observer learning did occur between the fourth and sixth elementary-school grades. In another recent experiment (Marx and D. W. Witter, 1972) performers repeated *both* correct responses and errors more frequently than did observers on a training trial immediately following a test trial (even though no overall difference in number of correct responses occurred). It was concluded that observer superiority tends to occur when the higher frequency of error repetition by performers disrupts sequential response, as presumably occurred in the early experiments described. It may safely be stated at present that the direction of superiority varies with the task characteristics, though the exact nature of these differences still has to be worked out empirically.

4 In a famous study J. S. Calvin, E. A. Bicknell, and D. S. Sperling (1953) demonstrated that rats that were repeatedly but briefly put in distinctive cages during periods of high hunger drive ate more than did a control group when fed in such cages later. Apparently the distinctive cues had acquired secondary motivating properties supplementing those of the primary drive. Since that time many researchers—P. S. Siegel and M. R. MacDonnell (1954), A. K. Myers and N. E. Miller (1954), I. Greenberg (1954), B. B. Scarborough and F. E. Goodson (1957), D. Novin and N. E. Miller (1962), T. C. Howard and F. A. Young (1962), and W. Pieper and Marx (1963)—have failed to find supporting evidence. The hypothesis that cues associated with the presence or increase of consummatory drives will acquire motivating properties remains extremely tenuous. Apparently there is insufficient change in the character of drive input for cues in the environment to become associated with it: The increase in hunger or thirst is too gradual. Furthermore, not only is the drive a diffuse state that moves with the organism, but also there are few discrete and emphatic stimuli in the environment that can become associated with whatever shifts in drive input may take place.

5 There have been approximately twenty different experiments on this topic since the pioneer study by H. W. Coppock in 1950. In 1961 R. C. Beck reviewed the basic data on the problem and concluded that the results were still equivocal,

but in the last few years some experimenters appear to have overcome some of his objections. W. W. Wenrich and D. D. Cahoon (1965) obtained positive results when a light and a clicker were used as S^D (discriminative stimuli) in a bar-press, shock-termination design. In another study by E. E. Lawler (1965), which closely resembled that of Goodson and A. Brownstein (1955), an effort was made to test with a secondary motivator (a buzzer that had been paired with shock during training) present. Positive results were obtained, but the secondary motivator did not seem to have the predicted effect. There seem to have been no studies in which subjects were tested with primary drive present. O. H. Mowrer (1960) believes that such a study is critical if definitive results are to be obtained, particularly as the studies that have demonstrated secondary reinforcement in consummatory drive termination have all been conducted with primary drive present.

6Many researchers have questioned I. P. Pavlov's (1927) claim that the conditioned response cannot result from backward conditioning (presentation of the unconditioned stimulus before the conditioned stimulus). Four early studies, by S. A. Switzer (1930), H. M. Wolfe (1932), A. L. Bernstein (1934), and W. F. Grether (1938), produced results indicating that Pavlov was incorrect. But two other early studies, by H. Cason (1935) and J. M. Porter (1938), as well as five recent ones, by A. Spooner and W. N. Kellogg (1947), M. E. Fitzwater and M. N. Reisman (1952), R. A. Champion (1962), L. J. Kasmin (1963), and M. A. Trapold, M. Homzie, and E. Rutledge (1964), yielded results supporting Pavlov's statement. For example, Spooner and Kellogg ran six groups of human subjects in 100 trials of a finger-withdrawal experiment. They discovered that in the first twenty trials responses were 20 percent conditioned in the backward-responses and simultaneous-conditioning groups, in the next forty trials 10 percent, and in the remaining trials less than 5 percent. These results appear to indicate that backward and simultaneous conditioning produce decremental, or extinction, effects, exactly the reverse of forward conditioning.

7There is some evidence of the motivating effects of positive cues. The sight of pellets apparently activates the hoarding response even in sated rats (Marx, 1950). Mowrer (1960) has argued that the sight of food triggers a "hunger fear" and that this fear, rather than hunger itself may be responsible for the hoarding behavior of rats. W. J. Brogden (1942) found that dogs trained to lift their paws for food continued to do so even after they were sated and would not eat. In our own laboratory we found that rats run significantly faster when "primed" with a secondary reinforcer just before running; in a similar study E. L. Wike and A. Casey (1954) found that the mere presence of food in the goal box motivated rats to run faster and more consistently, even though the animals were sated. Actually, only slight consideration suggests that every secondary reinforcer must also by definition be an activator. There are now more than 200 studies demonstrating that secondary reinforcers can be used to slow the process of extinction, occasion the learning of new responses, or change the subjects' orientation. By any or all these criteria it can be immediately observed that additional motivation is an implicit property of secondary reinforcers. Such motivational increment seems dramatic only when it can be demonstrated once the primary drive has been alleviated.

8Can the approach properties of a cue be demonstrated when the appropriate drive input is not present? Experimental data on this point remain somewhat equivocal. Miller (1951) reported that a chimpanzee trained to beg for tokens to earn bananas would not do so when sated. A study reported by D. E. Wooldridge (1963) demonstrated that a rat with electrodes implanted in its hunger-reward center would stimulate itself when hungry but not when sated. J. L. Brown (1956) and R. C. Miles (1956) both found that, though drive level is not important in development of secondary reinforcers, it is significant in subsequent use of these reinforcers; that is, rats that were not hungry pressed the bar for a tone or a light far fewer times than did hungry ones. W. K. Estes (1949) discovered that hungry rats do press a bar when thirsty but that sated rats press no more often than do controls. In similar experiments W. B. Webb (1949) and C. M. Brandauer (1953) demonstrated that rats initially trained in bar pressing when hungry, whose training had then been extinguished under varying degrees of thirst but with food satiation, pressed more frequently the longer they had been deprived of water. Webb and I. J. Goodman (1958) trained hungry rats to press the bar for food. Then the rats were fed and put back into the training box for five minutes, during which bar presses were recorded. The box was then flooded, and it was discovered that the need to escape from the water resulted in a significant increase in the number of bar presses.

References

Allport, G. W. The eidetic image and the after image. *American Journal of Psychology*, 1928, 40: 418-425.

Bandura, A. Social learning through imitation. In M. R. Jones (ed.), *Nebraska symposium on motivation.* Lincoln: University of Nebraska Press, 1962.

Bandura, A., and Huston, A. C. Identification as a process of incidental learning. *Journal of Abnormal and Social Psychology*, 1961, 63: 311-318.

Bandura, A., Ross, D., and Ross, S. A. Imitation of film-mediated aggressive models. *Journal of Abnormal and Social Psychology*, 1963, 66: 3-11.

Bandura, A., and Walters, R. H. *The social learning of deviant behavior: A behavioristic approach.* New York: Holt, Rinehart and Winston, 1963.

Beck, R. C. On secondary reinforcement and shock termination. *Psychological Bulletin*, 1961, 58: 28-45.

Berelson, B., and Steiner, G. A. *Human behavior: An inventory of scientific findings.* New York: Harcourt Brace Jovanovich, 1964.

Bernstein, A. L. Temporal factors in the formation of conditioned eyelid reactions in human subjects. *Journal of Genetic Psychology*, 1934, 10: 173-197.

Boycott, B. B., and Young, J. Z. Reversal of learned responses in *Octopus vulgaris* Lamarck. *Animal Behavior*, 1958, 6: 45-52.

Brandauer, C. M. A confirmation of Webb's data concerning the action of irrelevant drives. *Journal of Experimental Psychology*, 1953, 45: 150-52.

Brogden, W. J. Non-alimentary components in the food-reinforcement of conditioned forelimb-flexion in food satiated dogs. *Journal of Experimental Psychology*, 1942, 30: 326-335.

Brown, J. L. The effect of drive on learning with secondary reinforcement from the primary drive. *Journal of Comparative and Physiological Psychology*, 1956, 49: 254-260.

Bruner, J. S., Mandler, J. M., O'Dowd, D., and Wallach, M. A. The role of overlearning and drive level in reversal learning. *Journal of Comparative and Physiological Psychology*, 1958, 51: 607-613.

Calvin, J. S., Bicknell, E. A., and Sperling, D. S.　Establishment of a conditioned drive based on the hunger drive. *Journal of Comparative and Physiological Psychology*, 1953, 46: 173-175.

Capaldi, E. J., and Stevenson, H. W.　Response reversal following different amounts of training. *Journal of Comparative and Physiological Psychology*, 1957, 50: 195-198.

Cason, H.　Backward conditioned eyelid reactions. *Journal of Experimental Psychology*, 1935, 18: 599-611.

Champion, R. A.　Stimulus-response contiguity in classical aversive conditioning. *Journal of Experimental Psychology*, 1962, 64: 34-39.

Coppock, H. W.　An investigation of secondary reinforcing effect of a visual stimulus as a function of its temporal relation to shock termination. Unpublished doctoral dissertation, University of Indiana, 1950.

Darby, C. L., and Riopelle, A. J.　Observational learning of monkeys. *Journal of Comparative and Physiological Psychology*, 1959, 52: 94-98.

Dawson, B., and Foss, B. M.　Observation learning in budgerigars. *Animal Behavior*, 1965, 13: 470-474.

Ebbinghaus, H.　*Memory: A contribution to experimental psychology*. Trans. by H. A. Krueger and C. E. Bussenius. New York: Columbia University Teachers College, 1913.

Estes, W. K.　Generalization of secondary reinforcement from the primary drive. *Journal of Comparative and Physiological Psychology*, 1949, 42: 286-295.

Fitzwater, M. E., and Reisman, M. N.　Comparison of forward, simultaneous, backward, and pseudo-conditioning. *Journal of Experimental Psychology*, 1952, 64: 211-214.

Goodson, F. E., and Brownstein, A.　Secondary reinforcing and motivating properties of stimuli contiguous with shock onset and termination. *Journal of Comparative and Physiological Psychology*. 1955, 48: 381-386.

Greenberg, I.　The acquisition of a thirst drive. Unpublished doctoral dissertation, University of Pennsylvania, 1954.

Grether, W. F.　Pseudo-conditioning without paired stimulation encountered in attempted backward conditioning. *Journal of Comparative Psychology*, 1938, 48: 91-26.

Hicks, D. J.　Imitation and retention of film-mediated aggressive peer and adult models. *Journal of Personality and Social Psychology*, 1965, 2: 97-100.

Hillix, W. A., and Marx, M. H.　Response strengthening by information and effect in human learning. *Journal of Experimental Psychology*, 1960, 60: 97-102.

Howard, T. C., and Young, F. A.　Conditioned hunger and secondary rewards in monkeys. *Journal of Comparative and Physiological Psychology*, 1962, 55: 392-397.

Hull, C. L.　*Principles of behavior: An introduction to behavior theory*. New York: Appleton, 1943.

Kasmin, L. J.　Backward conditioning and the conditioned emotional response. *Journal of Experimental Psychology*, 1963, 56: 517-519.

Klüver, H.　An experimental study of the eidetic type. *Genetic Psychology Monographs*, 1926, 1: 71-130.

Krueger, W. C. F.　The effect of overlearning on retention. *Journal of Experimental Psychology*, 1929, 12: 71-78.

Lawler, E. E.　Secondary reinforcement value of stimuli associated with shock reduction. *Quarterly Journal of Experimental Psychology*, 1965, 17: 57-62.

Marx, M. H. A stimulus-response analysis of the hoarding habit in the rat. *Psychological Review,* 1950, 57: 80-91.

Marx, M. H., and Marx, K. Observation vs. performance in learning over the fourth to the sixth grades. *Psychonomic Science,* 1970, 21: 199-200.

Marx, M. H., and Witter, D. W. Repetition of correct responses and errors as a function of performance with reward or information. *Journal of Experimental Psychology,* 1972, 92: 53-58.

Miles, R. C. The relative effectiveness of secondary reinforcers throughout deprivation and habit-strength parameters. *Journal of Comparative and Physiological Psychology,* 1956, 49: 126-130.

Miller, N. E. Learnable drives and rewards. In S. S. Stevens (ed.), *Handbook of experimental psychology.* New York: Wiley, 1951.

Miller, N. E., and Dollard, J. *Social learning and imitation.* New Haven: Yale University Press, 1941.

Mowrer, O. H. *Learning theory and behavior.* New York: Wiley, 1960.

Myers, A. K., and Miller, N. E. Failure to find a learned drive based on hunger; evidence for learning motivated by "exploration." *Journal of Comparative and Physiological Psychology,* 1954, 47: 428-436.

Novin, D., and Miller, N. E. Failure to condition thirst induced by feeding dry food to hungry rats. *Journal of Comparative and Physiological Psychology,* 1962, 55: 373-374.

Pavlov, I. P. *Conditioned reflexes.* Trans. by G. V. Anrep. London: University Press, 1927.

Peiper, W. and Marx, M. H. Conditioning of a previously neutral cue to the onset of a metabolic drive: Two instances of negative results. *Psychological Records,* 1963, 13: 191-195.

Porter, J. M. Extinction of an acquired response as a function of the interval between successive non-rewarded trials. *Journal of Comparative Psychology,* 1938, 26: 261-270.

Postman, L. Retention as a function of degree of overlearning. *Science,* 1962, 135: 666-667.

Pubols, B. H., Jr. The facilitation of visual and spatial discrimination reversal by learning. *Journal of Comparative and Physiological Psychology,* 1956, 49: 243-248.

Reid, L. S. The development of noncontinuity behavior through continuity learning. *Journal of Experimental Psychology,* 1953, 46: 107-112.

Rosenbaum, M. E., and Arenson, S. J. Observational learning: Some theory, some variables, some data. In E. C. Simmel, R. A. Hoppe, and G. A. Milton (eds.), *Social facilitation and imitative behavior.* Boston: Allyn and Bacon, 1968.

Scarborough, B. B., and Goodson, F. E. Properties of stimuli associated with strong and weak hunger drive in the rat. *Journal of Genetic Psychology,* 1957, 91: 257-261.

Siegel, P. S., and MacDonnell, M. R. A repetition of the Calvin-Bicknell-Sperling study of conditioned drive. *Journal of Comparative and Physiological Psychology,* 1954, 47: 250-252.

Spooner, A., and Kellog, W. N. The backward conditioning curve. *American Journal of Psychology,* 1947, 60: 321-334.

Switzer, S. A. Backward conditioning of the lid reflex. *Journal of Experimental Psychology,* 1930, 13: 76-97.

Trapold, M. A., Homzie, M., and Rutledge, E. Backward conditioning and UCR latency. *Journal of Experimental Psychology,* 1964, 67: 387-391.

Underwood, B. J. Studies of distributed practice. 12. Retention following varying degrees of original learning. *Journal of Experimental Psychology,* 1954, 47: 294-300.

Warren, J. M. Reversal learning by paradise fish *(Macropodus opercularis). Journal of Comparative and Physiological Psychology,* 1960, 53: 376-378.

Warren, J. M., Brookshire, K. H., Ball, G. G., and Reynolds, D. V. Reversal learning by white leghorn chickens. *Journal of Comparative and Physiological Psychology*, 1960, 53: 371-375.

Webb, W. B. The motivational aspect of an irrelevant drive on the behavior of the white rat. *Journal of Experimental Psychology*, 1949, 39: 1-4.

Webb, W. B., and Goodman, I. J. Activating role of an irrelevant drive in the absence of the relevant drive. *Psychological Reports,* 1958, 4: 235-238.

Wenrich, W. W., and Cahoon, D. D. Note on secondary reinforcement using a discriminative stimulus from an aversive stimulus. *Psychological Reports,* 1965, 16: 1242-1244.

Wike, E. L. *Secondary reinforcement: Selected experiments.* New York: Harper & Row, 1966.

Wike, E. L., and Casey, A. The secondary reward value of food for satiated animals. *Journal of Comparative and Physiological Psychology*, 1954, 47: 441-443.

Wolfe, H. M. Conditioning as a function of the interval between the conditioned and the original stimulus. *Journal of Genetic Psychology,* 1932, 7: 80-103.

Wooldridge, D. E. *The machinery of the brain.* New York: McGraw-Hill, 1963.

6
Focalization

In Chapter 3 we defended the view that various transmitting mechanisms (whether specialized receptors, free nerve endings, or fluids) are being activated during every moment of an individual's life and that each of these mechanisms introduces sensory components into the integration matrix. As reacting to all such information bits would impose unresolvable complexity, we observed in Chapter 4 how fusion and structuring simplify the organism's effective environment and the manner in which information is encoded. But, as a function of learning (see Chapter 5), the organism once again suffers an impossible information overload. Not only are fused sensory components being continually imposed, but also thousands of encodes are potentially available. Simultaneous reaction to all such inputs would be not only impossible but also completely unadaptive (see Chapter 2); some kind of focusing mechanism therefore becomes prerequisite to effective behavior. Apperception,[1] as we use the term here, is the process by which inputs from sensory receptors or memory are brought into focus in a given moment.

The importance of apperception in our theory cannot be overemphasized. Without it neither primary nor secondary encoding could occur, and apperception of memory residuals encompasses all thought behavior. Furthermore, as we shall argue more fully in Chapter 7, apperception provides the immediate occasion for most, though not all, overt behavior.

Apperception is both completely automatic and lawful, without doubt the most highly refined homeostatic process that has emerged during evolution. Hence the first postulate of apperception.

What is brought into focus constitutes the most equilibratory outcome of the interactions among materials from both sensation and memory at any given moment.

This postulate is a logical extension of the basic postulate of process, that all activity, whether overt or internal, tends immediately toward equilibrium.

What are the variables that determine which component within the integration matrix will be brought into focus at any given moment? This question is crucial to adequate understanding of the behavior of complex organisms. In the following discussion, we shall try to pinpoint some of these variables and to indicate, at least in a general way, how they contribute to continuing apperception.

The Influence of Structure

Even as a riverbed determines the direction in which water will flow to produce the greatest balance of all the forces at work, so the structure of the organism influences the particular course of apperception that will be most equilibratory. It accounts, for example, for the fact that pain is more readily brought into focus than are other inputs of comparable intensity. Some critics of homeostatic theory have argued that the simple fact that we apperceive pain—which is essentially a powerful disequilibratory input—refutes the homeostatic theory. Why, they ask, would disequilibrium in any of its various forms—hunger, thirst, pain, the agony of unrequited love—be brought into focus at all if apperception tended toward equilibrium, as postulated in our theory? The answer is simple. The organism has been structured by the confluence of evolutionary circumstances in such a way that disequilibrium (in the form of experiental input) is thrust into the integration matrix so pervasively that the most equilibratory response *is* to focus on it. An individual may apperceive pain, an on-rushing tiger, the burning of a loved one, or hideous hallucinations (see Chapter 8).

It should be emphasized, however, that many components of input interact dynamically to determine which particular focus will be most equilibratory at any given moment. Structure determines that pain will be introduced into the integration matrix and that under ordinary circumstances such input will be brought into focus. Yet, if there is powerful competing material, like input constituting extreme anger, it might be apperceived instead of pain, and, if a particular memory residual is sufficiently pervasive, both anger and pain may be displaced. Therefore, though we maintain that apperception is the most equilibratory outcome of all dynamically interacting experiental materials, the structure of the organism powerfully affects the nature and direction of this resolution.

The Apperceptual Mechanism

The mechanism of apperception reflects, of course, the way in which the organism is structured. Curiously, we know little about this mechanism. Here are some unanswered questions. Can we apperceive more than one input component at one time?[2] In our previous discussion of this issue (see Chapter 2) we deduced that some focusing mechanism must have evolved to ensure that the organism would respond not simply to one input at a time but also to the component most pertinent to its survival at any given moment. We pointed out that simultaneous response to many inputs would result in nonintegrative and thus nonadaptive behavior. This analysis implies that apperception is a singular process, which may, however, fluctuate rapidly among inputs.

Sometimes it seems that apperception is very specific, focusing only on a minute component, whereas at other times it seems to encompass a "blob" composed of many different items. Is all apperception actually of single components but so rapid in its fluctuations that it *seems* to include a variety of components simultaneously? Or is apperception a multichannel system after all? We believe it is a single-channel system, that as one component is brought into focus at a given moment all others are effectively blocked out.

This probablility implies a neural mechanism that "cuts out" particular components as others are brought into focus, as some experimental evidence also suggests. In 1956 R. Hernández-Péon, H. Scherrer, and M. Jouvet implanted an electrode in the cochlear nucleus of a cat and found that a noise near the cat's cage produced a discernible spike in recordings from the electrode. They then presented the cat with inputs from other modalities. In one instance it was allowed to observe a glass beaker containing live mice, and in another the odor of fish was blown into the cage. Under these conditions the cat immediately became alert and at the same time the brain-wave spikes from the continuing sound decreased in magnitude! Apparently input from the visual or olfactory modalities was jamming the auditory components. Even if we accept the view that apperception operates on a single channel, so that only one input component can be brought into focus at any particular moment, two critical questions remain: How "big" is the component? How long is the moment? Let us consider these questions separately.

In our discussion of input fusion in Chapter 4, we suggested that the development of phenomenological unities is a function of the contiguous imposition of sensory bits, after which the person tends to apperceive not the separate components but the composites. The size of any given composite is determined by the degree of fusion among inputs from the situation being apperceived. Although the encode of a chair may be a composite of many discrete sensory elements, it has assumed unity, as far as apperception is concerned. The amount of fusion from primary encoding thus determines the "size" of the component that will thenceforth be apperceived. But, it may be objected, the individual need not apperceive the chair as a global phenomenon; he may focus on any of the many inputs that characterize his encode of it. Nevertheless, the chair is typically apperceived as a unit, and this unit is broken down only with effort and expenditure of time. Even when apperception encompasses many components, it is still assumed to be unitary. There is apparently a direct relationship between loss of detail and the breadth of the field brought into focus; when any particular aspect of the field comes under scrutiny, however, it, rather than the field, becomes central. Gestalt psychologists have called this shift the "figure-ground rivalry" and have devised many ingenious examples to demonstrate it.

How do we determine the "size" of an input component? It would be better to leave this question to future speculators and researchers, for its complexity is staggering; let us attempt a tentative first step toward answering it: The "size" of a given input component is whatever is apperceived. Regardless of the circularity implicit in this statement, it does offer some small possibility of empirical testing. If a human being is briefly exposed to a room filled with various items and is then asked what he has seen in the room, he will be able to list with some accuracy items like chairs, tables, and pictures, for he will recall totalities, rather than their individual characteristics. But the crux of the problem is revealed in even this simple example: Not only does the extent of fusion that has previously taken place determine what the person sees, but also the intrusion of language complicates both encoding and recall (see Chapter 7).

Although we suggest that apperception operates through a single channel, it may fluctuate rapidly between inputs. The speed of such fluctuation is the major factor responsible for erroneous conclusions that more than one component can be focalized simultaneously. There is a growing body of experimental evidence suggesting that apperception can fluctuate many times a second. In one experiment it was found that subjects could remember both a given form and its color when the form was presented tachistoscopically only once for an interval exceeding one-twentieth of a second. But, when the exposure period was less, the subject tended to be able to identify color or form. Actually, however, the maximum speed of apperceptual shift remains an open question.[3]

We are, of course, speculating about the upper limits of the speed of fluctuation. Obviously, apperception does not shift that rapidly under most ordinary conditions; if a particular input is sufficiently intense it may dominate apperception for an extended period.

Although few experiments have been aimed at discovering the nature of the apperceptual process, recent advances in equipment, particularly refinements in tachistoscopic instruments, suggest that many of the questions considered here may soon be answered with some degree of objectivity. Our own discussions suggest the following corollary.

As the duration of the exposure period becomes shorter, the tendency to apperceive single units will become greater until the point at which, when a number of items are presented, only one can be recalled.

As we assume a necessary relationship between apperception and encoding (see Chapter 5), this corollary can be tested—provided that the encode in question lasts long enough to allow recall. When techniques have become sufficiently refined to permit accurate measurement of the speed of apperceptual fluctuation, then the most troublesome issue of "size" of an input component can be resolved by presenting varied materials *at that speed,* and testing what the subject recalls.

What is the nature of the apperceptual mechanism? Any inferences about the physical process itself are undoubtedly premature. But certain general hypotheses, which the reader may consider questions, about its operations can be stated. It appears that the process is cyclical, somewhat analogous to the "sweep" of a radar scope but much more rapid. Accordingly, there may be a relationship between the rapidity of apperceptual fluctuation and the frequency of the hypothetical cycles, suggesting that the upper limit of apperceptual change would be fixed by the cycle frequency. But what kind of cycle? Perhaps a reverberating neural circuit of the Hebbian variety. If it could be isolated from the other potentials continually emanating from the brain cortex, some evidence might be gathered from brain-wave recordings.

We might jump to the conclusion that there is an intimate relationship between the processes accounting for lower absolute thresholds for pitch and flicker fusion, on one hand, and for the apperceptual mechanism on the other. But we are hard put to find any similarity other than the critical frequencies themselves. The lower thresholds for pitch and flicker fusion are both related to emergence of continuity in sensory input, whereas apperception is related to fluctuation toward inputs already present in the integration matrix. The difference is between how input is introduced and which variables determine whether or not it will be in focus. Indeed, central to our view of apperception is the notion that it focuses on components already potentially available within the integration matrix. But the mere fact that a component is present is little guarantee that it will be brought into focus. Both flicker fusion and the lower pitch threshold result from reverberatory overlap and may occur either in conjunction with or independent of apperception.

We might also leap to another equally incorrect conclusion: that apperceptual fluctuation is tied to eye movements. There is certainly a relationship between the focus of the eyes and the component in the visual field being apperceived, but these two factors can vary independently. Although the eyes may be focused on an object straight ahead, some component in the periphery of the visual field can be centered in apperception. Conversely, an input from the periphery may remain in focus while the eyes move through a relatively complete arc.

Structurally Imposed Predispositions

There are, however, certain variables in the structure of the organism that do influence apperception, which brings us to the second postulate of apperception.

The particular component (regardless of its inclusiveness) of sensation or memory that is in focus at any given moment is always the one that has provided the most enduring and relevant survival information in the total history of the organism (both as species and as individual).

An examination of certain characteristics of the evolutionary context should help us to pinpoint those variables that influence the process of focalization. What were some of the input characteristics particularly important to survival, of such significance that facile and rapid response to them was a survival imperative? The term response is used advisedly here because in a real sense apperception is the first and most fundamental adaptive response that the organism can make.

There is certainly a relationship between an organism's proximity to a predator and the danger involved. As there is also a correlation between the closeness of an item and the size of its visual image, we may predict that a "larger" input will more likely be apperceived than will a smaller one. There is also a relationship between proximity of an object and the amount of energy emanating from it; a more intense input will thus come more readily into focus than will a less intense one. Movement is another variable that has always had critical survival significance; this characteristic should therefore have corresponding importance in determining the course of apperception. Discreteness, or contrast, is another important variable: Other organisms have always been critical to survival, and, as their edges set them off from the background, the variable of discreteness should have great influence on which component in the integration matrix will be in focus. As the approach of the predator typically produces successions of similar sounds, repetition is also of enduring importance to survival and should thus have critical influence on apperception. Repetition of input increases the likelihood of its being brought into focus; but the influence of repetition has limitations. Repeated inputs over a short period have survival significance, but over an extended period they may block other vital information. Fortunately, sensory adaptation (see Chapter 7, note 2) helps to free the apperceptual mechanism from the dominance of prolonged repeated stimulation. We shall encompass all these variables in one corollary.

When other factors are constant, the greater the "size" (intensity, movement, repetition, discreteness) of a particular input, the greater will be the tendency for that input to be brought into focus in apperception.

Because vividness mirrors the importance of input for survival, we may predict that certain kinds of input will come more readily into focus than will others: Pain will be more easily apperceived than will thirst and thirst more easily than hunger. It is even fairly probable that certain specific inputs through a given modality will have a greater potential if they have had unique and enduring significance for survival. Red, the color of blood, is probably more readily brought into focus than is any other color.

Influence of Prior Encoding

Learning depends upon apperception, but it also affects the subsequent course of apperception. In the adult human being we find a complex network of associations and counterassociations that have been established by contiguous presentation of countless sensory inputs. The apperception of one component of a pair will trigger immediate focusing on the other, assuming, as does Hebb, that contiguous presentation of sensory inputs actually occasions structural changes in the organism.

When other factors are constant, the probability that a given sensory or memory input will be apperceived is a direct function of the number of contiguous presentations between that input and the one that immediately preceded it in focus.

This corollary encompasses not only apperceptual fluctuation from sensory input to encode and the reverse but also shifts from one encode to another. It suggests that apperceptual fluctuation is a continuous process, that encode chains follow one another and are disrupted briefly by sensory components that may initiate other encode chains, that there may be rapid alternation between encodes and sensory inputs, and that a series of sensory components may occur in rapid succession. This view is exactly our own and one that seems particularly applicable to the "mental life" of the individual. Apperceptual fluctuation is homeostatic, in that it follows the most equilibratory path among all the myriad components from memory and sensation that are dynamically interacting during every waking moment of an individual's life. Associations between input components may then be viewed as "equilibratory paths," and each such path may determine the course of apperception as long as some other input does not disrupt the chain and initiate another.

Apperceptual fluctuation typically follows the same sequence as does the input imposed; it is much easier to say the alphabet forward than backward. Once language and its sequential rules are learned, the order in which different encodes follow one another will become more fixed. As various inputs are fused and the composites come to be represented by encodes, more and more abstract "thinking" becomes possible. We note in passing that the structural change assumed to underlie an association has no representation in experience; members of the Würzberg School spent many years searching for it without success. The "equilibratory path" simply helps to determine which input components will follow one another.

One variable that influences the course of apperception—contrast—cuts across both inherited and learned predispositions. In dealing with the influence of structure, it is probably best to designate contrast by the term "discreteness," but, in dealing with learning, "novelty" seems more appropriate. A familiar situation is, by definition, less dangerous than an unfamiliar one. The simple fact that the organism has lived sufficiently for a circumstance to become familiar supports this assertion. Danger lies in the unfamiliar, and when a novel input intrudes into sensory materials from a commonplace situation, it tends to be immediately brought into focus.

When other factors are constant, the greater the novelty of a given input, the greater is the likelihood that it will become the focus of apperception.

In certain instances the input from one sense modality constitutes only a small proportion of what is ordinarily imposed by the given set of circumstances. For instance, an individual may see only part of a human face or a component of a motor car. The tendency then is to apperceive the encode of the total situation immediately afterward, as a function of past fusion. The term "redintegration" has been adopted by experimental psychologists for the "total responses" of organisms to partial cues; the Gestalt concept of closure, to the extent that it can be demonstrated, is presumably a function of the apperception of such fused residuals and of the unity-constancy phenomenon discussed in Chapter 4. When exposed to the chin of Winston Churchill, a human being would respond not to the chin per se but to the total encode representing Churchill. We can now state two further interdependent corollaries.

When other factors are constant, the more frequently the inputs designating a particular item have been apperceived, the more likely a partial presentation is to occasion focusing on the fused encode.

When other factors are constant, the greater the tendency for a partial presentation to result in focusing on a fused encode, the more likely it is that the partial presentation will be apperceived as the total item.

Influence of Background Input

It is a rare moment in which an individual is not experiencing some kind of disequilibrium. Hunger, anxiety, guilt, fatigue, subtle moods, and pervasive fears are only part of the input that serves as background to the endless procession of sensory components from ears, eyes, and other organs. Depending upon persistence, intensity, and pervasiveness, such background input influences the direction and speed of apperception.[4] This influence would be predicted from an evolutionary frame of reference. Background input reflects the fact that certain process systems of the body are moving toward hazardous imbalance.

As the immediate welfare of the organism is threatened specifically in the area represented by the input, it is essential that this input affect apperception and therefore behavior. When an organism is deprived of water, there is pervasive and continuing experience of thirst. As thirst results from deprivation and as survival is contingent on its alleviation, the organism is structured so that such background input will become the predominant factor determining action under circumstances of deprivation.

What establishes the relationship between disequilibratory input and other components in the integration matrix? Although innate factors may predispose apperception in certain directions (as implied in Clark L. Hull's first postulate and in S. Freud's object of the primary process), learning undoubtedly plays the dominant role. The input from a given need state is not very different (except in quality and persistence) from input from more obvious sense modalities. Therefore, the same principles of learning (see Chapter 5) that account for establishment of associations between components from the eyes and ears should also explain associations between disequilibrium inputs and input from other sources. When the input from any given need comes into focus, encodes previously associated with it tend to follow in apperception.

Background input not only helps to determine which memory residuals will be in focus; it also more indirectly influences which sensory components will be apperceived. When an individual apperceives hunger, he will immediately tend to focus on the encodes of previous eating situations. If similar sensory inputs are present in the integration matrix, this material will also tend to be apperceived. Not only memory residuals but also sensory components are dominated by the background input from a need state.

Apperception tends to be "flooded" by disequilibrium input and to be coerced along pertinent channels until it is eliminated. Although competing material may be in focus briefly, the continued presence of disequilibrium input in the integration matrix determines that it will return to focus as apperception fluctuates. Each return initiates and sustains apperception of pertinent encode chains and appropriate sensory inputs. When drive input is not present, apperception fluctuates continuously among the components perpetually intruding from other transmitting mechanisms.

Unless an innate relationship between drive input and certain encodes or sensory components exists, which seems doubtful, at least in human beings, learning must occur before apperception becomes "need centered." If an organism has had no experience with a particular food or one even remotely similar to it, the input from it will not be brought into focus even when the organism is hungry.

We shall now try to develop some testable corollaries of motivation. It should be remembered that the "spur" to action of any kind is neither the number of hours of deprivation, as the neo-behaviorists insist, nor an underlying physiological state, as physiological psychologists assume. Rather, it is the input from the condition of deprivation, surfeit, and visceral transmission. It must be admitted that deprivation of an organism produces conditions that activate transmitting mechanisms and that such activation constitutes a requisite physiological state for experience—but the effective determinant of activity is the apperceived disequilibrium input. An increase in hunger may be correlated with an increase in general activity, and such activity may be potentially related to underlying physiological variables, but the actual determinant of action is the experience of hunger.

Effects of Disequilibrium Input

As we have previously indicated, the course of apperception apparently constitutes the most equilibratory resolution possible among the dynamically interacting components within the integration matrix. Apperception is thus a homeostatic process, in which continual shifts compensate for introduction of different inputs.

The input from deficit, surfeit, and visceral transmission is both persistent and pervasive; we could therefore predict its high potential for dominating apperception. Apperception is "need centered" because the input from the need serves as continuing background, constantly occasioning focusing on associated materials. Apperceptual fluctuation between disequilibrium input, memory residual, and sensory component is both rapid and continuous.

Three corollaries can be derived from this discussion.

The more intense the disequilibrium input, the greater will be the tendency for previously associated experiential materials to follow in apperception.

For example, as hunger increases in intensity, it will tend to be in focus, but there will also be a greater tendency for memories of food to follow in apperception. Furthermore, the tendency to apperceive related sensory inputs will also increase. A hungry organism will thus not only be prone to apperceive memory residuals of food but will also tend to focus on sensory materials similar to such memory residuals. Conversely, a hungry organism will tend not to apperceive materials within the integration matrix that have not been associated with hunger in the past. In fact, because apperception is a unitary process, the hungrier an organism happens to be, the less it will tend to apperceive extraneous stimulation of any kind.

The more intense the disequilibrium input, the less will be the tendency for extraneous components to be apperceived.

We have just mentioned that continuing disequilibrium input occasions memory residuals previously associated with such input. Furthermore, sensory materials similar to memory residuals tend to be apperceived.

The more ambiguous the sensory input, the more likely such components are to be apperceived in relation to the existing disequilibrium state.

A hungry organism will therefore tend to apperceive food in an ambiguous situation, whereas one that is sexually deprived will tend to apperceive sexual items in the same situation. We believe that two primary variables account for this tendency: first, similarity between the ambiguous situation and the encodes previously associated with the drive input and, second, the relative intensity of such input.

Although a relationship between disequilibrium input and focalization on previously associated materials could be predicted, when such input becomes extremely pervasive it may completely flood apperception and block out even relevant encodes and sensory components. Examples of apperceptual flooding by disequilibrium input can easily be cited. The continuing presence of a hot iron against some part of the body, the sensory repercussions of sexual orgasm, and the input from visceral transmitting mechanisms (commonly called "anxiety") in neurosis are only a few. In such circumstances very little rational behavior can occur, simply because the essential encodes cannot be apperceived. Fortunately for adaptation, this kind of condition rarely lasts for any length of time (except in neurosis; see Chapter 8).

Influence of the Autocept

The most important motivational system for both thought and overt behavior is the autocept. We recall from our discussion in Chapter 4 that the autocept comprises fused memory representations and is a need system with far-reaching implications. When incompatible inputs threaten the integrity of the self, powerful visceral changes generate the disequilibrium required for action.

The constellation of memory residuals composing the autocept, as well as input from threats to the integrity of this system, are always potential for apperception. The inputs from other need systems fluctuate according to relative deprivation and surfeit, but those from the autocept are permanently accessible. It is true that components from this source may vary in apperceptive potential as other inputs are thrust into the integration matrix, but even so they persist in the background. All experience, whether of memory or senses, is tied to the self system, the degree depending upon how much it served as recurrent input when the self was emerging and becoming structured.

When the activity of the organism, of whatever kind, is sustained by disequilibrium from threats to the structure of the self, it is said to be "volitional." This term does not imply an element of free will arising from the autocept; in fact, it implies the opposite. The autocept enters into activity much as any other disequilibratory system does, and the behavior resulting from its influence is no less lawful.

What are the relative influences of the autocept and other drive inputs on the continuing process of behavior? An example will clarify the problem. In certain circumstances an individual can choose to expose himself to continued drive input. He can go hungry for long periods or perhaps put his hand on a hot stove. If action is the most equilibratory resolution of all the factors dynamically interacting within the integration matrix, holding one's hand to a hot stove may be the most equilibratory possible response at that moment. As paradoxical as this reasoning may seem, the disequilibrium introduced by pulling away the hand is greater than that occasioned by leaving it on the stove! A fairly accurate estimate of the cohesiveness of a self system might be obtained by putting it in conflict with another pervasive input. A relationship between a child's age and his ability "voluntarily" to withstand varying intensities of shock would be predicted.

The Light-Shift Model

A relatively simple model may help to clarify our view of the influence of disequilibrium input on the continuing process of apperception. Let us assume an ordinary room filled with many kinds of objects, each with particular reflection characteristics. Let us also assume that we can flood this room with light: either white light from a constant source or light of any color that can be beamed from a projector. If the room is flooded only with white light (analogous to input from the autocept) everything in the room will stand out with equal clarity, but if we flood the room with red light as well (analogous to experiential input synonymous with a disequilibrium state like thirst) objects with reflection characteristics peculiar to that particular wave length will stand out, whereas the others will fade into the background. Each time that the color of the light is changed (or the particular input is shifted) different classes of objects (analogous to materials in the integration matrix) will become dominant, and others will be deemphasized.

This model may also clarify the relative influence of the autocept and other need systems of the individual: The more intense the white light that pervades the room, the less will be the influence of any given hue that may be introduced. Similarly, the apperceptions and consequent behavior of an individual with a highly integrated autocept (see Chapter 8) will be less dominated by input from one of the other need systems.

Internal Locomotion

In Chapter 2 internal locomotion (thinking) was defined as the most functional adaptation attribute yet evolved. By "moving around" in the "harmless" surrogate world of memory residuals, an organism can resolve potential problems threatening to its continued existence before it is exposed to them in reality. The organism can apply all its past experiences in related situations to particular adaptation problems.

We noted in Chapter 3 that some similarity between the encode and the initial sensory input must exist if the "internalized symbolic world" is to be functionally representational, yet there must also be sufficient difference between them to prevent confusion.

In Chapter 4 we argued further that, although initial input may consist of discrete elements, if they are presented together repeatedly they can become fused into phenomenological wholes. As a child matures and learns to use language, such unities become associated with particular written and spoken symbols. Thinking involves sensory bits, fused memory residuals, and symbol encodes. "I" may thus think of a particular cow, the concept cow, or the word "cow."

Thinking, then, is nothing more than fluctuation of apperception among available encodes and as such is a completely automatic and lawful process. Apperception is always the most equilibratory response possible to the myriad components dynamically interacting within the integration matrix, and when the components brought into sequential focus consist of encodes, thought is taking place.

The course of thought tends to follow equilibratory paths developed through secondary encoding (see Chapter 5), but any given sequence rarely lasts long. Sensory input typically intrudes on apperception and initiates other chains of encodes, or visceral changes occasioned by focusing on particular encodes may disrupt the series. Indeed, as we shall see in Chapter 8, certain encodes or encode chains may acquire sufficient disequilibrium potential to prevent completely their being brought into focus.

Pleasurable Feedback and Thought

Does apperception of memory residuals previously associated with pleasure input actually introduce equilibrium into the integration matrix? Is it not pleasant to think about food when we are hungry? It certainly seems to be. But from what source is such pleasure derived? How does it affect the continuing thought process?

Let us take up each of these questions in turn. Pleasure, as we suggested in Chapter 3, apparently occurs when certain systems are returning to equilibrium. There are no specific receptors for pleasure; it must be produced by excitation of a still undetermined central process, which is somehow activated by movement toward equilibrium in other systems. If pleasure can be introduced by sheer apperception of a memory residual, such focalization must either directly activate the appropriate central process or produce changes that activate it (as when apperception of the encodes of sexual partners occasions tumescence in the male, with consequent experiential feedback). Certain memory residuals (previously associated with pleasure input) do undoubtedly have the potential for occasioning "pleasurable" feedback, but does such input affect thought? Apparently yes. We often savor certain encodes; in fact, there is a tendency for such encodes to follow one another in apperception, as in daydreaming. Not, however, that thinking can be *initiated* by equilibrium any more than overt behavior can. The loss of pleasure input when the activity (overt or internal) is terminated provides the disequilibrium that sustains it.

Memory residuals capable of introducing pleasurable feedback are said to have "positive valence," whereas those that produce disequilibrium feedback have "negative valence." Thinking, though it always follows the path of greatest equilibrium, is frequently sustained and directed by perceptual shifts in valence, which result in sequential apperception of encodes; the disequilibrium arising from each apperception motivates continuation of the process.

Unpleasant Feedback and Thought

Apperceptual fluctuation synonymous with thinking can also be initiated and sustained by continuing and pervasive input from a primary or secondary drive state. Such general disequilibrium enters the "thought process" and lends continuity and direction. When an organism is hungry this input persists within the integration matrix and is continually brought into focus as the apperceptual process fluctuates. Apperception of this continuing and qualitatively distinct input alters the equilibrium potential of all available components, so that memory residuals previously associated with such input can be more readily brought into focus. We do not mean that "need dominated" thinking fails to follow associational paths. Rather, as a function of background input, it involves use of constellations and sequences of memory residuals previously associated with hunger.

The disequilibrium occasioned by a threat to the integration of the autocept may also lend impetus and direction to thought. If a person's deepest religious beliefs are threatened, powerful anxiety is introduced, and memory residuals related to defense of the threatened point of view are more readily apperceived.

All internal activity is thus lawful and automatic, whether wandering "freely" as in fantasy or dreams, directed toward goals as in hunger, or "volitional" as when the self system provides the requisite disequilibrium for focusing. The process of thought is the most equilibratory resolution of the dynamically interacting components within the integration matrix at any given moment.

Secondary Reverberations

We must now consider a process so ephemeral that it would be tempting to ignore it were it not for its systematic importance and vital contribution to adaptive behavior. Probably because it is transitory, it is difficult to classify precisely and thus raises a perplexing organizational problem. Where should it be discussed? It is essential to perceptual fusion and so perhaps should have been included in Chapter 4 (Primary Encoding); it has been considered a type of memory by certain investigators and this designation might argue for its treatment in Chapter 5 (Secondary Encoding). It is related to the problem of input so could well have been discussed in Chapter 3. We have placed it here because neither its character nor its function could be adequately described without the foundation provided up to this point.

Some investigators have labeled this elusive process "primary memory" (Waugh and Norman, 1965); others (Hebb, 1949; Hellyer, 1962) have used the term "short-term retention." N. C. Waugh and D. A. Norman (1965) and D. E. Broadbent (1958) are convinced that it is different from ordinary memory; A. W. Melton (1963) argues that there is only one memory system and that distinctions between short-term and long-term memory are completely arbitrary. We agree with the first point of view, but we prefer the term "secondary reverberations" to "primary memory."[5]

When a transmitting mechanism is activated a sensory component is introduced into the integration matrix. But even after the activation has been terminated sensory input continues for approximately one-twentieth of a second. We are convinced that such continuation reflects an extremely transitory influence of the same process that produced the sensation in the first place. These reverberations, which we call "primary," account for the lower threshold for pitch, flicker fusion, and perception of movement (see Chapters 3 and 4).

We now come to another kind of reverberation, which though derived from activation of transmitting mechanisms, lasts longer and produces less clear input than does primary reverberation. Every human being has had the experience of making an error in speech and then recognizing it afterward. How is he able to catch himself? Apparently an "echo" of the previous speech sounds reverberates for some time after the speech itself has been uttered. As apperception fluctuates, such "echoes" may be brought into focus and errors thus determined and corrected. The corrective functioning of such secondary reverberations is by no means infallible. A professor may use an inappropriate word in the enthusiasm of his lecture and remain unaware of his mistake until he notices the peculiar expressions of his students. He may then experience a few moments of real panic as he tries to remember exactly what he has just said. Fortunately, the apperceptual monitoring of the input from secondary reverberations allows most such errors to be caught and corrected.

How should we classify such echoes? Are they memories? Perhaps, but if we classify them as memories, then primary reverberations should also be classified that way. It seems more appropriate to call them simply "secondary reverberations." They accompany our every experience, and apperceptual monitoring of the input arising from them provides a perpetual check on all activities. Indeed, without such monitoring it is doubtful that effective speech could occur. Meaningful speech must depend largely upon continuity between what has just been said and what is being said. Apperceptual fluctuation relative to secondary reverberations permits such continuity and provides a synthesis that makes speech meaningful and even possible. What variables determine that some input from secondary reverberation will be apperceived? The same ones that account for apperception of any input within the integration matrix. In a blooper like the commentator's "For a refreshing taste experience, try Bupert's Rear," the error stands out among the secondary reverberations, first, because it deviates from what the person has meant to say and, second, because of embarrassment arising from the error itself.

Secondary reverberations may have a related and perhaps even more important function: to provide short-term storage for input until the single channel
of apperception is clear enough to handle it. A critical cue may thus influence
behavior even when it is no longer present.

Still another contribution of secondary reverberations is basic to the emergence of such phenomenological wholes as trees, houses, motocepts, and autocepts and also resolves a logical dilemma of our theory. The reader may have
noticed that fusion is said to occur when inputs are introduced *simultaneously*
(see Chapter 4). But, if apperception can focus on only one component at a
time, how can different inputs be presented simultaneously? The dilemma is
resolved by an assumption that fusion is not contingent on apperception but
results from overlap in the input from secondary reverberations. Many different
secondary reverberations can introduce inputs into the integration matrix simultaneously, and then there is a tendency for fusion to occur. Fusion is thus
"preapperceptual" and can occur whenever inputs exist simultaneously within
the integration matrix. We may also surmise that strict simultaneity of stimulation is not required for fusion. As secondary reverberations last perhaps four
or five seconds (see note 5), the input from one stimulus may overlap that from
another, even though the stimuli may be presented several seconds apart.

Summary

Apperception is always the most equilibratory outcome of the interaction among
materials from memory and sensation at any given moment. It provides simplification for organisms burdened by increasing information overload and is necessary because effective behavior must have a single direction; the fact that organisms are structured as units ensures that responding simultaneously to multiple
inputs would be unadaptive. Apperception is another manifestation of the
evolutionary imperative that increasing complexity must always be compensated
for by greater adaptability. Complexity may bring with it increased potential
for survival but only when its disadvantages are neutralized. Even as the movement of an amoeba between two lights is in the direction that best resolves
their tropistic effects, so the fluctuation of apperception inevitably tends toward
the most equilibratory resolution of those forces present within the integration
matrix at the moment.

We view apperception as the direct and necessary occasion for all secondary
encoding; it is synonymous with thinking when it involves encodes and with
sensing when the inputs in focus are derived from the various modalities. As
learning develops, apperception tends to follow associational paths but is at the
same time responsive to background disequilibrium that is in perpetual flux
within the integration matrix. Apperception of inputs may alternate with great
rapidity, and the mental life of the individual typically consists of sequences of
encode chains interspersed with inputs from the various transmitting mechanisms of the body.

Apperception is the ultimate mediating process. Without it nothing can be learned; unless encoded input reenters apperception it can neither become part of the thought process nor influence overt behavior. Between input and behavior stands apperception, the highest refinement and the most functional outcome of the evolutionary struggle. It is the attribute underlying man's most subtle reasoning and his rudest skill. We must now turn to the next and most difficult problem, that of overt behavior. We shall attempt to show how apperception precedes adaptive behavior and makes it possible.

Notes

[1]Interest in apperception is as old as man's concern about his own workings. By the name "attention" it has remained an enduring problem since Aristotle (Bakan, 1966), who thought of it as a single channel. More recently D. O. Hebb (1949) posited a central storage system into which different stimuli can enter through different channels simultaneously. J. F. Herbart (1882) developed a very reasonable theory (aside from his unfortunate use of mathematics), in an effort to pinpoint the variables accounting for emergence of a given idea into awareness. He postulated, somewhat tentatively to be sure, that perhaps two memories can be apperceived simultaneously. G. H. Mowbray (1953) took the view that, as the period of presentation becomes shorter and shorter, fluctuation between inputs becomes progressively more difficult, so that, at least when complex cognitive phenomena are involved, attention is unitary. When very simple inputs (like letters, numbers, and three-letter words) are involved (Mowbray, 1954), however, he apparently believes that attention can be multichanneled. D. E. Broadbent (1957) is probably the leading exponent of the single-channel view and certainly the theorist who offers the clearest conceptualization of the problem. He believes that attention is analogous to a Y-shaped funnel, with two branches larger than the central portion. The branches represent sensory sources, whereas the central portion represents the direction of attention. Although several bits of sensory input can enter the branches at the same time, only one can enter the central channel of the funnel at any given moment.

This brief review has not begun to do justice to all the investigators who have had something to say about the capacity of attention. For an intensive treatment of the subject, we recommend P. Bakan's excellent and most readable book (1966).

[2]How many items can attention (apperception) include? We tend to assume only one, if the critical period is sufficiently short (approximately one-twentieth of a second). But several researchers since W. S. Jevons (1871) have investigated the range of attention without any preconceptions about an absolute refractory period. Jevons threw varying numbers of beans on a tray and found that he could take in as many as eight at a single glance. Using a tachistoscope (as in most studies of attention span) J. Cattell (see Dennis, 1948a & b) concluded that the human being can attend to six and possibly eight dots at a time. W. W. Fernberger (1921) believed that there is an intrinsic tendency for subjects to group dots as the number grows larger and time interval shorter; he probably discovered the phenomenon of "subitizing." Behaviorists like W. S. Hunter and M. Sigler (1940) and I. J. Saltzman and A. R. Garner (1948) tried to study the effects of other variables on attention span and concluded that training, knowledge of the number of items, size of the visual field, and viewing distance are

all related to the number of dots that can be recalled after a single exposure. The process of subitizing was first named by E. L. Kaufman and his colleagues (1949). They claimed that a subject can recognize six or fewer items immediately. When more than six are presented, he will attend to them less quickly and accurately and will tend to estimate the total number of items presented. Research by R. W. Gardner and R. Long (1962), P. Fraisse and E. Vurpillot (1956), and J. W. Kaswan (1958) further lengthened the list of variables supposed to affect the attention span. These variables include duration of presentation time, information permanently stored, level of attentiveness, spatial grouping, intensity of items, size of visual field, viewing distance, character of input, absence of recent inputs, sense modality used, and number of sense modalities involved. J. Adams (1962) and L. Creamer (1963) introduced the variable of "set," concluding that, as expectancy increases, the period of fluctuation of attention decreases to the point at which more than one item can be brought into focus at once.

What can we conclude from this abundance of research? As tachistoscopes and designs have improved, a preponderant body of evidence seems to support the notion that attention operates through a single channel. Other variables may affect its span but only when the exposure time is longer than the refractory period. This conclusion has been responsible for the recent tendency of investigators to switch to a single-channel hypothesis (see notes 1 and 3) and to seek to measure the refractory period. G. A. Miller (1956) reviewed one-dimensional experiments on several modalities and concluded that the concept of limited channel capacity seems valid when all pertinent variables are carefully controlled. We still have not answered the question of the size of the apperceived unit, nor has anyone else. Research on this problem will be difficult but not impossible. It must concentrate on the variables that cause fusion of individual inputs and on factors that determine whether the wholes or the components will be apperceived. We believe that discovery of the process of subitizing is a step in this direction.

3 Research on the speed of apperceptual shifts probably began with the work of F. W. Bessel (1823) (see Boring, 1950), inspired by miscalculations at the Greenwich Observatory. Although there were various notions to explain the personal equation, attention variables doubtless accounted for at least part of it. In 1885 Von Tschisch designed the first psychological experiment specifically focused on attention shifting; he discovered that a person cannot tell at which point on a clock's face a moving pointer is located when a click is sounded. The sound apparently jams the visual input, so that the person tends to report the number indicated by the pointer just before the click, rather than during it.

From the turn of the century until quite recently research on attention was centered on its span (see note 2), but during the past twenty years there have been many experiments—and speculations—on the length of the refractory period. R. Davis (1956; 1957) found evidence for a single-channel system, using both multidimensional and unidimensional stimuli. He posited a refractory period of about 100 milliseconds. C. W. Tellford (1931) and M. Vince (1940) also found evidence of a refractory period. Recently M. Schmidt and A. B. Kristofferson (1963) conducted an experiment on the hypothesis that sensory systems consist of independent channels that can be attended to only one at a time. They obtained a positive linear function between length of time intervening between variable stimuli and correctness of responses and found mean refractory periods of 63.8 and 66.4 milliseconds. In 1966 I. Reed found a significant decrement in bisensory learning that can be expressed as a linear function of the amount of switching required for successful performance; on this basis he concluded that switching attention requires about 170 milliseconds. E. Brussell (1967) used a modified complication clock with colors instead of numbers on the face and found a linear relationship between amount of negative displacement and the speed at which the pointer rotated; as the speed increased the subject tended to see the pointer farther behind its actual position when the click sounded. When displacement in millimeters was translated into milliseconds, the average for apperceptual shift between visual and auditory inputs was 56 milliseconds. Although this study controlled both direction of movement and position of pointer (an improvement over other complication-clock studies), it failed to rule out eye movements and the possibility of visual lag. We have now designed an experiment that should control these variables. Instead of a complication clock, a tachistoscope will be used; it allows precise manipulation of both intertrial intervals and duration of exposure. Certain visual materials (like colors) will be presented in rapid succession for short periods, and the subject will then be asked to name the color presented when a click is sounded. Eye movements will be controlled, for the subject will be staring at the same spot when each color is projected. To control for visual lag, one group of control subjects will be instructed to name at random some of the colors flashed on the screen. A sound sensor will pick up the subject's voice and record which color was actually being exposed when the choice was made. Although this design is not perfect —for even the decision to "choose now" in the control group may introduce a complication—it should yield a fairly precise estimate of the speed of apperceptual fluctuation between inputs from different modalities. We predict that the period of such fluctuation will be approximately 50 milliseconds.

[4]What is the evidence that background disequilibrium input influences the course of apperception? Again there is a fundamental difference in terminology. Most contemporary researchers and theorists talk about the influence of "central determinants" (Bruner and Goodman, 1947) on perception. But use of the term "perception" in this context seems inappropriate. Motives, needs, moods, sets, and so on do not influence perception. Perceptual fusion and structuring are fixed and remain relatively stable, regardless of transitory central states; apperception, not perception, is influenced. Let us consider some of the studies that have been conducted. In general they all follow the same format: The experimenter establishes the subjects' "operant" level of apperception under normal conditions and then determines how much a given need, set, or mood alters this level. R. N. Sanford (1936; 1937) was the pioneer. He demonstrated that hungry subjects would make "food words" out of word stems (for instance, "me--" would be completed as "meal" or "meat") more often than did subjects who were not hungry. E. M. Siipola (1935) used a tachistoscope to demonstrate that when subjects were told to see terms related to animals or travel, this *set* would influence the manner in which they responded to a group of ambiguous words flashed for one-tenth of a second. C. Leuba and C. Lucas (1945) found that different moods (anxious, happy, and critical) significantly influenced the responses of hypnotized subjects to ambiguous pictures.

There have also been many studies of the influence of personality variables. Typically they involve verbal tests, as used by L. Postman, Bruner and E. McGinnies (1948); space-orientation tests, as in a study by H. A. Witkin and his colleagues (1954); or projective devices like the Rorschach and Thematic Apperception tests, as discussed in a symposium edited by Bruner and D. Krech (1950). In general, these studies support the view that background input—whether needs, values, emotions, or various ephemeral personality variables—may influence the course of apperception. Such influence continues to be investigated, and several studies have been published (see Bartley, 1958). We reiterate that "perception" is a misnomer in this context. The only central determinant that can influence perception is prior learning (see Chapter 4, note 1). Background input influences the course of apperception but has little, if any, effect on either fusion or structuring.

5 Why do we accept the notion that two different mechanisms account for secondary reverberation and ordinary memory? The experimental evidence appears to support this distinction, but more important from a systematic point of view, the common occurrence of information overload suggests that some mechanism must have emerged during evolution to allow preliminary storage before exposure to the single channel of apperception.

An experiment by Broadbent (1954) has provided convincing evidence of a dual retention mechanism. He wanted to know whether or not subjects could remember material presented on a channel to which they could not attend immediately. He presented three pairs of digits, one of each pair to each ear, and asked the subjects to recall as many digits as they could. They were able to recall all six, but they repeated all the digits fed into one ear *before* those fed into the other. It was impossible for the subjects to alternate between the two ears when the digits were presented more rapidly than one in each ear per second. Broadbent repeated this experiment (1956), using simultaneous input to eye and ear and obtained essentially the same results. He concluded that, in order to recall the second set of three digits, subjects had to have "stored" them while the first set of three digits was being identified. It appears that secondary reverberations keep available inputs that have not yet been apperceived and stored permanently.

An experiment by E. Averbach and G. Sperling (1960) sheds light not only on the existence and duration of such secondary reverberations but also on their relation to apperception. They thought that, if they could measure what was immediately available at the time of exposure, they might discover that subjects take in considerably more than the typical experiment on recall suggests. They showed subjects three rows of items for brief periods and then immediately afterward indicated which one of the three they were to recall. As the subjects did not know in advance which row would be required, their report on that row allowed an estimate of the total information available at the moment. If they recalled two-thirds of it, Averbach and Sperling reasoned that two-thirds of the entire display was represented. Using this technique, they found that subjects retained two or three times as much information as had been suspected from direct-recall studies. They also demonstrated that this "extra" information decays very rapidly. If the subjects were delayed even one second before being told which row to recall, much of the information was lost. Averbach and Sperling concluded, first, that visual intake is rapid and many items can be stored briefly before they decay and disappear, and, second, that the central "read out" procedure is much slower and probably handles items successively.

The question of how long such secondary reverberations continue immediately arises. An experiment by A. M. Treisman (1964) allows us some reasonable estimates. She introduced two messages to her subjects simultaneously: one in the left ear, the other in the right. In order to ensure that one message would be attended and the other ignored, she instructed all subjects to repeat aloud the message coming into one ear and to ignore the message fed into the other. E. C. Cherry (1953), who originally developed this design, had previously found that subjects could report nothing specific about the ignored message but could remember general changes like a shift from English to German or from a man's to a woman's voice. Treisman's design involved a subtle addition. She fed the same message into both ears but fed the message to be ignored sometimes behind and sometimes ahead of the other. When the message to be attended led the message to be ignored by about 4.3 seconds, the subjects noted their identity spontaneously. But, when the other message led, recognition of their identity did not occur until the interval was only 1.3 seconds. Why was the reverberation longer in one instance? One reason is that, when the message to be attended led, it received emphasis from the verbal repetition of each word. Furthermore, the true delay was not really 4.3 seconds; it was the interval between the subjects' verbal reports of the message to be attended and the input of the other message. Now we come to an interesting conclusion: The reverberation of the attended (and repeated) message was about three seconds (assuming about one second to repeat each word), whereas the reverberation of the unattended message was only about one second. This result suggests either that emphasis on the message to be attended intensified the reverberation or that apperception itself caused accentuation. Ingenious experiments will be required to answer this question. Once apperception takes place, the input from the reverberation is integrated into permanent memory. Under such conditions it will be difficult, if not impossible, to determine to what extent recall is based on secondary reverberations and to what extent it is a function of the ordinary memory process.

References

Adams, J. Test of the hypothesis of the psychological refractory period. *Journal of Experimental Psychology,* 1962, 64: 280-287.

Averbach, E., and Sperling, G. Short term storage of information in vision. E. C. Cherry (ed.), *Information theory.* London: Butterworth, 1960.

Bakan, P. *Attention: An enduring problem in psychology.* Princeton: Von Nostrand, 1966.

Bessel, F. W. *Astronomische Beobachtungen.* Königsberg: Academia Albertina, 1823.

Boring, E. *A history of experimental psychology.* New York: Appleton, 1950.

Broadbent, D. E. Role of auditory localization and attention in memory span. *Journal of Experimental Psychology,* 1954, 47: 191-196.

Broadbent, D. E. Successive responses to simultaneous stimuli. *Quarterly Journal of Experimental Psychology,* 1956, 8: 145-152.

Broadbent, D. E. A mechanical model for human attention and immediate memory. *Psychological Review,* 1957, 64: 205-215.

Broadbent, D. E. *Perception and communication.* New York: Pergamon, 1958.

Bruner, J. S., and Goodman, C. D. Value and need as organizing factors in perception. *Journal of Abnormal and Social Psychology,* 1947, 42: 33-34.

Bruner, J. S., and Krech, D. (eds.). *Perception and personality–A symposium.* Durham, N.C.: Duke University Press, 1950.

Brussell, E. The speed of attentional fluctuation as indicated by progressive increase in negative displacement, DePauw University Library, unpublished manuscript, 1967.

Cattell, J. The influence of the intensity of the stimulus on the length of the reaction time. In W. Dennis (ed.), *Readings in the history of psychology.* New York: Appleton, 1948.

Cattell, J. The time it takes to see and name objects. In W. Dennis (ed.), *Readings in the history of psychology*. New York: Appleton, 1948.

Cherry, E. C. Some experiments on the recognition of speech with one and two ears. *Journal of the Accoustical Society of America*, 1953, 25: 975-979.

Creamer, L. Event uncertainty, psychological refractory period and human data processing. *Journal of Experimental Psychology*, 1963, 66: 187-194.

Davis, R. The role of attention in the psychological refractory period and human data processing. *Journal of Experimental Psychology*, 1956, 8: 24-38.

Davis, R. The human operator as a single-channel system. *Quarterly Journal of Experimental Psychology*, 1957, 9: 119-129.

Fernberger, W. W. Preliminary study of the range of apprehension. *American Journal of Psychology*, 1921, 32: 121-133.

Fraisse, P., and Vurpillot, E. L'effet de l'orientation de l'attention sur le détendue du champ d'appréhension. *Année Psychologique*, 1956, 56: 433-436.

Gardner, R. W., and Long, R. Cognitive controls of attention and inhibition: A study of the individual. *British Journal of Psychology*, 1962, 62: 381-388.

Hebb, D. O. *The organization of behavior*. New York: Wiley, 1949.

Hellyer, S. Supplementary report: Frequency of stimulus presentation and short term decrement in recall. *Journal of Experimental Psychology*, 1962, 64: 650.

Herbart, J. F. *Lehrbuch zur Psychologie*, Hamburg: G. von Hartenstein, 1882.

Hernández-Peón, R., Scherrer, H., and Jouvet, M. Modification of electrical activity in cochlear nucleus during "attention" in unanesthetized cats. *Science*, 1956, 123: 331-332.

Hunter, W. S., and Sigler, M. The span of visual discrimination as a function of time and intensity of stimulation. *Journal of Experimental Psychology*, 1940, 26: 160-179.

Jevons, W. S. The power of numerical discrimination. *Nature*, 1871, 3: 281-282.

Kaswan, J. W. Tachistoscopic exposure time and spatial proximity in the organization of visual perception. *British Journal of Psychology*, 1958, 49: 131-138.

Kaufman, E. L., Lord, M. W., Reese, T. W., and Volkman, J. The discrimination of visual number. *American Journal of Psychology*, 1949, 62: 498-525.

Leuba, C., and Lucas, C. The effects of attitudes on descriptions of pictures. *Journal of Experimental Psychology*, 1945, 35: 517-524.

Melton, A. W. Implications of short-term memory for a general theory of memory. *Journal of Verbal Learning and Verbal Behavior*, 1963, 2: 1-21.

Miller, G. A. The magical number 7, plus or minus two: Some limits on our capacity for processing information. *Psychological Review*, 1956, 63: 81-97.

Mowbray, G. H. Simultaneous vision and audition: The comprehension of prose passages with varying levels of difficulty. *Journal of Experimental Psychology*, 1953, 46: 365-371.

Mowbray, G. H. The perception of short phrases presented simultaneously for visual and auditory reception. *Quarterly Journal of Experimental Psychology*, 1954, 6: 86-92.

Postman, L., Bruner, J. S., and McGinnies, E. Personal values as selective factors in perception. *Journal of Abnormal and Social Psychology*, 1948, 43: 142-154.

Reed, I. E. Sense modality switching in relation to learning. *Dissertation Abstracts*, 1966, 27: 965-966.

Saltzman, I. J., and Garner, A. R.   Reaction time as a measure of span of attention.   *Journal of Psychology,* 1948, 25:   227-241.

Sanford, R. N.   The effects of abstinence from food upon imaginal processes.   *Journal of Psychology,* 1936, 2:   129-136.

Sanford, R. N.   The effects of abstinence from food upon imaginal processes: A further experiment.   *Journal of Psychology,* 1937, 3:   145-159.

Schmidt, M., and Kristofferson, A. B.   Discrimination of successiveness: A test of a model of attention.   *Science,* 1963, 113:   112-113.

Siipola, E. M.   A study of some effects of preparatory set.   *Psychological Monographs,* 1935, 46:   28-37.

Tellford, C. W.   Refractory phase of voluntary and associative responses.   *Journal of Experimental Psychology,* 1931, 14:   1-35.

Treisman, A. M.   Monitoring and storage of irrelevant messages in selective attention.   *Journal of Verbal Learning and Verbal Behavior,* 1964, 3:   449-459.

Tschisch, W. von.   Prior entry and attention.   *Philosophical Studies,* 1885, 2:   603-634.

Vince, M.   Rapid response sequence of the psychological refractory period.   *British Journal of Psychology,* 1940, 40:   23-40.

Waugh, N. C., and Norman, D. A.   Primary memory.   *Psychological Review,* 1965, 72:   89-104.

Witkin, H. A., Lewis, H. B., Hertzman, M., Mackover, K., Meissner, P. B., and Wapner, S.   *Personality through perception.*   New York: Harper & Row, 1954.

7

Reaction

An evaluation of the labors of many contemporary theorists in experimental psychology might lead us to conclude that learning is the principle that accounts for most behavior, but that conclusion would simply be incorrect. Certainly much of the behavior of most mammals has been learned, but, once learning has occurred, the process itself ceases to play an important part in activity. During any given day of a human being's life, most of his behavior involves using what he has already learned, mainly during infancy and childhood. The problem of understanding behavior thus centers not on the learning process per se, but on the variables that determine which of the kinds of behavior already in the individual's repertory will be used.

This discussion leads to affirmation of a principle that has been implicit in the development of the theory in the preceding chapters: that activity, of whatever kind, is always an outcome of the variables interacting at each given moment. This point seems obvious, but it has been much discussed and more misunderstood. Our view of contemporaneous causation does not underestimate the importance of historical variables. Indeed, we accept that an historical approach—at least at present—is the most feasible method of determining which variables influence activity at any given moment. Following Kurt Lewin

(1935), we believe that past learning may have effects that intrude on time present and that anticipations of the future may influence current behavior. Neither the past nor the future is operative in itself, however; rather, it is the effects and the anticipations of the future that influence present behavior. Time past and time future are thus both contained in time present. If we wish to understand those variables that are currently operating, we must use an historical rather than a contemporaneous approach as was Lewin's emphasis. When we insist that most behavior has little to do with learning, therefore, we do not imply that it is not critical in determining action, but we do insist that it is the effects of the process and not the process itself that are important.

With these observations out of the way, we shall turn reluctantly to discussion of overt behavior. It seems paradoxical that those aspects of the organism that seem most readily open to assessment are also those that have most tenaciously defied integration into our theory. Overt behavior, though traditionally accepted as the source of "objective" data in psychology, is the outcome of the processes that we have been discussing. Between the input and output lies process, and it is this process to which we must look if we are to understand the role of behavior in the total economy of the adapting organism —not an easy task, as will become apparent as we proceed.

The Motocept and the Motor Threshold

The postulate of process states that all behavior, whether overt or internal, tends immediately toward equilibrium. Overt behavior is thus considered homeostatic, even as thought is considered homeostatic, as we discussed in Chapter 6. Overt behavior, except that included under the headings "reflexive" and "instinctive" follows apperception and is assumed to be a direct outcome of it. But at what point does it take place? It is one thing to surmise—as we do—that apperception is the functional antecedent of most overt behavior and quite another to explain plausibly which particular apperceived component occasions overt action and when this reaction occurs. For example, a human being may indulge in considerable thought about a given problem before any discernible behavior takes place. At what point in this process of thought is overt behavior initiated? Furthermore, an individual may apperceive many sensory components in sequence without overt response. To which one will he respond and at what point? What accounts for the lag between apperception and action? Before these questions can be considered, we must examine several factors on which overt behavior is contingent.

Fusion and the Development of the Motocept

In the newborn infant behavior is diffuse and undifferentiated. As time passes maturation and learning combine to facilitate development of coordination and refinement of specific motor skills. The integration of body movements requisite to exercise such skills depends upon a fusion process similar to that described in relation to perceptual phenomena (see Chapter 4). Body activity produces hundreds of similar, recurrent, and discrete sensory inputs, conditions already postulated as necessary and sufficient for the occurrence of fusion. From such fusion a phenomenal body experience emerges, much as a phenomenal self or a phenomenal tree emerges; this unity, which we call the "motocept," underlies all integrated and coordinated movement. After fusion has occurred the particular sensory components that constitute the motocept are not apperceived separately, as long as there is no interference with coordinated action. The individual sensory-feedback components peculiar to any skill like typing thus become fused in phenomenological unities as practice continues. Only at the outset are other, "corrective" sensory components (as from vision and touch) required for effective performance. With practice the skill becomes automatic: The individual components become subordinated to the fused totality, and the "crutch" cues from other modalities are no longer necessary.

The majority of the motor skills that will be used during an individual's lifetime have already developed by the time that he is three or four years old. The sensory inputs derived from such activities as eating, walking, grasping, and talking—to mention but a few—are soon fused into motocepts comprising the feedback components unique to each particular set of movements.

The survival function of such fusion is considerable. It facilitates the emergence of precise skills that can be exercised with the least possible expenditures of energy. It provides the basis for such exercise without the necessity for focusing on each individual sensory component and thus reduces apperceptual overload. Furthermore, as such fusion allows relatively automatic responses, it frees the apperceptual process so that other inputs can be brought into focus more readily.

Overt Behavior and the Motor Threshold

Examination of the newborn child permits the inference that a motor threshold actually exists, as well as some insight into its nature. We assume that the infant's integration matrix is continually bombarded with sensory input from the various body receptor systems and that apperception (albeit of a crude variety) of such input is in perpetual (except during sleep) process. Yet overt behavior does not occur until the intensity of this apperceived input reaches a particular level. This is called the "motor threshold." We assume that, once this threshold has been crossed, behavior will inevitably follow.

In our view *three* thresholds are important: the sensory threshold, which is crossed when the activation of a transmitting mechanism introduces sensory input into the integration matrix; the apperceptual threshold, which is crossed when one of the many components present within the integration matrix is brought into focus; and the motor threshold, which is crossed when apperceived input occasions overt behavior.

Consideration of what happens when an organism goes to sleep gives us
further insights into the nature and functioning of these three thresholds. In
sleep both the sensory and motor thresholds are apparently raised. The input
from the various receptor systems of the body is essentially shut out, so that
apperception relative to such material simply does not occur (unless it is extremely intense). Apperception of encodes during sleep also does not ordinarily
cause behavior because of the elevated motor threshold.

A Digression on Dreams

As dreams consist of nothing more than sequential apperception of encodes
during sleep, this topic should perhaps have been considered in Chapter 6. But
a discussion of thresholds is so essential a precursor to an evaluation of dreams
as such that we have delayed consideration of them until now.[1]

During sleep the input from any transmitting mechanism sufficiently intense
to cross the elevated sensory threshold may initiate a dream. The resulting encodes, which constitute the dream, are those previously associated with such
input. If an individual has input from a distended bladder, he may dream of
going to the bathroom or of finding a place to urinate. If he has input corresponding to the sex drive, he may dream of sexual behavior perhaps even to the
point of orgasm. Any sensory input, regardless of its source, *may* initiate and
sustain the direction and symbolism of the dream if it is sufficiently intense to
cross the elevated sensory threshold—but not necessarily! It must also be sufficiently intense to cross the apperceptual threshold, for it is apperception of
both the initiating input and the resulting encodes that shape the dream.

But how can dreams be so jumbled and haphazard, so "nonvolitional" so
free-wheeling and quasilogical if they are initiated and sustained by some enduring sensory input? Surely dream symbolism would have greater continuity and
would more closely approximate the person's experiences in reacting to such
input in the past. According to this statement, the hungry person should
always dream of food and the sex-deprived person of sex. But in dreams there
are a "flitting" quality, lack of continuity and direction, a tendency toward
scrambling of symbols, and fluctuation from one topic to the next.

Nevertheless, dreams are exactly as we would predict from the perspective
established in this book. The free-ranging and quasilogical character of dreams
partly results from the absence (except for that small proportion that is intense
enough to cross the elevated threshold) of the apperceptual coercion ordinarily
imposed by sensory input. The symbolism of dreams is thus liberated to follow
associational paths that may be either ordinary or bizarre, depending upon
circumstances to be described later.

Even more important, the direction and continuity provided during the waking
state by the autocept (volitional motivation) are greatly reduced by the elevated
sensory threshold; input that is ordinarily monitored for awareness of self and
accounts for volitional activity is essentially excluded. Therefore most dreams

unfold as automatically and as uncontrollably as if the dreamer were watching television. As the influence of the autocept is absent, the sequence of encodes may move in directions completely at variance with those that would be followed if the person were awake; strange, even terrifying combinations of symbols may occur, or the person may be involved in bizzare and repugnant activities.

A man sometimes dreams of his children burning or of tornadoes or floods. Does this mean, following Freud, that there is some wish for such catastrophe? We do not think so. Often people go to sleep with high levels of generalized anxiety or fear, which on occasion may cross the elevated sensory threshold to initiate a dream sequence. Dreams about catastrophe are exactly what we would predict (see Chapter 5). Images related (either because of actual experience, stories, or anticipations) to inputs of fear and anxiety would naturally arise again when these inputs intrude across the threshold. But sometimes a person dreams about something that is normally repugnant to him, such as homosexual activity or an incestuous relationship. Do such dreams imply an impulse toward such activity? Once again a simpler explanation seems feasible. If a person goes to sleep harboring feelings of freefloating guilt, whatever the basic cause, the symbols that arise would, according to our view, be those that had been associated with this input in the past. But why doesn't such input, whether anxiety, fear, or guilt, produce the same image sequences (thought) while we are awake? Because then the effects of the autocept are present. During sleep the autocept or "I" that normally directs and limits the onward march of apperceptual flux is missing, locked feebly behind the elevated sensory threshold.

To complicate the problem of continuity even further, each encode apperceived during the dream occasions varying degrees of visceral change that result in further pervasive input repercussions. Such input may cross the elevated sensory threshold to break up a symbol sequence or initiate a new one. Small wonder, then, when all things are considered that dreams are so far outside logic, so evanescent, so uncontrollable, and often so terrifying.

The erratic behavior of the somnambulist takes on meaning when we understand that he is probably responding not to sensory input, which has been "shut out," but to apperceived memory residuals that are sufficiently intense to cross the elevated motor threshold. It seems reasonable to assume (as we shall discuss later in detail) that somnambulistic behavior involves the use of motor skills relative to which the motor threshold has been lowered because of continued practice. Talking and walking, which are two of the most intensively practiced and thus most highly refined motor skills, would thus be high in the hierarchy of dream-initiated motor responses.

The Lag between Apperception and Overt Behavior

Before learning the time lapse between apperception and action is minimal. A baby who is hungry or has stomach pains will react immediately with the few diffuse responses in his repertory. The lag between apperception and overt response in lower animals is also typically brief, though, as a function of innate mechanisms, the response may be quite discrete and functionally appropriate. But, as learning proceeds, more and more aspects of the organism's world become internalized so that a greater number of variety of "internal locomotions" relative to a given imposed circumstance become possible. Such internal locomotion, like overt movement, takes time, and it is this time that accounts for the lag between apperception and overt behavior.

Learning and Lowering the Motor Threshold

In the human infant, except for reflexive behavior, the motor threshold appears to be at approximately the same level, regardless of the source of the apperceived input. Intensity alone seems to be the major determinant of action, and once the motor threshold has been crossed behavior is diffuse and undifferentiated. But, as the infant matures, learning plays an increasingly important part in activity: Motocepts emerge and become associated with apperceived encodes and sensory components. Hence the following corollary;

The lowering of the motor threshold is a direct function of the number of times that a given apperceived input (whether encode or sensory component) has been followed by a particular overt response.

Automatic reactions are direct indications of the lowering of the motor threshold. In learning speech there is such a lowering of the motor threshold between certain apperceived encodes and their verbal counterparts that each encode is immediately and effortlessly followed by the appropriate verbal sound: the barrier between "to think" and "to speak" has been reduced so far that thought alone can occasion the spoken work. The expert typist can continue to copy material from a page while carrying on a conversation with another person. The motor threshold between the visual word and the manual response has been lowered so far that the relationship between them proceeds automatically, with only occasional apperceptual monitoring for precise behavior. When there is close correspondence between certain inputs and particular motor responses, the two may actually become fused, as has evidently happened in certain children who insist that a given word is somehow identical with the thing that it designates. Many eight- or nine-year-old children will maintain that a rose could not have been called anything other than a rose.

Most complex organisms are born with relatively low motor thresholds between certain inputs and particular motor responses. The reflexes fall into this category; an intense light will occasion pupillary contraction, a blow on the patellar tendon a knee jerk, the sudden application of a traumatic stimulus to the skin a specific withdrawal response. Apperception is not required for these responses. Such reactions are the ultimate in automatic behavior, but so are certain highly practiced habits that we often find in human beings. When skills are highly refined, apperception ceases to be a crucial antecedent to behavior; the motor threshold is lowered so far that a whole complex series of reactions may unfold with only occasional apperceptual monitoring. It is in these relatively automatic, highly practiced skills that the similarity between learned and innate motor responses is most apparent; the essential difference is that in the former the lowering of the threshold is a function of practice, whereas in the latter the threshold is low to begin with.[2] The extent to which the motor threshold has been lowered as a function of practice and the degree to which an activity has become automatic can be experimentally determined.

The more a given motor skill has been practiced, the greater will be the subject's ability to learn a new habit while simultaneously performing that motor skill.

Accordingly, a skilled typist will find it easier to learn a list of nonsense syllables while typing than will one less practiced in the art, and individuals forced to sort cards while learning nonsense syllables will find the latter task less difficult as they become more skilled at the first.

Response Variety and the Motor Threshold

What kinds of responses reflect the first lowering of the motor threshold and when? We know that the reflex arc initiates withdrawal reactions when the individual is suddenly exposed to a traumatic stimulus. We also know that a hungry infant will exhibit sucking responses when his cheek is stimulated and a grasping response when something is placed in his hand. These examples seem to constitute rudimentary prototypes of movement "away from" and "toward" that develop in later life. When learning enters the picture, as discussed in Chapter 5, these incipient responses occur not only to direct application of the appropriate stimuli but to cues as well.

The grossest of the homeostatic responses of which an organism is capable involve movement of the entire body toward or away from some critical circumstance. Such gross reactions can be occasioned by many different inputs: pain, excessive heat, excessive cold, and presence of food, warmth, or water. Such inputs, regardless of their apparent diversity, have become tied to the same general response. On the other hand, there are many examples of discrete motor reactions that will, after continued practice, occur automatically but *only* when quite specific input comes into focus. A hungry organism will exhibit automatic eating responses only when food is in its mouth and drinking responses only when both thirst input and that derived from water are apperceived. The motor threshold for gross movements "away from" and "toward" thus may be lowered for many different inputs, whereas the threshold pertinent to such discrete responses as eating and drinking is crossed only when certain specific and appropriate inputs are brought into focus. The observation makes sense from an evolutionary point of view: The only adequate responses to a multitude of different environmental situations (composed of dangers or food sources) are movements of the entire organism either "away from" or "toward." Such gross movements are functional in a wide variety of situations, whereas specific responses are much more limited in their applications and are therefore likely to become associated with quite discrete and circumscribed environmental circumstances.

Once a given motocept has emerged, its individual components tend to remain fused and to resist separation: It is difficult for an individual to alter a motor activity that has been very much practiced. That is why it is more difficult for a person who has picked up "bad habits" to learn to type or play golf correctly than it is for someone who has had no experience with these activities at all. Adults who learn new languages almost invariably inject into that language certain inappropriate motocepts that may persist for years as interfering accents. Motocepts provide a kind of motor constancy that though it is extremely functional, nevertheless imposes a degree of inflexibility that may result in negative transfer. This fact is not remarkable. We have already noted (see Chapter 4) that the unconscious coercion of primary encoding produces an enduring tendency toward constancy in perception and in the autocept. It should not be surprising to find a parallel phenomenon in behavior when the requirements for fusion (recurrent presentation of similar input components) have been fulfilled.

The Autocept and Overt Behavior

The autocept (see Chapter 4) is not only a fused unity arising from integration of similar and recurrent components, it is also a "need system" with major implications for behavior. When the organization of the autocopt is threatened, secondary disequilibrium (anxiety or guilt) is introduced into the integration matrix. Behavior activated and sustained by such disequilibrium is said to be "volitional." As the autocept emerges early in the individual's life and frequently occasions action, the threshold between the input from this system and most overt behavior is lowered somewhat. The input from the autocept therefore not only takes precedence over that from other sources but also occasions behavior so easily as to be automatic.

Let there be no mistake about our implications here. We assume that most behavior is initiated and sustained by input from threats to the autocept. When "I" decide to pick up a pencil, the act of doing so is equilibratory in that it allows the structure of the autocept to remain relatively more intact than if "I" did not. We may wonder why no disequilibratory input can be discerned before such actions. But we must remember that the motor thresholds between many behaviors and disequilibratory input from the autocept have been lowered by means of many contiguous presentations. The automatic quality postulated would typically obtain, and a crucial mark of it is the relative freedom from apperception. If "I" decided to pick up a pencil and found that "I" could not do it, the disequilibratory input from threats to the autocept would be much more apparent.

This discussion suggests that much human behavior is volitional. But that does not mean that behavior is occasioned by some kind of "free will." Precisely the opposite. Let us return to the postulate of process, that all activity, whether overt or internal, tends toward equilibrium, and reconsider the manner in which the autocept contributes to behavior. The autocept, like other constant outcomes of primary encoding, maintains as much organization and structure as circumstances allow; there is an enduring tendency toward equilibrium. Sufficient deviation from balance occasions introduction of input that in turn initiates either overt or internal behavior, which persists until tolerable integration is regained.

Such behavior not only appears to be volitional; there actually also seems to be a component of "freedom" attached to it. Curiously one major argument for "free will" is based on this observation. Several polemicists have argued that, as we have the phenomenal experience of freedom when we choose between two alternatives or persist in some patently odious activity, there must be some free agency that determines our behavior in such instances. Two factors seem to be involved: the "feeling of freedom" at the moment of choice and the ability to persist in activity that apparently produces needs rather than reducing them which contradicts homeostatic theory. Let us consider these points individually.

Certainly there can be little doubt that man does have a phenomenal experience of freedom of choice. But we insist that this experience at the so-called "moment of decision" is a by-product of the shift from activity sustained by other disequilibrium input to that arising from threats to integration of the autocept. This feeling of freedom is, however, much more than the experience of a moment; it can continue through the course of volitional action. "I" can remain constantly aware of the feeling of freedom all the while that "I" am directing and energizing internal or external activity.

The point is that the "I" that has the power to direct the course of action *is* the autocept. But what is the source of the "feeling of freedom"? The following analysis may help to answer this question. Let us begin by asking the opposite question: Under what circumstances do we have the feeling that our behavior is "predetermined" or not free? Certainly when there is external coercion or irresistable need. In such examples we would answer the question "Why did you do that?" with "Because I was forced to," "Because I was afraid," "Because I was hungry," and so on. The relationship between the particular circumstance, or input, and the resulting behavior is apparent to us.

But what about behavior motivated by the autocept? The encode "tree" is derived from concurrent sensory particulars fused in a global phenomenon; in much more complex fashion the myriad individual sensory and valence components of the autocept have become lost in the larger representation. A determination of which particular aspects of this system occasion action thus becomes impossible. The self is experienced as a functional unity. When a person's behavior is occasioned by disequilibrium within this system and he is asked why he takes particular action, he will probably answer, "Because I wanted to." This answer reveals that the impetus for action has been derived from the system under discussion. In our view, such activities are just as lawful as are those occasioned by coercion or needs. The individual may do what he wills, but he cannot *will* what he wills, for the autocept is the "willing" agency, and it is itself a lawful product. We do not deny, of course, the *experience* of freedom of choice, but we do insist that this experience is derived from the fusion of the many components in the autocept.

But, according to our theory, is not the very existence of the experience of freedom evidence that it is functional in the total behavioral economy of the organism? Does not this evidence imply that "free will" is a characteristic of the human being? The answer to the first question is "maybe," but to the second question it is "no." It is entirely possible that the experience of freedom so common in human beings is functional and that it evolved just as did other attributes because it is functional. But this experience does not mean that man actually has free will. Most men believe that colors are inherent in the objects they see. We certainly agree that such erroneous inferences may be functional, but they *are* erroneous. We also agree that man has a feeling of freedom and even assent to the notion that it may be functional, but we insist that such affirmations have little to do with the question of whether man actually is free.

Effects of Conflict on the Motor Threshold

In the discussion so far we have suggested that overt behavior occurs automatically once the motor threshold has been crossed. But the level of the threshold is a function not only of the frequency with which a given input has been associated with a particular response; it is also affected by the presence of competing inputs that have been associated with other behavior. During practically all waking moments of an individual's life many different inputs are being apperceived sequentially and some of them have been previously associated with incompatible responses. It is thus possible for an individual to apperceive sequentially two different inputs, one of which has previously been associated with "approach" behavior and the other of which has frequently occurred just before "aversive" responses. Under such circumstances the motor threshold for both kinds of behavior will be raised. When apperception is fluctuating between inputs that have been associated with different and incompatible responses conflict results, and it is to the problem of conflict that we now turn.

One of the simplest examples of conflict occurs in the newborn child. If he is hungry, the stimulation of his cheek will occasion head movements toward the side stimulated. When both cheeks are stimulated the child will move his head from side to side. We may surmise what is taking place: The inputs from both sources of stimulation are present in the integration matrix, and apperception is fluctuating between them. As the input from one cheek is brought into focus, movement in the prescribed direction is initiated, but when the input from the other cheek comes into focus it cancels the first action and initiates the opposite movement and so on. The demonstration of oscillation does of course depend upon relative shifts in the intensity of stimulation: As the child moves his head left, the right cheek must be stimulated more intensively in order to initiate both apperception and the opposite movement. Oscillation is also contingent on the amount of sensory adaptation that has already taken place.

In a superbly controlled study, J. P. Nafe and K. S. Wagoner (1941) not only demonstrated the rate of adaptation but also gained insight into the mechanism responsible for sensory input. They found that a weight placed on the skin's surface does not sink immediately, it sinks gradually but increasingly slowly until a critical rate is reached. As long as movement is at a rate above this critical level the subject feels pressure, but when it falls below the critical level the subject feels no pressure. Adaptation has taken place. Many different kinds of persistent stimuli cease in this way to introduce sensory components into the integration matrix, and the apperceptual process is thus freed from the coercion of inputs that no longer have adaptive significance.

All conflict between two kinds of approach behavior follows the general pattern of this example, but usually learned rather than innate responses are involved. Such "approach-approach" conflict is quite unstable. As apperception presumably varies with input intensity and as distance from a circumstance and intensity of input derived from it are related, the immobility found in an approach-approach conflict situation will soon be disrupted. As the individual moves farther from one stimulus circumstance than from the other, input from the former will be less intense and therefore less likely to be apperceived whereas the opposite conditions will obtain if it moves farther from the latter circumstance, unless the intensity of the input is varied to compensate for the shift.

What happens when behavior is triggered by two different inputs arising from the same circumstance, one of which occasions behavior "away from" and the other behavior "toward"? Then, as apperception fluctuates, the organism is first impelled toward and then away from the same situation. An animal that eats food that burns its mouth offers an elementary example of such conflict. A thirsty individual finally driven to drink salt water is a slightly more complex example. In both instances two different inputs occasion two different responses that are incompatible yet derived from the same circumstance.

This kind of conflict is typical of overt behavior. As sequential apperception of the myriad components available within the integration matrix occurs, many of the inputs brought into focus are associated with incompatible responses above the threshold. During any particular period a fair number of "approach-avoidance" conflicts should arise from the continuing process of apperception itself. To which of the apperceived components of such a conflict will response be made?

When motor thresholds are equal, behavior will be occasioned by the most intense of various apperceived inputs.

In the classical studies of approach-avoidance conflict by J. S. Brown (1948) oscillation was noted at the point at which approach and avoidance gradients crossed. They crossed when the subject organism had moved far enough from the critical situation so that fear became less intense than hunger. Brown demonstrated experimentally that if either input was increased, the point at which oscillation occurred would vary correspondingly. If both inputs were increased proportionally, then oscillation would occur more rapidly, indicating that dynamic tension within the system had also been increased. It should be noted that the oscillation that can be demonstrated in an approach-avoidance conflict is another example of the fulcrum phenomenon (see Chapter 2) characteristic of behavior once a dynamic equilibrium between antithetical inputs has been achieved.

We have been assuming that the motor thresholds relative to precipitating inputs have been equal. Obviously they rarely are in actual behavior: The thresholds between inputs and behavior vary according to the number of contiguous pairings that have occurred. If we could hold the intensity of two inputs constant, the behavior with the lower threshold would always occur.

When inputs associated with two incompatible responses are equal in intensity, the sequence of input and behavior with the lower threshold will predominate.

If rats were given 50 trials in the left arm of a T maze under water deprivation and 100 trials in the right arm under food deprivation, we could predict that they would choose the right arm when the two inputs (thirst and hunger) were equal in intensity. This hypothesis, of course, would be difficult to test, simply because little research has been conducted on equating input intensities. Yet the general implications of this corollary could be evaluated experimentally without too much difficulty: All that would be necessary would be to demonstrate that both the level of deprivation and the number of training trials can affect behavior differentially when the other is held constant.

Such an experiment would involve two different primary disequilibrium inputs, thirst and hunger; it therefore raises a complication implicit in the preceding discussion. The variables of input vividness and input intensity confound the design. Future researchers may develop approaches that will permit us to determine the relative influences of these two input characteristics, but it will probably be some time before we can say how much thirst or hunger is equal to how much pain.[4]

It is from threats to the organization of the autocept that the most profound conflicts arise in the human being. If an input initiates thought that threatens the integrity of the autocept, anxiety and guilt may be extremely disruptive (see Chapter 8). Although powerful antithetical components are typically required before behavior disruptive to autocept organization will occur, there are limits to their resistance. Only rare individuals could withstand the precise torture techniques developed by the Nazis in World War II. Usually after only a brief experience of their shock devices, even the most loyal individual would make pronouncements contrary to his most cherished principles and values. But, when certain precepts have been sufficiently integrated into an autocept, an individual will endure hunger or thirst until death, rather than violate them. While the author was a prisoner of the Japanese during World War II, survival was literally contingent on scrounging food from any and every possible source. Yet a number of Roman Catholic priests suffered death rather than violate principles that they had incorporated into their essential selves. Incidentally, the disequilibrium introduced by the threats to the autocept that such behavior occasioned in many others was less pervasive than was hunger and thirst.

Fortunately for the adaptive integrity of behavior, there is usually an overlap of activities that reduce other disequilibratory inputs and those required for continuation of autocept integration. Even when there is conflict, input from the autocept typically takes precedence, for, because of the low motor threshold, very little disequilibrium from this source is required to initiate and sustain action.

Whether or not a given input occasions behavior counter to the organization of a particular autocept is predominantly a function of its intensity and its pervasiveness. But behavior is also affected by the kinds of material that have been fused in the autocept and by the degree of integration that has taken place. Behavior that might be extremely disruptive to one autocept could be only incidental or even "strengthening" to another (see Chapter 8).

Although the unraveling of several given input-apperception-output chains might reveal great differences in the precise steps involved, they generally follow the same sequence. Let us assume that the critical input in this example is hunger. First, it is brought into focus; then associated encodes enter apperception, followed in rapid succession by valence input that has become attached to these encodes. These encodes combine with the hunger input to determine what further encodes and external input will also be apperceived. It is usually only after the various inputs pertinent to the basic disequilibrium have come into focus that behavior results. The entire process sketched here may occur in less than a second. If conflict variables are involved, however, fluctuation of apperception may cause a considerable time gap between the initial input and the overt reaction.

The major point of course is that, although overt behavior is a lawful outcome of apperception, a great many lawful apperceptions typically intervene between the precipitating input and the initiation of overt behavior. The essential difference between our position and that espoused by certain behaviorists becomes apparent. E. R. Guthrie's early work, for instance, supposedly revealed that behavior will result when a stimulus that has preceded it in the past is presented again (assuming that no interference has occurred).[5] Our view is far different. First, we believe that an imposed stimulus may or may not introduce input into the integration matrix; even if it does, such input may not be apperceived; and if it is apperceived it may still not occasion an overt reaction. In order for a reaction to occur, the stimulus must occasion an input, which must be brought into focus, and then it must also be sufficiently intense to cross the motor threshold.

Discrimination: Generalization and Language

Two major characteristics mark the increasing complexity of evolved species: the number and variety of energies to which the organism can respond and the number and variety of responses that can be made. The amoeba can respond to only a small number of energy shifts and only in limited ways. In higher mammals the variety and distribution of receptors provide for potential sensitivity to a remarkable range of energy changes. Not only does each modality have certain dimensions that may be divided into a multitude of just noticeable differences, but also the possibility of interaction and combination increases almost to infinity the number of sensory inputs that can be introduced. Furthermore, the skeletal and muscular structure of the mammal provides the basis for an appreciable increase in possible different kinds of behavior.

But the increase in possible responses has not kept pace with the expanding sensitivity of the organism. Even in the primates, in which motor dexterity has reached a pinnacle, the variety of behavior, as great as it is, does not begin to match the variety of possible inputs. This observation applies to the entire phylogenetic scale; sensitivity has progressed "geometrically," whereas reactivity has increased only "arithmetically." One of the critical adaptation problems generated by developing complexity has been to make a relatively small range of possible behavior suffice for the much greater range of energy shifts to which the organism is sensitive.[6]

In this context the adaptive contributions of the antithetical processes of generalization and discrimination become apparent: The organism must develop, either through inherited mechanisms or through learning, the capacity to respond to different inputs in the same fashion. Yet it must also continue to respond differently to input variations pertinent to its survival. Discrimination provides the basis for differential response by allowing more facile adjustment to the environment, whereas generalization ensures common responses when differential behavior is not significant for survival. Both learned and unlearned behavior mechanisms may be viewed as compromises between the unresolvable complexity of total discrimination and the nonfunctional oversimplification of generalization. An organism's behavior must always fall between these two extremes: one that would require a different response to each stimulus variation, regardless of how slight, and another that would involve giving exactly the same response to all stimuli. The process of generalization allows reduction of what would otherwise be overwhelming complexity, whereas that of discrimination ensures that energy shifts important for survival will occasion appropriate responses.

Both discrimination and generalization are essential mechanisms in every living entity, from the simplest cell to the most complex mammal. An amoeba will make the same general type of response to varying intensities of light, but the fact that a gradient of behavior does exist is evidence of crude discrimination. An herbivorous animal will make the same response (eating) to a variety of plants, but it will not make this response to other animals. A horticulturist will respond to a given item as a rose regardless of whether he tastes, sees, feels, or smells it, but he will not make the same response to any other flower. A bigot faced with a wide variety of black people might respond with thoughts that they are "shiftless and untrustworthy" but fail to make this response to white people.

This list could, of course, be extended indefinitely, but, limited though it is, it gives some indication of the universality and variety of both generalization and discrimination. Both were intrinsic to the first life element, and both remain fundamental to the highest products of evolution.

From an operational point of view both discrimination and generalization are easy to define. Discrimination is an organism's ability to respond *differently* to two or more different stimuli; generalization is its ability to make the *same* response to two or more different stimuli. But we cannot stop here. Although the character of both processes remains ostensibly the same as we move up the phylogenetic scale, the mechanisms that occasion them change markedly as organisms become more complex.

In Chapter 2 we suggested that the course of evolution can be charted according to the emergence of mechanisms allowing more facile differential responses. Now we may emphasize that techniques for more appropriate discriminations and generalizations are implicit in differential responses; they may even be considered critical indicators of the relative adaptability of any given organism or species, whether gross avoidance and approach responses or subtle speech variations are in question.

We may begin by emphasizing an obvious point that has been much overlooked. There are always limits to both generalization and discrimination. When energy fluctuations are too minute for receptors to distinguish them, the organism will respond to both alike. The human ear, for instance, cannot discriminate between two tones of 1,000 and 1,001 cycles per second respectively; it must therefore respond to both as if they were the same. This type of generalization reflects the limitations of the system; when discrimination *cannot* occur generalization is bound to occur.

Even when discrimination does occur, however, the organism may respond in the same way because no alternative response exists within its repertory, circumstances have placed it in a behavioral strait-jacket, or the almost universal application of certain gross responses makes generalization appropriate. A deer will run from such diverse circumstances as fire, a man, and a predatory animal, but the response reflects not failure of discrimination but a limited behavioral repertory and the general functional contribution of running away. A rat in a straight alley maze may continue to run toward the goal box even though the stimulus characteristics of the box have been greatly altered. What else can it do? If disequilibratory input is continuously introduced into the integration matrix, the rat will continue to run, regardless of the changes in the stimulus characteristics of the maze.

The discrimination potential of any organism is thus limited by the range of qualitatively different inputs that can be introduced; generalization, on the other hand, is always affected by the range of responses available. This point has been much confused. Discrimination cannot be defined operationally without the concept of differential behavior, but the absence of differential behavior does not guarantee that discrimination has failed to occur.

We shall now try to classify various mechanisms of discrimination and generalization, suggesting that much of the confusion surrounding these topics arises from the assumption that similar behavior reflects similar processes.

Inherent Mechanisms

Although discrimination is necessarily limited by the resolving power of a receptor system, it is also abetted by certain intrinsic differences between such systems. As we discussed at length in Chapter 3, the inputs from different transmitting mechanisms have characteristically different qualities. The organism (at least the mammal) is constructed so that intrinsic and unlearned discriminations among such inputs as pain, hunger, thirst, cold, hot, sound, and light automatically occur (assuming that the inputs have been apperceived). Not only does such intrinsic discrimination characterize input from different modalities, it is also implicit in the various dimensions of each receptor system. There is a qualitative difference between the inputs of pitch and loudness, hue and brightness, sweet and sour; for that matter, there are discriminable differences between points along a single dimension that exceed the threshold. Any energy change that transcends this threshold is discriminated if it is apperceived. It is true that we must generally infer this kind of discrimination, for the apperception that both defines and demonstrates it occurs internally. Yet that such discriminations do occur can be checked by casual introspection on the variety of inputs typically apperceived during each waking moment. The contributions of the structuralists and of those who still study problems of psychophysics and psychological scaling are further evidence of the universality of such discriminations. Not only are sensory inputs apperceived, the differences between them are also apperceived. This process is a kind of intrinsic discrimination.

Our discussion suggests some of the sensory components that may be introduced into the integration matrix. Not only does each transmitting mechanism present qualitatively different sensations, but each dimension within a modality also provides unique input that can be broken down into a multitude of "just noticeable differences." When we also consider the novel components that may be derived from the combinations and interactions of such material, the number of potential inputs becomes astronomical—and so, incidentally, does the number of potential intrinsic discriminations.

When we turn from apperceptual shifts to overt behavior, we find that inherent mechanisms are still represented, including some that are present in human beings. All reflexes and instinctive sequences are based on inherited discriminations; they are initiated more easily by certain stimuli than by others, and the receptors that produce them are usually quite specifically located. Furthermore the stereotyped sequence of responses that defines instinctive behavior can be triggered and sustained only by certain appropriate stimuli, and other stimuli will have little or no effect. Birds' responses to the hawk shape, for example (see Chapter 2, note 3), also fall into the general category of inherited discriminations. This mechanism seems remarkably specific, for chickens respond when the moving shape is similar to that of a hawk but not when the moving shape gives the appearance of a duck. Indeed, all innate behavior mechanisms involve intrinsic discrimination, for specific stimulation is a universal requirement for their demonstration.

Learned Mechanisms: Perceptual

When learning enters the picture of generalization and discrimination, both processes become much more complex. The resolving power of the receptor system inevitably sets the limits of discrimination, but the inputs into the integration matrix do not remain discrete. The primary encoding process (see Chapter 4) soon occasions emergence of phenomena located in three-dimensional space. The fusion responsible for this emergence is a kind of generalization mechanism, for it provides for the inclusion of large numbers of discrete inputs in a single functional unity to abet common responses. Size, shape, and brightness constancies (basic outcomes of primary encoding) are also generalization mechanisms. Although the actual physical image projected on the retina fluctuates markedly as distance varies, the object is perceived as of the same size because of size constancy. Brightness and shape constancy operate in the same way. Despite fluctuations in the shape projected in the retina, a window is seen as rectangular, a plate or a saucer as round, and a piece of coal as black, regardless of the amount of light actually reflected from it.

Again we encounter the functional antagonism between discrimination and generalization. Size, shape, and brightness constancy, as well as the emergence of phenomena, actually work *against* discernible shifts in input. Individual cue variations are obscured: A rotating square blackboard moving toward a light source will be perceived as a single form, even though its retinal shape, brightness, and size are changing moment by moment. The constancies, then, are excellent illustrations of the principle that the adaptation of any organism must always be a compromise between generalization and discrimination. In perceptual generalization individual cues are fused in functional unity allowing particulars that might have survival significance to become lost in the totality. But without such generalization the organism's chance for survival would be reduced by the sheer multitude of inputs imposed.

Very seldom, except perhaps in the laboratory, does an organism react to energy changes on a single dimension alone. More often, indeed almost always, it responds to fluctuations in perceptual characteristics of phenomena that inevitably reflect changes on a number of dimensions interacting in various ways. We respond *not* to shifts in tone or light frequencies but to global phenomena of which particular stimulus dimensions are simply part of larger complexes of cues. The crucial point is that these cues have actually lost their individual characteristics and become fused in the total phenomenon.

Furthermore, not only are individual cues thus submerged, but also it is the context within which this fused totality occurs that usually determines the manner in which it is perceived. For example, when we wish to guess the size of a man, we measure him against items in the environment around him. The producers of monster films are expert in the art of altering context to create unusual perceptual responses. A chameleon rarely generates fear, but viewed among diminutive trees and buildings it may seem frightening indeed. The stimulus characteristics of the lizard do not change, but the perceived size shifts dramatically because of manipulations of the context.

Even at this juncture, most experiments on generalization and discrimination that have been conducted seem inappropriate. Typically they have been limited to variations on single dimensions in constant context. But in an actual life situation the organism almost always responds to variations in whole phenomena, and these variations are more often than not "discriminated" according to alterations in context, rather than to changes in the phenomena themselves. This problem appears even more critical when we examine the basis for most of the generalizations and discriminations that account for behavior in complex mammals, particularly human beings.

Learned Mechanisms: Conceptual

When a common response is produced by some mediating encode, we can speak of conceptual generalization. In any such circumstance two or more qualitatively different inputs are occasioning apperception of the same encode, which in turn provides the basis for response. In classical conditioning the common response of salivation was produced by both the bell and the sight of meat powder, but it was the encode of the meat powder that mediated and actually occasioned this response (see Chapter 5). In the same way, it is the completely disparate inputs from tasting, feeling, or smelling a particular object that may result in the common response of "apple"—but only if they are mediated by the encode of that particular fruit. It does not matter that the inputs may be remarkably dissimilar; if they occasion the apperception of the same encode, the same response will occur (assuming that the motor threshold is crossed). When an appropriate intermediate encode (whether a word or a fused residual) is present, the inputs characteristic of many items can be represented by a single term; canines, regardless of variations in size, color, shape, and general configuration, occasion the same response "dog." Once again we have an example of the remarkable simplifying power of generalization. Not only are individual sensory cues fused in the phenomenon of each dog, but the differences between these various pehnomena are also fused in the general response "dog," which represents them all.

Many conceptual discriminations are not based on variations in the sensory input characterizing a given object. The fusion process, the constancies, and the emergence of mediating encodes often prevent this eventuality. Lions are an example. Once the sensory input characteristic of this animal has been apperceived, the encodes summarizing experience with lions follow immediately in apperception. The ensuing response is contingent not on the input itself but on the context within which the lion comes into focus. If the lion is perceived as far away (and context determines perception of distance), very little response may occur. If it is perceived as close, the response may be immediate flight. But, if the lion is perceived as close but in a cage, the response may be approach. In actual life situations the organism thus often reacts to contextual cues, rather than only to discrete shifts in the stimulus characteristics of the item.

All conceptual generalization, then, depends upon one or more encodes that mediate between a vast variety of inputs and some common responses. Many of these encodes represent various input items, but there are others that do not represent similarities or common features in the input per se. Rather, they are derived from recurrent *contrasts*, relationships, and processes among the inputs.

The Emergence of Language. The development of language offers one of the clearest examples of the lowering of the motor threshold. As has often been observed, before a child can use a particular sound he must first have practiced it at length during the "babbling" stage of language development.[7] The inputs derived from tongue and lip movements are thus fused into motocepts long before the child has actually begun to use language to convey precise meaning. Even while such motocepts are being established, the process of lowering the motor threshold is underway. After much practice the motor threshold between a visual image and the motor response that produces a sound may be so low that the child can make the sound automatically when the image is presented. For example, each time that the child's visual image "dog" is followed by the word "dog" the motor threshold between them is lowered and the encodes representing both also become more firmly established. Once established, either encode (or the predicted fused encode), if apperceived, can occasion the motor responses essential to utterance of the word. The child may even say the word "dog" when neither the visual image or the sound is presented. Apperception of the encode alone is sufficient for utterance of the word.

Speech, then, is simply the emission of sounds, produced by motocepts that have previously become associated with particular encodes. In effective speech the encode must always precede the motocept that occasions vocal sound. When speech has been much practiced it may proceed smoothly with minimum delay, each utterance being preceded briefly by the apperception of the appropriate encode. Thought and speech are thus remarkably similar; thought involves sequential apperception of encodes, whereas speech includes occurrence of the motocepts that have been previously associated with such encodes.

Although language may be as diverse as are the cultures of the earth, the words used always represent certain recurrent common features in the experience of a people. But every language system represents only a small portion of the inputs that the individual may experience. Any word, regardless of its specificity, is always a summary and no matter how many qualifying terms we may use, distortion is one inevitable outcome of language. Women can vary on a continuum of beauty, but we have no continuum of terms to represent each such variation. There are ugly women and beautiful women and very ugly women and very beautiful women. We can, of course, make still finer distinctions but not a great many. And so it is with all our experiences: An almost infinite number of inputs must be represented by a limited number of sounds. Any human being is capable of billions of discriminations, but even the most learned man can probably use fewer than 10,000 words.

In the evolution of a language there is thus a tendency to represent the greatest possible amount of experience with the least possible number of sounds. If we consider the English suffix "ing" we can marvel at the broad category of experience subsumed under this single sound. If we put it at the end of certain other sounds, it stands for "taking place," whether we mean talking, walking, killing, or loving. Indeed "ing" has mighty generalizing power—but no more than do many other sounds that condense human experience into categories that make communication possible. The familiar eight parts of speech, which most of us hated in school and which more of us have since forgotten, are remarkable examples of the manner in which overwhelming complexity is reduced to order and simplicity. In each instance the principle of reduction involves representing by a single term a wide band of man's experience, which regardless of its variety, has common features. A noun, according to one grammar book, "is the name of something you can taste, touch, see or hear." Nouns thus stand for categories of sensory input sufficiently common and stable to be represented by particular sounds. There are common nouns and proper nouns, singular nouns and plural nouns; most of the latter are created by simply adding "s." With a muted hissing sound we thus subsume the vast category of "more than one." Pronouns, too, contribute to reduction. "It," for instance, can stand for *any* idea or place or thing.

Because much of human experience is of change, every language must have sounds to represent flux. Verbs not only fulfill this function, they also indicate the "when" of such a change. Again we see the inclusive power of a single sound. If we put "will" before certain other words, we indicate the future; if we add "ed" to the same words, we indicate the past. Nouns and pronouns represent static inputs, but verbs indicate process, and the particular kind of verb tells us whether this process was, is, or will be.

Certain sounds have the function of partially alleviating the bluntness and imprecision of language. Both adverbs and adjectives permit expression of some small part of the infinite shades and gradations of our experience. Adjectives break "things" down into finer categories; they tell us "what kind," "which one," "how many." They lend concreteness to nouns and pronouns. They tell us that there are "several" reasons why the "blue" eyes of "that" woman are "beautiful." Adverbs do for verbs what adjectives do for nouns and pronouns. They represent the characteristics of process, the how, when, where, and how much of action.

Components of experience never occur in isolation. They are always related to other items in time and space. And, although there are many ways in which "things" can be related, only a few prepositions represent them all. When we consider "above" or "in" or "upon," we realize again how few sounds represent vast segments of our experience. We shall survey without mentioning introjections, which represent different emotions by certain sounds.

We have not intended to provide a review of the intricacies of the English language. Any sixth-grade grammar book can do that. But we have tried to demonstrate a point that most of us fail completely to see when we endure this study in childhood: The variety of man's experience includes certain recurring characteristics, processes, and relationships, and language represents them.

As use of language emerges in the little child, the varied character of his experience must be funneled into the limiting categories of specific sounds. The encodes that accumulate and thus summarize the common and recurring features of man's experience make communication through such sounds possible. But speech can begin only when the thresholds between certain encodes and motocepts produced by fusion of input from movements of vocal cords, mouth, and tongue are low enough to allow utterance of appropriate sounds smoothly and with minimal hesitation.

The process of speech always follows the same general sequence, but there may be slight alterations in the various steps. It is typically initiated by some sensory input sufficiently competitive with all other components of the integration matrix to cross the apperceptual threshold. Immediately after focusing on such input the encode summarizing the person's experience with similar input is apperceived; it is followed by associated encodes. If somewhere in this sequence of rapid fluctuations the motor threshold between encodes and appropriate motocepts is low enough, verbal sounds will be emitted. If the encodes succeeding one another in apperception embody associational chains, then the resulting sounds will convey meaning and logic.

We note again (see Chapter 6) that secondary reverberations (sensory feedback) play a vital role in the organization of speech.[8] While sounds are being uttered there is constant apperceptual monitoring of these reverberations. Should some discrepancy between encode and uttered sound occur, as when a person means one thing and says another, monitoring would allow correction. More important for language continuity is the rapid fluctuation of apperception among precipitating input, appropriate encodes, resulting sounds, and secondary reverberations; this fluctuation provides for the continuing synthesis without which effective language would be impossible.

In general, then, the use of language to communicate is contingent on apperception of encodes associated with particular verbal motocepts. But in much speaking, especially among educated people, a dual transposition is required. Before a sound can be uttered it is often necessary to translate an extremely abstract encode, or "blob," into concrete memory residuals. Much of our thinking does not involve discrete and specific encodes that have previously been associated with particular verbal sounds. Rather, it may consist of residuals subsuming entire experiences or total perspectives, for which specific sounds are unavailable in the response repertory of the individual. When such "blob" encodes are involved thought may proceed extremely rapidly simply because particulars need not be brought into focus, but verbalizing such thinking poses a problem: There are *no* sounds to represent such broad conceptual categories, and the notions implicit in them must be attached to specific encodes before verbal responses become available. Anyone who has studied foreign language has experienced the laborious process of dual translation, of thinking in his native tongue, then translating into the new language before finally and haltingly uttering sounds. The translation of "blobs" into encodes sufficiently discrete to have verbal representation is much more common but at times no less burdensome.

The critical reader may object that this analysis neglects at least one fundamental attribute of speech, its volitional character. The speaker is almost always aware that "he" is both uttering sounds and directing them. This view is essentially correct. The autocept provides the input that gives both momentum and direction to speech except when the person is under extreme duress or is talking in his sleep. The motocepts responsible for speech sounds have been associated with the input from the autocept on so many different occasions (beginning with the babbling phase of language development) that the threshold between this input and speech movements has been almost eliminated. This lowering accounts for the fact that most if not all language utterance, even though it may proceed quite rapidly and apparently automatically, still appears volitional to the speaker. If a person talks in his sleep, talks aloud to himself while immersed in some problem, or is driven to verbalization (a rare phenomenon) by extreme pain or grief, the volitional character is missing; when he remembers it later it seems strange indeed.

The responses that occasion language sounds seem unique, but they are not. The movements of the vocal cords and mouth that produce such sounds are different from other responses in only three respects. They may be varied rapidly, they usually produce sound, and the vocal cords that produce the sound are always handy. But, even as the motor threshold between particular sensory inputs or encodes and certain vocal cord movements can be lowered, so can that between such components and other responses. Indeed, if a sufficient variety of sounds were uttered, any behavior could take over this function of the vocal cords. Human beings can learn to communicate by means of the manually produced sounds of drums, telegraph keys, or musical instruments.

Many people have tried to teach chimpanzees to talk, apparently with little success until quite recently. Possibly the vocal utterances of primates are *inherently* correlated with certain types of input, as is so of birds and dogs. If so, the "speech trainers" of chimpanzees are trying to override intrinsic (and thus interfering) relationships. The chimpanzee's inability to learn to speak may reflect response, rather than cortical incapacity.

This conclusion is strongly suggested by a recent demonstration by D. Premack (1970): A chimpanzee can learn to use a series of clearly distinguishable forms in a manner reminiscent of the symbolic manipulations commonly assumed to be restricted to human beings. Through a series of small but orderly increments of reinforcement, each step deftly shaped, Sarah soon not only mastered a vocabulary of more than 100 words, she was also able to use verbs, adverbs, adjectives, and some relatively abstract concepts appropriately.

Actually, in most subhuman species inability to learn to speak is probably cortical. The adaptive function of language is so great that any species with the capacity for it would probably have developed it, unless countermechanisms interfered. It is true that many organisms can emit and respond to signals, but usually the nature of the stimulus and response are genetically fixed.[9]

In conceptual generalization both the benefits of simplification and the handicaps of failure to discriminate are extreme, and, when spoken or written words enter the picture, both tendencies are further accentuated. In the adult human being the number of information bits (measured by sensory inputs and encodes) is markedly increased. Generalization is a vital simplification mechanism that allows the application of language, yet with generalization there is typically a loss in discrimination. Language limits in varying degrees (depending upon the number of terms available) the "reality" of the individual; we have only one word for rice, but the Chinese have many. The most unfortunate consequence of such overgeneralization is the stereotypes that characterize the language patterns of most of us.

Response Cessation

Two factors may be involved in every circumstance of cessation of response: reduction in performance and loss of learning. Let us illustrate with a simple example. A rat trained in a Skinner box will continue to respond for a fairly prolonged period after the magazine has ceased to deliver food pellets. Why does it eventually cease to respond? The input of hunger may still be present; as long as it is apperceived and is sufficiently pervasive to cross the motor threshold, response should continue. And indeed it would if other components did not intrude into apperception and occasion incompatible behavior. As the rat continues to press the bar, fatigue increases and comes into focus, in direct proportion to its intensity. When it is apperceived, the motocepts associated with it in the past are triggered. These "resting" responses are incompatible with the press response, and behavior at the bar is thus reduced in frequency. But fatigue is not the only intrusive input during extinction. If a barrier interferes with demonstration of a motocept, secondary disequilibrium—anger—may be introduced in the integration matrix. When it is apperceived new behavior like an "attack response" tends to occur and to compete with smooth performance at the bar. As attacks typically involve "moving toward" behavior, anger may for a time actually bring about an increase in activity at the bar, but, as it becomes more intense, specific "aggression" behavior like biting and scratching tends to predominate, and these responses are almost directly incompatible with pressing the bar.

Such interference may explain response cessation, but what about "unlearning?" In our view, whenever responses other than the bar press occur in the situation, they, rather than the bar press, become associated with input from the Skinner box. As "to be apperceived is to be encoded" (see Chapter 5), the visual inputs from the experimental apparatus become associated with behavior that interferes with the bar press: The sight of the bar no longer occasions the bar press but only the incompatible responses. Loss in performance thus reflects apperception of inputs that occasion competing behavior, whereas loss of learning results from association of interfering inputs.

But why does the animal finally leave the bar and move to some other area? Because, as prior associations between external input and the bar-press response are severed, the anger produced by abortive and interfering behavior is reduced and ceases to be apperceived. Furthermore, after sufficient rest, fatigue is also reduced to the point at which it ceases to influence behavior. As these extraneous inputs are no longer in competition, hunger can once again predominate in apperception, and the rat will respond to such input with the next most appropriate behavior in its repertory.   Indeed we may suggest another hypothesis:

The rate of extinction varies inversely with the number of pertinent alternative responses available.

We can thus predict that a rat's response to a given goal box will be extinguished faster if another one in which it has been given a certain amount of training is accessible.

A similar explanation accounts for extinction in classical conditioning.   It will be recalled that repeated presentation of the metronome without the meat powder eventually failed to arouse salivation in I. P. Pavlov's dog. We believe that the response itself was not extinguished; it simply no longer occurred to the metronome. Once again interference seems to be the crucial factor. Our explanation of classical conditioning (see Chapter 5) included the notion that it depends upon the sound of the metronome, which occasions apperception of the food encode, and that as long as the sound and this encode remain associated conditioning will remain operative. But, when the meat powder is no longer presented with the metronome, other inputs that interfere with the food encode become associated with the sound. When the metronome is sounded, these inputs, rather than the food encode, come into focus and extinction takes place.[10]

Discussion

Although we still have the problem of malfunctioning to consider, the essential logic of the theory is complete. It is perhaps appropriate that the statement of the postulate of reaction should come at this juncture, for not only does it summarize the basic notions presented in this chapter, it also restates, with only slight modifications the postulate of process developed in Chapter 1. It thus demonstrates the coherence of both the logic and the development of our theory. The postulate of process is:

All overt or covert activity serves the immediate function of impelling the organism toward equilibrium.

The similarity between this postulate and the following postulate of reaction is obvious.

The overt act that occurs at any given moment is always that one that provides the greatest probability of maintaining optimal equilibrium in terms of the structure of the organism as derived from heredity and altered through learning.

This statement restricts the postulate of process to overt behavior. It also reflects the postulate of inference.

Every nonintrinsic attribute that has remained characteristic of a species for an enduring period contributes (or once contributed to) the survival of the organism.

The postulate of reaction demonstrates what the perceptive reader has perhaps noticed all along: that the two fundamental postulates of the theory are actually interlocked. The process or attribute that abets survival potential must make this contribution by increasing the facility with which the organism can maintain or regain the equilibrium necessary for life. In the postulate of reaction we find the two complementary lines of logic, the one based on homeostatic theory, the other on evolutionary theory, coalescing. In order for an organism to adapt, it must be a homeostatic negative-feedback system, whether we are speaking of primitive motile life or a human being. Down the entire tortuous path of evolution the attribute that has been incorporated because of its survival value has also been the one that has permitted more effective resolution of disequilibrium.

Summary

Overt reactions are contingent on two fundamental processes: development of the motocept and lowering of the motor threshold between such motocept and some apperceived input. In reflexive and instinctive behavior the motor thresholds between specific inputs and particular behavior are low to begin with, but for most activities series of contiguous occurrences of input and response are necessary before the thresholds can be lowered. The lower the threshold between input and response, the more automatic the resulting behavior is. This point is most apparent in frequently practiced habits and actions occasioned by disequilibrium within the autocept. Conflict occurs when two or more inputs associated with incompatible responses are apperceived in sequence. Although apperception is single channeled and many input components are always competing for focalization, extreme conflict is relatively uncommon; fortunately for adaptive behavior, the same circumstances rarely introduce two different inputs associated with incompatible responses. All motor activity produces feedback components that are continually monitored to provide information on the continuity and process of behavior. Such feedback is particularly important in speech; the secondary reverberations resulting from utterances allow the synthesis necessary for effective use of language. Language emerges according to the same principles as does any other behavior. Certain inputs (encodes that have been previously associated) have simply become correlated with motocepts that produce sounds when they are triggered. Cessation of response occurs when an input associated with an alternative response predominates in apperception; unlearning of a response occurs when the association between the particular input and the response in question is cancelled by interfering components.

Notes

[1] Many theories about the origin of dreams have been proposed, from the ancient notion of divine prophecy to Sigmund Freud's concept of wish fulfillment (1953). Other theories have included C. S. Jung's idea that dreams are repre-

sentations of archetypal truths (1953), Alfred Adler's notion that they are antic-ipations (but not prophecies) of the future (1956), and Wilhelm Stekel's belief that they are attempted resolutions of conflict (1943). Recently L. S. Kubie (1961) has suggested that sleep imposes sensory isolation on the sleeper; con-tact with reality is broken, and the sleeper—in order to maintain a coherent en-vironment, as well as his perceptual and cognitive organization—must hallucinate, or dream.

In the past two decades two methods have been used in attempts to discover the natures of dreams. C. S. Hall has statistically evaluated more than 10,000 dreams described by "normal" people and has arrived at the following conclu-sions: Dream settings are commonplace; 85 percent are about other people, 43 percent about strangers (usually symbolic of familiar people); men dream about men twice as much as about women, whereas women dream equally about both sexes; 34 percent of dreams involve motion of some sort; in dreams hostile acts greatly outnumber friendly ones; and 64 percent of the emotions experienced are unpleasant. Hall (1951) thus formulated the theory that dreaming is think-ing that occurs during sleep, that abstract ideas are then converted into visual images, and that dreaming is typically egocentric, centered on one's problems and hopes.

The second approach has involved electroencephalogram (EEG) readings of rapid eye movements (REMs). In 1957 W. C. Dement and N. Kleitman discov-ered that eye movements during sleep have a definite connection with dreams. Hall (1966) has reported that adults usually have four or five separate periods of REMs during the night. The first occurs about an hour after a person falls asleep and is very short; they then occur approximately every ninety minutes, and the final one may last as long as an hour. B. Berelson and G. A. Steiner (1964) report that dream time is usually "realistic": The elapsed time in the dream approximately matches the duration of the actual dream behavior. REMs have been observed in many mammalian species, and one investigator mentioned by Hall (1966) found results implying that monkeys dream with visual images. Hall also reports that cats deprived of REM sleep by the destruction of a small area of the brain manifest bizarre behavior culminating in total exhaustion and death. Along the same lines Dement (1960) has found that, when a human sub-ject is prevented from dreaming, attempts at dreams are more common. There were four or five attempts the first night, ten the second, and thirty the third. The subject's daytime behavior during the experiment was irritable, anxious, and tense, marked by inability to concentrate and lapses of memory. A sharp increase in appetite and weight gain were also observed. Dement (1965) later reported that infants demonstrated high percentage of REMs and suggested that dreaming may be necessary to normal development. In an earlier study Dement and E. A. Wolpert (1958) had found that body movements during REM periods tend to signal changes in dream activity. In the same study they observed that external stimulation apparently has little effect either in causing REM periods or in reports of dreaming.

Studies of nonrapid eye movement (NREM) periods have also yielded informative results. J. Kamiya (1961) and A. Rechtshaffen, D. R. Goodenough, and A. Shapiro (1962) found that most sleep talking occurs during these periods. F. Snyder (1967) observed that reports after NREM periods were fragmentary, whereas reports after REMs were long and detailed Rechtschaffen, P. Verdone, and J. Wheaton (1963) reported that REM dream content probably involves much more vivid and elaborate imagery and emotion. It also includes more physical activity and is more distorted and implausible, whereas NREM periods closely resemble loose conceptual thought.

2The simple fact that the same withdrawal response can be made *both* volitionally and reflexively suggests that there may be two areas of motor control: one probably in the cortex and the other in lower (cerebellar, extrapyramidal, or spinal) centers, perhaps in the spinal cord itself. It also suggests that, in learning a motor skill, control is gradually transferred from the cortical center to one lower in the brain stem, as more and more kinesthetic inputs become synthesized into a functional unity. According to this logic, the motocept would involve organization of the neural elements underlying the particular skill in a center relatively independent of the higher area of control.

A. J. Deutsch and D. Deutsch (1966) have discussed a brain model remarkably similar to the one suggested here. Basing their logic on the work of R. Jung and R. Hassler (1960), they have deduced that voluntary movement requires development somewhere in the cortex of a "spatial-temporal" template of the specific acts of a skill. While the skill is being learned, corresponding instructions are represented in lower centers. Once the kinesthetic inputs have been organized, the lower center may become dominant, so that highly practiced skills become automatic. While the act is being performed the cortex receives continuous feedback from kinesthetic and vestibular receptors; if this "reafferent" copy does not correspond to the central pattern, corrections can be introduced by the higher center. The Deutsches have also suggested that this control of specific skills by lower centers relieves the cortex of direct involvement in innate routines and well-learned skills so that it can concentrate on mastery of new skills.

The survival significance of both learned and unlearned reflexes is emphasized in both these models. In both instances some essential behavior comes to be represented subcortically, so that it can be demonstrated automatically, precisely, and rapidly. Let us consider a few reflexes of the human being: The sucking reflex provides food, the grasping reflex provides (or did at one time) support, reciprocal innervation is basic to walking, the blinking reflex protects the eyes, the cough reflex keeps the breathing apparatus free of congestion. All these behaviors have been so important to survival for so long that the neurology underlying their performance is centered below the cortex. Such behavior is similar to that connected with motocepts (indeed could well be called "inherited" motocepts), except that the integration of essential components does not occur through learning but is transmitted genetically.

The similarity between the processes of organizing inputs into motocepts and of determining perceptual fusion and structuring is also clear. The major difference is that in the former *behavior* fundamental to the solution of particular survival problems becomes automatic (either genetically or through learning), whereas in the latter certain critical relationships and consistencies in the environment are automatically (either genetically or through learning) imposed on sensory input. It is curious that a kind of cortical, or voluntary, "override" can be manifested in all these instances. That is, we can, when necessary, volitionally direct the course of walking, or we can see the window as trapezoidal, rather than as rectangular. Of course, the more specific and fixed a motocept or percept becomes, the greater is the difficulty in overriding it and the more indefinite and ineffectual is the volitional control.

3There are two mechanisms that help to liberate the organism from the domination of a continuing stimulus: sensory adaptation and habituation. They free the individual from having to make responses that serve no function, and thus they enter actively into the resolution of many conflicts.

Sensory adaptation, as described by B. Berelson and G. A. Steiner (1964), arises directly from properties of the individual receptor cells that initiate sensory impulses. The term specifically means becoming accustomed to certain sensations, accommodation to a certain level of stimulation. Under conditions of constant stimulation, the experience becomes less intense.

By contrast, habituation refers to the diminution of specific behavior patterns, rather than changes in the sense organs. A. Manning (1967) has described it as the simplest form of learning, involving the loss of old responses, rather than acquisition of new ones. P. Marler and W. J. Hamilton (1967) have further distinguished it from sensory adaptation by noting the recovery rate: Recovery from habituation usually takes minutes, hours, or even days, whereas sensory adaptation usually disappears within seconds.

As it is so easy to demonstrate sensory adaptation (for example, visual adaptation whenever a person enters a dark room), not many experiments have been conducted on it. Many studies, however, have been aimed at explaining habituation. As early as 1906 H. S. Jennings discovered that habituation occurs in the sea anemone *Aiptasia annulata*. He found that when a drop of water falls on the animal it contracts; after this sequence has been repeated two or three times it fails to contract.

Birds are frightened by scarecrows when they are first placed in a field, but, as as the stimulus becomes familiar, they no longer react (Manning, 1967). Manning describes that turkeys make escape responses to any large moving thing but that they rapidly cease to respond to familiar objects. R. Hinde (1954), studying the chaffinch's mobbing response, found that the extent of habituation to a frightening experience varied with the length of time since the stimulus had been removed. If it had been presented at short intervals, the chaffinches habituated rapidly. Intervals of thirty minutes or longer brought the response up to 50 percent of its initial level but never higher.

G. Humphrey (1933) has demonstrated habituation in the withdrawal of tentacles in response to mechanical shock in the snail (*Helix albolabris*). G. M. Hughes and L. Tauc (1963) found that nerve cells of the mollusk *Sphysia* showed habituation. J. H. Hollis (1963) discovered that the pupae of the mealworm become habituated to electric shock after a median of twenty trials. G. Horn and R. M. Hill (1964) found that a small region in the midbrain of the rabbit exhibits attenuation in activity with repetition of stimuli. Some cells were sensitive to input from one modality, others to several. Sixty-three of seventy-two cells showed decreases in responsiveness as the stimulus was repeated, though a novel stimulus still elicited strong responses. R. Hernández-Peón and J. Brust-Carmona (1961) planted electrodes in the brain of a cat. Activity clearly occurred in the cochlear nucleus when a tone was played in the cat's ear. When the tone was played at two-second intervals, the response diminished, but a tone of a different frequency revived the response to its initial level.

Habituation has also been demonstrated in human neonates. A. K. Bartoshuk (1962a; 1962b) studied heart-rate acceleration and found that, once infants had ceased to respond to an eight-second tone that changed from low to high frequency, a tone whose frequency changed in the opposite direction again elicited the response. T. Engen and L. P. Lipsitt (1965) found that, after the breathing response of human neonates to a mixture of odors had waned, it could be revived by only one of the components.

[4]A simpler design (and one that neutralizes the criticisms mentioned) involves association of two different visual inputs with two different and incompatible responses and then presentation of both inputs simultaneously. Human subjects would be placed before a panel that could present different colored lights of varied intensities; subjects would be trained to push a toggle switch in different

directions, depending upon the particular problem. In perhaps the simplest example they would be trained to push the toggle switch to the right when a green light appeared and to the left when a red light appeared. If both light-response combinations were given the same amount of training, we would predict that subjects would respond to the most intense light when both appeared simultaneously. If both lights had previously been of equal intensity, then subjects would probably respond to the light that had been associated with its response most frequently, for the motor thresholds would have been lowered in direct proportion to the ratio of associations prevailing during the training trials. The reader may object to this design on grounds that equal intensities would be difficult if not impossible to achieve. We believe that this problem is more apparent than real. To assume that two lights were of equal functional intensity it would be necessary only to find the particular value for each light that would result in a 50-50 split between left and right responses when both lights were given the same amount of training and then presented simultaneously.

5 In Guthrie's final statement of his theory (1959) a change has been introduced. He has suggested that his basic law of learning "a combination of stimuli that accompanies a movement will, on its recurrence, tend to be followed by that movement" be altered to read "What is being noticed becomes a signal for what is being done." Attention is thus added to his system. This kind of attention has two chief characteristics: the preliminary state of scanning, which involves systematic variation in receptor orientation to facilitate discovery of a given stimulus, and fixation that occurs when a particular cue is centered. We must not assume, however, that Guthrie has suddenly espoused a "centralistic" explanation of stimulus focusing. He has conceptualized attention as a set of responses that orient an organism's sense receptors toward certain stimuli; it is thus synonymous with responses like looking, listening, and so on. This view is certainly far different from our own, but it does reflect recognition of the problem implicit in all behaviorism. Why do stimuli not always stimulate?

6 As common responses to different stimuli are a universal phenomenon, the necessity for some kind of mediator is obvious. Some device must serve to funnel different stimuli into one response. One common device is emphasis on similarity of responses, rather than on similarity of stimuli. Contemporary researchers who have followed this orientation include C. N. Cofer and J. P. Foley, Jr. (1942), A. E. Goss (1958), H. H. Kendler and M. F. D'Amato (1955), N. E. Miller and J. Dollard (1941), and C. E. Osgood (1957). Indeed, early behaviorists like J. B. Watson (1920) and Guthrie (1952) toyed with the idea of "behavior-produced stimulation," and C. L. Hull (1943) used the concept "pure stimulus act" for much the same purpose. The stimuli said to be produced by such behavior are unobservable, which is rather amusing in view of those researchers' insistence on objective data. It is also curious that all response-similarity theories involve a stimulus-equivalence factor; that is, the stimuli produced by the common response are assumed to be equivalent. These response theories thus exhibit a stimulus orientation. The major difference is simply that in the one instance stimulus equivalence is assumed to exist in the external situation, whereas in the other it is said to arise from the common element of behavior.

Other theorists have relied on experiential mediators to account for the development of concepts. The classical Gestalt psychologists considered that modes of perception provide the primary basis for common responses to fluctuating physical stimulation, whereas neo-Gestalt theorists like Lewin (1935) and S. E. Asch (1952) have further emphasized the experiential dimension. Kendler, in his outstanding review of concept formation (1961), has noted a return to subjectivism, arising from the unlikely source of servomechanism theory. G. A. Miller, E. Galanter, and K. H. Pribram (1960) have emphasized, though somewhat humorously, the relationship between encoding mechanisms arising from cybernetics and so-called "memory residuals."

Although we find the need for some kind of mediator obvious, others have not. Hull (1920) turned to the stimulus-response pattern to explain the formation of concepts without postulating mediating processes of any kind. B. F. Skinner (1957) has followed this orientation and has provided perhaps the clearest statement of it. According to Skinner, any property of a stimulus that is present when a response is reinforced acquires some control over that response, and this control continues to be exerted when the property appears in other combinations. Through differential reinforcement, behavior may thus be brought under control of a single property or combination of properties or be freed from the control of any one property or set of properties. According to this point of view, concepts develop as a function of the differential reinforcement of particular behavior after the appearance of specific properties common to a class of stimuli. Statistical learning theory as represented by the work of L. E. Bourne, Jr., and F. Restle (1959), the learning-set research of H. F. Harlow (1959), and the theoretical formulations of J. J. Gibson (1959) follow the general orientation outlined by Skinner. All these theorists, eschewing inference of hidden explanatory devices, have endeavored to explain concept formation without resorting to mediating processes by emphasizing discrimination of common features as the essential mechanism.

[3]There has been a recent upsurge of interest in children's language development, and at present there are three popular theories to explain it: nativist theory (Chomsky, 1965; Lenneberg, 1964), imitation-reinforcement theory (Mowrer, 1960), and rule-learning theory (Berko, 1958; Brown and Bellugi, 1968; and Ervin, 1964).

The infant's first form of communication is crying, and before the age of three months he has learned that it brings relief and company. Babbling emerges at about this time; it involves repetition of all vowel and consonant sounds that the vocal system can produce (Osgood, 1953). Sometime around the twelfth month of life, when the child has gained some voluntary control of speech apparatus and recognizes that sound is communication, he says his first word, though his use of it is usually a parrot-like conditioned response (Baller and Charles, 1968). He speaks two-word sentences by the age of 18 months, has a vocabulary of 200 words by age two years, and can use several thousand words by the time that he enters school. The earliest words are likely to be nouns; verbs develop gradually, followed by adjectives, adverbs, and pronouns. S. M. Ervin and W. R. Miller (1963) found that by the age of four years the child could speak clearly and had already acquired the fundamentals of grammar. Curiously, girls develop in all aspects of language use faster than boys do (McCarthy, 1961).

J. Berko and R. Brown (1960) and J. J. Katz and P. M. Postal (1965) have studied the following categories of language responses: phenomes (vowels and consonant vocalizations), morphemes (the smallest meaningful combinations of sounds), rules of syntax and morphology (combinations of words to form larger structures), and semantics (meanings of words). These categories fit approximately the stages of language development.

When and how language use develops are thus not subjects of disagreement, but why it develops as it does is controversial. The nativist position has been expressed by N. Chomsky (1965), who remarked that the role of experience has been grossly exaggerated and that the child needs only to hear the language of his culture to learn it. O. H. Mowrer (1958; 1960) has stated the imitation-reinforcement view that a child learns to talk because verbalizations are associated with comfort and his mother's presence. This position has also been defended by Miller and Dollard (1941) and by A. W. Staats and C. K. Staats (1962). H. L. Rheingold, J. L. Gerwitz, and H. W. Ross (1959) found that reinforcement increased vocalization in three-month-old institutionalized children. The rule-learning theory has been formulated by R. Brown and U. Bellugi (1968), who argue that children cannot learn syntax solely through imitation, for they come up with too many novel sentence arrangements. Instead they believe that the child induces the general rules implicit in the speech that he hears, until eventually he can speak sentences that he has never heard.

[8] A universal characteristic of behavior is the intimate and immediate relationship between sensory input and action. In refined behavior like walking, typing, and talking, the reaction produces sensory input that is fed back into the system and perpetually monitored by the apperceptual process. Is the capacity to make rapid compensatory changes in behavior learned or innate? The baby wildebeest can be up and running ten minutes after it is born. Its ability to make compensatory adjustments to shifts in the terrain represented by visual input must be inborn; there must be a kind of "intrinsic feedback loop" between sensory input and motor responses. The same kind of loop must occur in many mammals, allowing complex behavior immediately or soon after birth. The research of E. Hess (1956) suggests that the relationship between sensory input and the pecking response in chicks is fixed and unalterable. He placed on chicks lenses that changed the perceived position of grain and found that little if any adaptation took place; the chicks pecked at the displaced image until they starved. There is evidence, however, that in many organisms learning soon contributes to the development of sensory-motor associations. R. Held reported (1965) that kittens that had been restrained from walking since their first exposures to light had inadequate visual control of their behavior and demonstrated that actual motor activity is essential if kittens are to develop sensory-motor coordination. As we move up the phylogenetic scale, intrinsic and inflexible sensory-motor relationships seem to disappear, and learned feedback loops tend to predominate. Many studies on perceptual adaptation (see Chapter 6, note 5) suggest that the primary encoding process in the human being is extremely plastic and may be altered by distortion of fairly short duration.

Most experiments that have interfered with the compensatory-feedback loop have disrupted the association between visual input and some motor response. But there is a growing number of experiments involving disruption of the association between sounds and motor responses. Most of them have distorted the usual temporal relationship between speech movements and the sounds produced by them, introducing a delay between utterance of a sound and the subject's hearing it. The first investigation of this type was conducted by B. S. Lee in 1950. Sound-resistant earphones were worn to prevent the normal conduction of speech sounds to the ears. The interval between speech and feedback from the earphones could be varied by adjusting the length of the tape loop running between the receptor and playback heads. All subsequent experiments have been based on essentially the same apparatus. The results of these studies confirm the view that continual apperceptual monitoring of speech sounds is essential for effective speech. Lee demonstrated that a subject would stop speaking or, if he attempted to maintain his normal speech rate, would begin to stutter. R. A. Chase and his colleagues (1959) found a marked increase in the intersyllable interval when auditory feedback was delayed, and G. Fairbanks (1955) discovered that the disruption was greatest when the delay was .2 second. W. R. Tiffany and C. N. Hanley (1956) found that the intensity of feedback material increased speech disruption, and Fairbanks (1955) and J. W. Black (1951) both reported marked increases in the intensity of the spoken word with feedback delay. Fairbanks and N. Guttman (1958) demonstrated that delayed feedback consistently caused decreases in total correct words and correct word rate, as well as increases in reading time and number of errors. They also found maximum disruption at a delay interval of .2 second.

In contrast to the frequent finding of rapid adaptation to in visual-motor disruption, there is little evidence that it occurs in the auditory-motor feedback loop. C. J. Atkinson (1953) found no evidence of improvement during relatively short practice intervals, and Tiffany and Hanley (1956) found no improvement in reading rate during prolonged practice periods, but they did find significant adaptation in fluency. There is also some evidence of adaptation in the rather prolonged aftereffects of delayed-feedback experiences. Black (1951) concluded that the decreased reading rate may continue for as long as 150 seconds after delay has been discontinued.

There seems little doubt that sensory feedback from motor responses is critical to effective performance of every commonplace skill. Such input appears to have two basic functions: guiding and monitoring. When a horse is running over difficult terrain there appears to be a literally reflexive relationship between his visual input and his motor responses, so that appropriate behavior is persistently and effectively guided. In speech behavior the reverberatory feedback appears to have little guiding function (as it occurs simultaneously with the response), but it does make a vital contribution to monitoring. This lack may account for the difference in plasticity between visual-motor and auditory-motor feedback loops. Plasticity in the latter would not be predicted for two reasons: No guiding function is involved, and adaptations of this type are never called for under natural conditions.

9P. Marler (1959) thinks that the communications systems of animals represent capabilities for transferring information essential to preservation and development. Animals living in environments in which visual and auditory communication is difficult have thus developed highly structured systems of tactile and chemical communication. For instance, the ant leaves behind it specific chemical substances to guide others to food and nests; it exudes another substance to feed immature ants and still another for behavioral sequences involved in disposing of the dead (Wilson, 1963).

Communication can serve many purposes, but in some species it is used for single purposes only. The flash patterns of fireflies convey sex identifications (Marler, 1959), as do the acoustic signals of arthropods (Dumortier, 1963a). K. von Frisch (1950) demonstrated that the honeybee's dance communicates the direction of food. In contrast, Marler and Hamilton (1967) have noted that the maximum repertories of birds and mammals are increasingly larger than those of lower vertebrates and invertebrates. T. G. Rowell (1962) has analyzed a graded system of nine sounds uttered by rhesus monkeys in agonistic situations only. R. J. Andrew (1963) has classified primate vocalizations as primitive or more highly developed, and S. A. Altmann (1965) has emphasized the additional communication value of posture and facial expression in primates.

Most animal vocalizations are specific to certain stimuli. The elephant seal pup calls immediately after birth to its mother, and the latter responds. If they are separated the vocalizations are repeated until they are brought back together (Bartholomew and Collias, 1962). J. Davis (1958) found that gonadal activity in the male rufous-sided towhee was correlated with the frequency of its singing. R. G. Busnel, B. Dumortier, and M. C. Busnel (1956) reported that male grasshoppers may remain silent for five days after mating before resuming song and readiness to mate again. R. D. Alexander (1960) has shown that the male cricket has six different sounds: for contact, courtship, courtship interruption, aggression, "post-copulation," and recognition. Bird song is usually the prerogative of the male and is typically associated with territorial defense, establishment and maintenance of of pair bonds, stages of the reproductive cycle, or some combination of these factors (Howard, 1920).

The vocalizations of similar species are usually quite different. Dumortier (1963b) has noted that the marked differences in the calls of male crickets presumably enable females to restrict their sexual responses to their own species. A. C. Perdeck (1958) demonstrated that the different songs of two closely related grasshopper species that live together play a crucial role in keeping them from crossbreeding. W. E. Lanyon (1963) found that sympatric male flycatchers have quite specific responses to song and that vocal behavior far outweighs external morphology in recognition behavior. G. Thielcke (1961) demonstrated that adjacent populations of the same species of tree creeper are clearly distinguished by "dialects." J. B. Falls (1963) found that in the ovenbird the interval between, rather than the order or loudness of, syllables is important for species recognition.

Although vocalizations among lower animals are generally unmodified by experience (Dumortier, 1963a), there is evidence that the same is not true among birds (Bremond, 1963). Marler and Hamilton (1967) have remarked that experience may lead to interspecies communication. Many finches form flocks of several species during the nonreproductive season; they can perform coordinated movements requiring interspecies exchange of signals (Marler, 1957).

[10]How does unlearning (extinction, or forgetting) occur, according to learning theories? Only two general approaches (or different combinations and versions of them) seem possible: interference and decay. Guthrie (1935) and Pavlov (1927) both believed that unlearning is an active process, but their notions of interference were quite different. Guthrie thought that the organism learned interfering responses in the experimental situation (that different responses became associated with the old stimuli), whereas Pavlov believed that continued presentation of the conditioned stimulus brought about a "central inhibitory state" that interfered with the response. Hull (1943) combined these points of view and suggested that reactive inhibition (similar to Pavlov's central inhibitory state) accounts for cessation of responses and that conditioned inhibition (similar to Guthrie's notion of interference) accounts for unlearning.

Other views of interference have focused on the input that occasions cessation of response. A. Amsel (1951) thought that the frustration arising from the removal of rewards introduces competing and interfering responses, and M. H. Marx (1960) believed that response cessation results primarily from a weakening motivational effect on the subject by a given stimulus. What causes this weakening? Perhaps, as Pavlov suggested, practice alone contributes to inhibitions or perhaps extraneous stimuli interfere with discrimination of the critical stimulus complex, so that the motivation previously produced ceases to occur.

This latter explanation leads to a discrimination view of unlearning, and there have been several related theories. E. C. Tolman (1932) set the stage for all of them: He argued that extinction occurs when an organism perceives that the goal object is no longer where it once was. When its expectation is not confirmed extinction occurs immediately. If the organism cannot be sure (if it fails to discriminate between a goal situation and no goal situation) that food will no longer be forthcoming in a particular circumstance, it may continue to respond for an extended period. This theory is essentially the same as Mowrer and M. H. Jones' discrimination hypothesis (1945), according to which any variable that makes it more difficult for the organism to perceive the difference between a reward and a nonreward circumstance will retard extinction.

This discussion only touches on some of the more important notions about interference. Within the confines of this approach to unlearning many concepts have been used: inhibition (retroactive and proactive), frustration, discrimination, changes in motivation, and relative availability of alternative responses. Varied interpretations have produced a plethora of research, the results of which typically support the implications of the experimenters' point of view.

By contrast, theories of "decay or disuse" have generated few experiments and appear to have less influence as time passes. This trend is not surprising when we consider that the only way to demonstrate decay would be to rule out all possibility of interference, an imposing task! But decay is not quite dead as a principle of unlearning. H. Ebbinghaus (1885) believed that the metabolism of the nerve cells gradually eradicates the changes produced by learning. As late as 1958 J. Brown staunchly defended this point of view as applicable to short-term memory; according to E. R. Hilgard and G. H. Bower (1966), even Skinner (1958) thinks that true forgetting is a slow process of decay with time.

We do not claim that the ideas of unlearning outlined in this chapter are particularly original. Perhaps we agree most closely with Marx, believing that an organism moves toward a positive cue because that cue produces a motivational increment; extinction must reflect more a change in motivation than a loss of learning. Our position also meshes closely with those of Hull and Amsel, for we accept the view that responses produced by removal of rewards (frustration, anger) are conditioned to the erstwhile rewarding situation. But while Hull and Amsel eschew experiential categories, we openly embrace them. Not only is sensory input the stuff of which memories are made, it is also what disrupts them once they have been established.

References

Alexander, R. D. Sound communication in Orthoptera and Cicadidae. In W. E. Lanyon and W. N. Tavolga (eds.), *Animal sounds and communications.* Washington, D. C.: American Institute of Biological Sciences, 1960.

Altmann, S. A. Social behavior of anthropoid primates: Analysis of recent concepts. In E. L. Bliss (ed.), *Roots of behavior: Genetics, instincts, and socialization in animal behavior.* New York: Harper & Row, 1965.

Amsel, A. A three-factor theory of inhibition: An addition to Hull's two-factor theory. *American Psychologist*, 1951, 6: 487.

Andrew, R. J. The origin and evolution of the calls and facial expressions of the primates. *Behavior*, 1963, 20: 1-109.

Ansbacher, H. L., and Ravena R. (eds.), *The individual psychology of Alfred Adler.* New York: Basic Books, 1956.

Asch, S. E. *Social Psychology.* Englewood Cliffs, N.J.: Prentice-Hall, 1952.

Atkinson, C. J. Adaptation to delayed side-tone. *Journal of Speech and Hearing Disorders,* 1953, 18: 386-391.

Baller, W. R., and Charles, D. C. *The psychology of human growth and development.* New York: Holt, Rinehart and Winston, 1968.

Bartholomew, G. A., and Collias, N. E. The role of vocalization in the social behavior of the northern elephant seal. *Animal Behavior,* 1962, 10: 7-14.

Bartoshuk, A. K. Response decrement with repeated elicitation of human neonatal cardiac acceleration to sound. *Journal of Comparative and Physiological Psychology,* 1962a, 55: 9-13.

——, Human neonatal cardiac acceleration to sound: Habituation and dishabituation. *Perception and Motor Skills,* 1962b, 15: 15-27.

Berelson, B., and Steiner, G. A. *Human behavior: An inventory of scientific findings.* New York: Harcourt, Brace Jovanovich, 1964.

Berko, J. The child's learning of English morphology. *Word,* 1958, 14: 150-177.

Berko, J., and Brown, R. Psycholinguistic research methods. In P. Mussen (ed.), *Handbook of research methods in child development.* New York: Wiley, 1960.

Black, J. W. The effect of delayed side-tone upon vocal rate and intensity. *Journal of Speech and Hearing Disorders,* 1951, 15: 56-60.

Bourne, L. E., Jr., and Restle, F. Mathematical theory of concept identification. *Psychological Review,* 1959, 66: 278-296.

Bremond, J. C. Acoustic behavior of birds. In R. G. Busnel (ed.), *Acoustic behavior of animals.* Amsterdam: Elsevier, 1963.

Brown, J. Some tests of the decay theory of immediate memory. *Quarterly Journal of Experimental Psychology,* 1958, 10: 12-21.

Brown, J. S. Gradients of approach and avoidance responses and their relation to level of motivation. *Journal of Comparative and Physiological Psychology,* 1948, 41: 45-465.

Brown, R., and Bellugi, U. Three processes in the child's acquisition of syntax. In N. S. Endler, L. R. Boulter, and H. Osser (eds.), *Contemporary issues in developmental psychology.* New York: Holt, Rinehart and Winston, 1968.

Busnel, R. G., Dumortier, B., and Busnel, M. C. Recherches sur le comportement acoustique des Ephippigères (Orthoptères, Tettigoniidae). *Bulletin Bioligique de la France et de la Belgique,* 1956, 90: 219-286.

Chase, R. A., Harvey, S., Standfast, S., Rapin, I., and Sutton, S. Studies on sensory feedback: The effect of delayed auditory feedback on speech and keytapping. *State of New York Residence Report.* New York: Columbia University, 1959.

Chomsky, N. *Aspects of the theory of syntax.* Cambridge: M.I.T. Press, 1965.

Cofer, C. N., and Foley, J. P., Jr. Mediated generalization and the interpretation of verbal behavior. 1. Prolegomena. *Psychological Review,* 1942, 49: 513-540.

Davis, J. Singing behavior and the gonad cycle of the rufous-sided towhee. *Condor,* 1958, 60: 308-336.

Dement, W. C. The effect of dream deprivation. *Science,* 1960, 13: 1705-1707.

——, Recent studies in the biological role of rapid eye movement sleep. *American Journal of Psychiatry,* 1965, 122: 404-408.

Dement, W. C., and Kleitman, N. The relation of eye movement during sleep to dream activity: An objective method for the study of dreaming. *Journal of Experimental Psychology,* 1957, 53: 339-346.

Dement, W. C., and Wolpert, E. A. The relation of eye movements, bodily motility and external stimuli to dream content. *Journal of Experimental Psychology,* 1958, 55: 543-553.

Deutsch, A. J., and Deutsch, D. *Physiological psychology.* Homewood, Ill.: Dorsey, 1966.

Dumortier, B. The physical characteristics of sound emissions in Arthropoda. In R. G. Busnel (ed.), *Acoustic behavior of animals.* Amsterdam: Elsevier, 1963a.

——, Ethological and physiological study of sound emissions in arthropoda. In R. G. Busnel (ed.), *Acoustic behavior of animals.* Amsterdam: Elsevier, 1963b.

Ebbinghaus, H. *Uber das Gedachtnis.* Leipzig, Duncker, 1885.

Engen, T., and Lipsitt, L. P. Decrement and recovery of responses to olfactory stimuli in the human neonate. *Journal of Comparative and Physiological Psychology,* 1965, 59: 312-316.

Ervin, S. M. Imitation and structural change in children's language. In E. H. Lenneberg (ed.), *New directions in the study of language.* Cambridge: M.I.T. Press, 1964.

Ervin, S. M., and Miller, W. R. Language development. In H. W. Stevenson (ed.), *Child Psychology.* Chicago: National Society for the Study of Education, 1963.

Fairbanks, B. Selective vocal effects of delayed auditory feedback. *Journal of Speech and Hearing Disorders,* 1955, 20: 333-345.

Fairbanks, B., and Guttman, N. Effects of delayed auditory feedback upon articulation. *Journal of Speech Research,* 1958, 1: 12-22.

Falls, J. B. Properties of bird song eliciting responses from territorial males. *Proceedings of the 13th International Ornithological Congress,* 1963, 1: 259-271.

Freud, S. *The Interpretation of Dreams.* London: Hogarth Press, 1953.

Frisch, K. von. *Bees: Their chemical senses, vision and language.* Ithaca: Cornell University Press, 1950.

Gibson, J. J. Perception as a function of stimulation. In S. Koch (ed.), *Psychology: A study of a science. Vol. 1. Sensory, perceptual and physiological formulations.* New York: McGraw-Hill, 1959.

Goss, A. E. Mediating responses and concept formation. Paper presented at the Symposium on Mediating Processes in Transfer of the American Psychological Association, Washington, D. C., 1958.

Guthrie, E. R. *The psychology of learning.* New York: Harper & Row, 1935.

——, *The psychology of learning.* Rev. ed. New York: Harper & Row, 1952.

——, Association by contiguity. In S. Koch (ed.), *Psychology: A study of a science. Vol. 2. General systematic formulation, learning and special processes.* New York: McGraw-Hill, 1959.

Hall, C. S. What people dream about. *Scientific American,* 1951, 184: 60-63.

——, *The meaning of dreams.* New York: McGraw-Hill, 1966.

Harlow, H. F. Learning set and error factor theory. In S. Koch (ed.), *Psychology: A study of a science. Vol. 2. General systematic formulation, learning and special processes.* New York: McGraw-Hill, 1959.

Held, R. Plasticity in sensory-motor systems. *Scientific American,* 1965, 213: 184-194.

Hernández-Peón, R. and Brust-Carmona, J. Functional role of subcortical structure in habituation and conditioning. In J. F. Delafresnaye (ed.), *Brain mechanisms and learning.* Oxford: Council for International Organizations of Medical Sciences Symposium, 1961.

Hess, E. Space perception in the chick. *Scientific American,* 1956, 195: 71-80.

Hilgard, E. R., and Bower, G. H. *Theories of learning.* New York: Appleton, 1966.

Hinde, R. Factors governing the changes in strength of a partially inborn response, as shown by the mobbing behavior of the chaffinch (*Fringilla coelebs*). 2. The waning of the response. *Proceedings of the Royal Society of Biology*, 1954, 142: 331-358.

Hollis, J. H. Habituatory response decrement in pupae of *Tenebrio molitor*. *Animal Behavior*, 1963, 11: 161-163.

Horn, G., and Hill, R. M. Habituation of the response to sensory stimuli of neurons in the brain stem of rabbits. *Nature*, 1964, 202: 296-298.

Howard, E. *Territory in bird life*. London: Murray, 1920.

Hughes, G. M., and Tauc, L. An electrophysiological study of the anatomical relations of two giant nerve cells in *Aphysia depilens*. *Journal of Experimental Biology*, 1963, 40: 469-486.

Hull, C. L. Quantitative aspects of the evolution of concepts, an experimental study. *Psychological Monographs*, 1920, 28: 85.

——, *Principles of behavior*. New York: Appleton, 1943.

Humphrey, G. *The nature of learning*. New York: Tontledge, 1933.

Jennings, H. S. *Behavior of the lower organisms*. New York: Columbia University Press, 1906.

Jung, C. J. The archetypes and the collective unconscious. In *Collected Works*, Vol. 9, Princeton: Princeton University Press, 1953.

Jung, R., and Hassler, R. The extrapyramidal motor system. In J. Field, H. W. Magoun, and V. E. Hall (eds.) *American physiological society handbook of physiology*. Baltimore: Williams and Wilkins, 1960.

Kamiya, J. Behavioral, subjective, and physiological aspects of drowsiness and sleep. In D. W. Fiske and S. R. Maddi (eds.), *Functions of varied experience*. Homewood, Ill.: Dorsey, 1961.

Katz, J. J., and Postal, P. M. *An integrated theory of linguistic descriptions*. Cambridge: M.I.T. Press, 1965.

Kendler, H. H. Concept formation. *Annual review of Psychology*, 1961, 12: 447-472.

Kendler, H. H., and D'Amato, M. F. A comparison of reversal shifts and nonreversal shifts in human concept formation behavior. *Journal of Experimental Psychology*, 1955, 49: 165-174.

Kubie, L. S. Theoretical aspects of sensory deprivation. In P. Solomon et al. (eds.), *Sensory deprivation*. Cambridge: Harvard University Press, 1961.

Lanyon, W. E. Experiments on species discrimination in *Myiarchus* flycatchers. *American Museum Novitates*, 1963, 2126: 1-16.

Lee, B. S. Effects of delayed speech feedback. *Journal of the Acoustic Society of America*, 1950, 22: 824-826.

Lenneberg, E. H. A biological perspective on language. In E. H. Lenneberg (ed.), *New directions in the study of language*. Cambridge: M.I.T. Press, 1964.

Lewin, K. *A dynamic theory of personality*. New York: McGraw-Hill, 1935.

Manning, A. *An introduction to animal behavior*. Reading, Mass.: Addison-Wesley, 1967.

Marler, P. Specific distinctiveness in the communication signals of birds. *Behavior*, 1957, 11: 13-39.

——, Developments in the study of animal communication. In P. R. Bell (ed.), *Darwin's biological works: Some aspects reconsidered*. New York: Cambridge University Press, 1959.

Marler, P., and Hamilton, W. J., III. *Mechanisms of animal behavior*. New York: Wiley, 1967.

Marx, M. H. Resistance to extinction as a function of degree of reproduction of training conditions. *Journal of Experimental Psychology*, 1960, 59: 337-342.

McCarthy, D. Affective aspects of language learning. *Newsletter Division of Developmental Psychology*. Washington, D. C.: American Psychological Association, 1960.

Miller, G. A., Galanter, E., and Pribram, K. H. *Plans and the structure of behavior*. New York: Holt, Rinehart and Winston, 1960.

Miller, N. E., and Dollard, J. *Social learning and imitation*. New Haven: Yale University Press, 1941.

Mowrer, O. H. Hearing and speaking: An analysis of language learning. *Journal of Speech and Hearing Disorders*, 1958, 23: 143-151.

——, *Learning theory and symbolic processes*. New York: Wiley, 1960.

Mowrer, O. H., and Jones, M. H. Habit strength as a function of the pattern of reinforcement. *Journal of Experimental Psychology*, 1945, 35: 293-311.

Nafe, J. P., and Wagoner, K. S. The nature of pressure adaptation. *Journal of Genetic Psychology*, 1941, 25: 323-351.

Osgood, C. E. *Method and theory in experimental psychology*. New York: Oxford University Press, 1953.

——, A behavioristic analysis of perception and language as cognitive phenomena. In *Contemporary approaches to cognition*. Cambridge: Harvard University Press, 1957.

Pavlov, I. P. *Conditioned reflexes*. Trans. by G. V. Anrep. New York: Oxford University Press, 1927.

Perdeck, A. C. The isolation value of specific song patterns in two sibling species of grasshoppers (*Chorthippus brunneus T. and C. Biguttulus L.*). *Behavior*, 1958, 12: 1-75.

Premack, D. The education of Sarah. *Psychology Today*, 1970, 4: 55-58.

Rechtschaffen, A., Goodenough, D. R., and Wheaton, J. Reports of mental activity during sleep. *Canadian Psychiatric Association Journal*, 1963, 8: 409-414.

Rheingold, H. L., Gerwitz, J. L., and Ross, H. W. Social conditioning of vocalizations in the infant. *Journal of Comparative and Physiological Psychology*, 1959, 52: 68-73.

Rowell, T. E. Agonistic noises of the rhesus monkey (*Macaca mulatta*). *Symposia Zoological Society of London*, 1962, 279-294.

Skinner, B. F. *Verbal behavior*. New York: Appleton, 1957.

Skinner, B. F. *Science and human behavior*, New York: Macmillan, 1953.

Snyder, F. In quest of dreaming. In H. A. Witkin and H. B. Lewis (eds.), *Experimental studies of dreaming*. New York: Random House, 1967.

Staats, A. W., and Staats, C. K. A comparison of the development of speech and reading behavior with implications for research. *Child Development*, 1962, 33: 831-846.

Stekel, W. *The interpretation of dreams: New developments and techniques*. New York: Liveright, 1953.

Thielcke, G. Stammesgeschichte und geographische Variationen des Gesanges unserer Baumlaufer (*Certhia familiaris L. und Certhia brachydactyla Brehm*). *Zeitschrift fur teirpsychologie*, 1961, 18: 188-204.

Tiffany, W. R., and Hanley, C. N. Adaptation to delayed side-tone. *Journal of Speech and Hearing Disorders*, 1956, 21: 164-172.

Tolman, E. C. *Purposive behavior in animals and men*. New York: Appleton, 1932.

Watson, J. B. Is thinking merely the action of language mechanisms? *British Journal of Psychology*, 1920, 11: 87-104.
Wilson, E. O. Pheromones. *Scientific American*, 1963, 208: 100-112.

8

Malfunction

When something goes wrong with a machine the first signs of malfunction are inevitably its failure to perform efficiently; its behavior deviates from the norm of effective operation established by those schooled in its various workings. The same observation applies to an organism: When a fair portion of its various kinds of behavior no longer fits the category established as "normal," then the appellation "abnormal" is applied, and efforts are made to alter this behavior so that it will closely approximate what is accepted as efficient operation. The difference between diagnosis of defects in men and machines is most apparent in the definitiveness of the relevant criteria. It is fairly clear what operating efficiency in automobiles means, but our bases for judging the relative efficiency of human performance are unclear and subject to disagreement. In evaluating the human mechanism, we have tended to fall back on a loose relativism, judging behavior always in terms of what is most commonly acceptable in a given context or a particular culture.

We disagree with such relativistic interpretations. Even as an absolute definition of malfunction can be formulated for automobiles or watches, so a definition of malfunction in human beings can be formulated. There is indeed no sharp distinction between normal and abnormal people; it is to behavior that we must turn if we are to classify an individual as either one. Furthermore, every person exhibits some behavior that calls for one designation and other behavior that fits the second. The mechanism that occasions mutilation of an ear may also provide the impulse for great paintings. Yet we are convinced that a universal definition of malfunction is possible, and to this task we now turn.

Where to begin is a problem. A human being is a totality whose smooth functioning is contingent on the efficient workings of myriad components and processes interacting dynamically. A breakdown anywhere may introduce disruptive reverberations that can engulf the entire system. If we are to understand malfunction, we must therefore look at the one *process* most basic to efficient operation. Otherwise we shall become lost in the complexity of the organism and make no progress at all.

We thus return to apperception. This mechanism has emerged as the critical one underlying adaptive behavior in higher organisms, and it is on this process that we must focus our examination of malfunction. Apperception is requisite for both encoding and overt responses, it must intervene between input and output if behavior is to be appropriate and effective. Most behavior, whether ordinary or bizarre, constructive or destructive, kind or cruel, is the direct outcome of this process. If there is some malfunction in behavior it must involve some disruption of apperception, for, as the individual apperceives, so will he behave. Apperception follows the path of greatest equilibrium relative to all the input components potentially available at each given moment. But in the abnormal individual we find that the equilibratory process of apperception leads to behavior that may have effects far different from those desired. That is, all activity is equilibratory but it may not be adaptive; when this gap becomes wide the designation of "abnormal" becomes appropriate.

It will be recalled (see Chapter 7) that disequilibrium input arising from threats to the integrity of the autocept initiates and sustains much apperceptual flux, which in turn precedes most behavior. If behavior deviates from what is ordinarily classified as normal, the autocept must be at least partly responsible. Let us consider.

Autocept Fusion and Malfunction

Each autocept emerges from the consistently recurring experiences of the individual. Its nucleus is in the continuing input from body functioning: sensations of eating and elimination, sensory reverberations from breathing and heartbeat, stimulation of particular tactual areas. Indeed, any sensory input that is imposed consistently will become integrated into the phenomenological unity called the "self" depending upon its relative intensity and frequency. The autocept emerges in much the same fashion as does the phenomenon "tree," originating in repeated sensory components but deriving its unity from the fusion tendencies intrinsic in the structure of the person.

But there is a fundamental difference between the autocept and such perceptual phenomena as trees and houses. All are derived from fusion of recurrent
sensory components, but, as has been demonstrated at Iowa State University,
misleading cues can dramatically threaten the integrity of perceptual organization
without introducing appreciable disequilibrium. Any circumstance that tends to
disrupt the existing organization of the autocept, however, will occasion powerful drive input. As we argued in Chapter 7, all volitional activity is motivated
by disequilibrium introduced in the integration matrix when the organization of
the autocept is jeopardized.

As all autocepts are derived from consistent and recurrent inputs, they vary
depending upon the kinds of experiences that have been predominant during the
life (particularly the early years) of each individual. It is true that the nuclear
selves (derived from elemental visceral, feeding, and elimination activities) of all
human beings are quite similar, but soon after a child is born a remarkable dis-
parity of inputs and a corresponding uniqueness of autocepts appear. For instance, sometimes the input from particular transmitting mechanisms (perhaps
hunger or anxiety) may provide the basic materials of a given system. An individual who has been perpetually hungry or anxious during his childhood will
have an autocept primarily composed of such pervasive input and associated
components. Such a person's literal statement of his own identity might well be
"I am hunger" or "I am anxiety." An individual who has been continually grat-
ified during his formative years will have an autocept comprising "pleasure derivatives" arising, for instance, from frequent eating or sexual stimulation. In
extreme examples there may be an almost complete overlap between such continuing materials and the autocept that emerges.

Whether or not a particular kind of input becomes central depends upon its
duration and relative intensity, as well as upon the age at which its components
were consistently introduced. It is also affected by the relative constancy and
character of *other* inputs during the period in question. Even if a child is perpetually hungry, hunger will be a less critical constituent of the emerging autocept if other consistent and pervasive materials were introduced at the same time.
The type of material that predominates in a given autocept will, of course, determine which *other* components will occasion threat and thus introduce disequilibrium input in the integration matrix.

An autocept, then, seems to develop in expanding concentric circles like the
growth rings in trees. There appears to be a relationship between a person's age
and the tendency to incorporate inputs: The younger the child, the greater will
be his orientation toward consistent experiences and the stronger will be his
tendency to integrate such materials. Many observers of very young children
have noted the latter's preference for stories and rhymes that they have often
heard before, and any parent who has raised a child with television will have
noted his great interest in oft-repeated commercials and his almost complete
lack of concern for regular programs.

When the autocept begins to dissolve, those aspects that were integrated last or were less effectively fused tend to give way first, and the individual will be forced to emphasize input essential to a more basic integration. As dissolution continues, he will indulge in more and more primitive and childlike behavior until, at least in theory, he returns to activities characteristic of a very early age. There is perhaps no disequilibratory input so prepotent and persistent as that when the autocept is dissolving and the drive to retain even a modicum of organization is strong.[1] Regressive behavior is thus a direct outcome of the drive to retain as much integrity of the autocept as is possible under the circumstances. It involves retrenchment through more fundamental integration "rings" until the individual may even demonstrate behavior typical of infancy.

This discussion (along with that in Chapter 7) suggests the critical role of the autocept in volitional behavior: When behavior deviates from the norm the problem may arise from this motivational system. Under typical circumstances volitional activity can proceed with minimal drive input—almost automatically, because the motor threshold has been lowered (see Chapter 7). But when organization of the autocept is profoundly threatened, powerful and pervasive input will result, and behavior may seem strange indeed. Behavior may also seem strange when circumstances have prevented the emergence of a well-integrated autocept, because the system that ordinarily provides the motivation for much behavior is not effective. But let us examine specifics. Throughout the following discussion the intrinsic tendency toward fusion of sensory input (emergence of the autocept) and maintenance of unit integrity (autocept cohesion) should be kept in mind.

Inconsistent Input and the Indefinite Self

What happens when experiences of a person have simply not been consistent, so that the autocept is poorly fused and does not encompass a clearly defined phenomenological unity? Let us consider a hypothetical example: an individual who as a child was placed in many different foster homes, in which treatment of him varied from extreme cruelty and privation to fawning adulation and overindulgence. This individual has developed an autocept from variable inputs, integrated along with the few consistent experiences that may have occurred along the way. He goes through life assuming different roles simply because he has no integrated self-system to provide identity and consistency; he does not know who he is and struggles incessantly to find out. The autocept of this person has a nucleus derived from the consistent input from body functioning, and only in relation to this nucleus are tendencies toward phenomenological integrity manifested. He thus indulges particularly in physical activities—eating, elimination, sex—in his search for identity. Furthermore, without a clearly defined and well-integrated autocept his potential for volitional behavior is limited. He is unable to forgo immediate gratification because his self system is insufficiently developed to compete with other materials in apperception.

This person remains a victim of his biological impulses. Two factors account for this condition. No clearly defined and well-integrated autocept exists to compete with the input of such impulses, and tendencies toward integrity implicit in all autocepts occasion emphasis on these very biological impulses because they are the only basis for identity that he has. We have just described the behavior of two kinds of individuals: psychopaths and small children. The latter have not had sufficient experience for mature autocepts to emerge, whereas the former have not been exposed to conditions that would allow them to emerge.

Overconsistent Input and the Rigid Self

Occasionally, the environment of an individual may generate pervasive input that is highly consistent and invariable. During his formative years the child may be subjected to intense and prolonged punishment. The input from such treatment—pain and guilt—may therefore constitute a fundamental aspect of the self-system that emerges. In later life this individual may actively seek punishment if the derivatives of such treatment have become integral to his autocept. We assume that the disequilibrium occasioned by the punishment will be less prepotent than that from dissolution of the autocept. The apperception of such pain and guilt would thus be the most equilibratory response possible under the circumstances.

Similarly *any* consistent and pervasive input introduced over a long period of time may become integrated into the autocept. An individual who has been overindulged during his formative years may be forced to seek pleasure in order to bolster the integrity of his autocept; one who has experienced powerful religious indoctrination may seek the input from various precepts and practices for the same reason.

We may infer that a person's behavior will be rigid and inflexible to the extent that a restricted set of inputs has been consistently and recurrently imposed during his formative years. If he has been indoctrinated in a given religion, the practices and precepts of that religion will become fused in his autocept and may indeed function as integral components. The statement "I am religious" could be changed to "I am religion," for in a real sense the input derivatives of religion become the central ingredients of his identity.

The autocept of even the so-called "normal" person partly comprises the "conformity demands" of society derived from consistent treatment accorded to him as a child. In our society it is considered "normal" to respect private property. As a recipient of a certain consistently imposed treatment, a representative of our society generally will not steal: To do so would threaten the autocept. The person would experience input in the guise of anxiety and guilt, which might be so powerful that behavior commonly considered "abnormal" would result.

It is enlightening to explore what might happen if an intensely religious person could no longer accept, because of antithetical input, the practices and precepts of his religion (and of himself). As practices (rituals) are typically imposed earlier and more constantly than are precepts, we would expect them to be more basic to the autocept. The defecting religious person would then first abandon the precepts, though the practices would remain. Many Roman Catholics who can no longer wholeheartedly accept the principles of their religion still participate in its rites simply because the latter are more integral to their autocepts.

We may also speculate on the circumstances that might occasion defection of an individual from the intellectual principles of a given religious position. As we explained in Chapter 6, apperceptual locomotion tends to follow equilibrium paths, as a function of learning (and perhaps of innate modes of structuring). Powerful disequilibrium is required to override the individual's tendency to think along such association paths. In order for a person to defect, then, the disequilibrium occasioned by "illogical" thinking (about religious precepts) must be greater than that imposed by disruption of the unitary self. The self system will then undergo transformation—but not without corresponding pervasive and lasting disequilibrium input (guilt and anxiety.) Furthermore, while the transformation is in process this person may go through a period in which his identity becomes vague and his ability in directed volitional activity is affected. Whether or not the autocept of this individual will ultimately undergo transformation depends upon the pervasiveness and duration of the two disequilibrium inputs. If the drive introduced by his overriding of the associational paths is greater than that occasioned by disruption of the self system, transformation of the self will occur. But if the reverse circumstances arise, equilibrium will be achieved only by distortion of the thought processes: Apperception of antithetical materials simply will not occur or will be warped to fit the existing structure.

The resolution of conflict between "self-system unity" and "logical thinking" does not usually occur in such either-or fasion. Rather, each system "gives" a little. The same compromise occurs when activities requisite for equilibrium among other primary or secondary need systems disrupt the autocept.

Let us consider what may happen when certain moral principles that have been integrated into the autocept conflict with resolution of basic biological drives, for example in sexual behavior. The individual may literally be unable to apperceive the input representing sexuality or to indulge in any activity (overt or internal) that has overtones of sexuality. On the other hand, if the sex drive is extremely powerful or circumstances demand sexual behavior, he may be forced to apperceive such material. The organization of the autocept is placed in jeopardy, and the consequent anxiety and guilt may be overwhelming. The integration matrix of this person may be flooded with such input, and its prepotence may occasion continuing apperception, even as an individual with a severe toothache can apperceive little else. Then the person will demonstrate the disorganized behavior often found in neurosis.

Several corollaries can be derived from this discussion:

The more consistent and recurrent experience is during the formative years, the more rigid the autocept that emerges will be and the more inflexible the individual's behavior will be.

The more a particular kind of experience dominates the formative years, the greater will be the individual's tendency to identify himself in terms of these restricted inputs.

The less consistent and recurrent the experience during the formative years, the less definite the autocept that emerges will be, and the greater will be the tendency toward erratic, inconsistent, and impulsive behavior.

The more an individual's recurrent experiences deviate from the norms of his society, the more alien and abnormal his behavior.

Regardless of how bizarre an act may seem, it is an outcome of apperception and is the most equilibratory response possible for a person at any given moment: As a person apperceives, so will he behave. Keeping this point in mind, let us now consider several apperceptual distortions that may underlie and explain deviant behavior that has been classified as abnormal.

Apperceptual Flooding and Jamming

Although apperception is the most equilibratory outcome of the interaction of many different components within the integration matrix, the structure of the organism determines that pervasive input will (except under very unusual circumstances) be brought into focus. As we have mentioned, an individual cannot help apperceiving the pain from an abscessed tooth or the disequilibrium (anxiety) arising from certain visceral changes. But, when such prepotent input continues for an extended period, adaptive behavior is less likely to occur because of apperceptual flooding. The responses of the individual become less appropriate as the intensity of the input increases. Rational action is curtailed simply because the encodes essential to it are *jammed* by the pervasive input, and quite predictably behavior becomes primitive and inappropriate. Of course, if a discrete response (like a withdrawal reaction, whether practiced or reflexive) is readily available in the person's repertory, it may occur, but otherwise behavior becomes disorganized.

When the integrity of the autocept is threatened, powerful disequilibratory input in the form of anxiety or guilt may flood apperception. The individual faces a terrible dilemma: The input cannot be escaped, but no appropriate response is available. If a hot iron were permanently attached to the skin, so that appropriate withdrawal reactions could not occur, we could predict that the individual would indulge in general flight, and that, if the intensity of the input were increased, he would simply writhe and scream. The pervasiveness and endurance of such input jams other components that might provide a basis for effective behavior. Intense and prolonged anxiety has much the same effect: As it increases, the activity level of the individual will go up, but the appropri-

ateness of his responses will decrease correspondingly. Even under these circumstances the individual is not totally without resources for adjustment. When the
pervasiveness of such input becomes too great, certain automatic control devices
are activated: control devices that either focus or jam the pervasive input, so
that at least quasi adjustment can be achieved.

Input Focusing

When disequilibratory input is free-floating, as it always is when the self-
system is threatened, it is by definition unattached to any particular circumstances. Avoidance responses are ineffective simply because the pervasive input
remains in the individual as he moves through the environment: Even though
flight may occur it brings no effective relief. Under such conditions an automatic quasiadaptive mechanism may operate: Free-floating input may be channeled and focused on some convenient object, activity, or situation.

This channeling tendency seems characteristic of all disequilibratory input
and is considered especially symptomatic of neurosis, primarily because of the
more dramatic examples reflecting this disorder. But the mechanism operates
in other areas as well. A baby first experiences hunger as free-floating; it is only
after learning has occurred that hunger becomes associated with certain types of
food. During adolescence free-floating sexuality may be focused on various ob-
objects, situations, or individuals, some appropriate and others less so. If anger
reaches a high level and persists unabated for long periods, it too may become
focused: Free-floating hostility may be objectified through diverse activities like
hate groups and scapegoating. Channeling of disequilibratory input is characteristic of human beings. We find it unadaptive only when the object seems inappropriate or when it produces negative social repercussions. Its adaptiveness
thus depends upon the appropriateness of the object, its effectiveness in reducing
disequilibratory input, and its repercussions for the individual and for others in
contact with him.

Channeling free-floating anxiety is certainly equilibratory and within limits and
may be effective in reducing the continuing pervasiveness of the input. An individual who focuses his free-floating anxiety on cats or some other convenient
object has made a quasiadjustment: Whereas the anxiety is always present, cats
are not and can be avoided. All phobias thus aid the individual to adjust by
introducing at least a modicum of control over an otherwise intolerable circumstance: They allow differential responses where none was possible before.

The mechanism of disequilibrium (anxiety and guilt) focusing is also basic
to certain types of obsession. The individual who fears that he is going to shout
an obscene word in church is funneling free-floating anxiety toward a specific
potential behavior that he can control. As long as anxiety or guilt is centered
on the possibility that he may commit such a specific indiscretion, the intoler-
ability of the free-floating input is reduced. The obsessive device is an equilibratory, though not an adaptive, mechanism.

This interpretation is also applicable to certain psychotic symptoms. The individual who is deluded that some agency or group of individuals is planning to harm him is very likely funneling free-floating input into this improbable but still possible eventuality. When guilt is the basic disequilibratory input such a delusion serves a double function: The free-floating guilt can be reduced through focusing and partially expiated through the punitive character of the delusion. Hideous hallucinations may also originate and function as a form of channeling. If anxiety or guilt is extreme, the individual may hallucinate an appropriate focusing circumstance; although his reactions may then be extreme, they may still be considered equilibratory. It is more equilibratory to apperceive a known demon than to endure the intolerable pervasiveness of an unknown devil.

Compensatory Jamming

As apperceptual flooding may become intolerable, some type of "cut out" mechanism—either for the disequilibrium input per se or for the circumstance that occasions disruption in the self-system—might be predicted. The child who whistles or sings loudly when frightened of the dark is indulging in this kind of gambit. The auditory input derived from vocalization intrudes into the integration matrix and disperses the threatening apperception; to the degree that the child focuses on his own voice, he cannot apperceive his fear. Jamming disequilibratory input by means of extraneous activity is relatively common and cannot be considered, except in extreme forms, indicative of malfunction. At least we hope not! The author, for instance, when faced with the anxieties of taking Ph.D. prelims, teaching several classes, participating in research, and supporting a family found himself repeating a particular slogan: "Ajax the foaming cleanser" intruded almost automatically as a continually reverberating encode chain. Obviously, as long as apperception was flooded by repetition of this slogan, the anxieties arising from heavy responsibilities could not come into focus.

Much of the ritualistic behavior common to human beings probably has a similar function. Compulsive behavior (like constant hand-washing) probably makes several contributions to adjustment, depending upon the circumstances and the individual. It may have a jamming function, a symbolic "undoing" function, or a function connected with maintaining integrity of the self-system as we shall see later.

Compensatory jamming is critical to adjustment when the organization of the autocept is in jeopardy. If the threat is extreme, either encodes or sensory input may be displaced to such an extent that they simply fail to come into focus. Apperception, we recall, is the most equilibratory response possible to all the materials available within the integration matrix at any moment. But, if a particular input were to threaten the autocept severely and thus to introduce correspondingly intense anxiety or guilt, the most equilibratory response possible could well be that of *not* apperceiving. Furthermore, if a given past experience has been sufficiently disequilibratory, the encodes of that experience may well never reenter apperception. What jams apperception? If such input were actually brought into focus, the integrity of the self system would be disrupted, with consequent disequilibratory input. Here a complex problem arises. Must the individual first apperceive the critical component before sufficient disequilibrium is introduced to jam further apperception of it? Perhaps. The apperception of the disruptive encodes may occur briefly and then be immediately jammed by the flood of anxiety or the flare response discussed in Chapter 3. More likely, however, as all encodes are associated to some extent, disruption of the encode chain may occur long before the critical component is apperceived. The more closely the "thinking" process approaches the critical encode, the greater will be the disequilibratory input, so that effective jamming could occur even before apperception.

In our view, what the Freudians have called "repression" is simply a failure to apperceive in circumstances in which we would be expected to do so. *There is no unconscious mind.*[2] Encodes vary in the amounts of disequilibrium that their apperception will cause. If these repercussions are too great the encode simply will not be brought into focus.

We may surmise that the relative tendency of a given encode to be apperceived will vary according to the general level of background disequilibrium; an individual with low anxiety may apperceive encodes that would not be brought into focus if his anxiety level were higher. When a person is anxious about passing his Ph.D. prelims he will tend not to indulge in behavior (internal or overt) that will raise his anxiety level. But once the exams have been passed, trouble can occur.

In our view such classical symptoms as fugue and multiple personality are both examples of input jamming, defenses against the disequilibratory input occasioned by disruption of the self-system. Both involve failure to apperceive certain encodes or encode systems; but in both a fundamental disruption of the self-system seems already implicit. In fugue the encodes essential to individual identity are not apperceived, whereas in multiple personality a fundamental cleavage in the autocept has apparently occurred.

How, then, can we insist that both fugue and multiple personality are mechanisms for defending the person against intolerable input derived from a loss in integration of the autocept? There are two possible answers to this question: Either actual cleavage in the autocept occurs, or such cleavage is only apparent. The first possibility implies that there is a point in the increase of disequilibrium when the fused self-system actually dissolves, at which disequilibrium occasioned by *continued* fusion is greater than that occasioned by cleavage. This notion suggests that such a cleavage is more likely to occur in an individual who happens to have had incompatible principles imposed during the formative years; an essential predisposition toward separation may thus have been implicit. The other interpretation, which we favor, assumes a distinction between actual cleavage and the "removal" of even large segments of memory from possible apperception. In both fugue and multiple personality the autocept remains intact, but certain constellations of encodes simply will not come into focus. In fugue the encodes essential to one level of identity cannot be apperceived because they would occasion a more basic disruption of autocept fusion. The extreme reaction would be predicted only under circumstances in which powerful disequilibrium would result regardless of which of two possible alternatives were taken. A man who loves his family and has been indoctrinated with the notion of familial responsibility might develop a fugue reaction if his specific family situation became intolerable. If he were to remain with the family, the disequilibratory input would be overwhelming; if he were to leave, it might be worse. Jamming the encodes essential to his identity would permit him to leave without suffering great guilt or anxiety.

A slightly different mechanism is involved in multiple personality. Incompatible encode systems become differentially available for apperception, but when the encodes intrinsic to one system are in focus, those constituting the other system are effectively jammed. Multiple personality is thus simply another type of defense against conflict. When enduring and pervasive inputs impel behavior disruptive to the integrity of a given autocept, such a symptom may emerge. A person with extremely strong sex drive who had been indoctrinated against all forms of sexual expression would be a candidate for this bizarre solution. While he was indulging in sexual behavior the encodes representing one identity would be effectively jammed; with reduction of the sex drive and the associated guilt, the alternative identity could emerge, with consequent jamming of the encodes comprising the other self. In Freudian terms a kind of reciprocal "repression" would obtain, in that, as one encode system became available for apperception, the other would be jammed and the reverse. In one sense, multiple personality is a remarkable adjustment mechanism: It allows the person to have his cake and eat it too.

Our discussion so far has dealt with encodes and encode systems, but it is apparent that compensatory jamming may apply to sensory input as well. If the input from a particular receptor system occasions sufficient threat to the integrity of the autocept, it may be effectively "cut out," so that it is simply not apperceived. If, for instance—and this example is common—a person who has been taught that the ultimate "sin" is to take the life of another person is placed in a situation in which killing is not only required but accepted by him as a responsibility, input jamming may occur. There are many examples in the psychological literature of soldiers who, when required to fire their rifles, found their trigger fingers or perhaps their entire hands suddenly paralyzed. We may surmise that the act of killing was simply so threatening that, on the very threshold of this act, the flood of anxiety from disruption of the autocept was sufficient to jam the input essential to its performance. The individual is thus rescued from an intolerable dilemma: the fact that for integrity of his autocept he must view himself as both a good soldier and a nonkiller. All so-called "conversion reactions" function to resolve such intolerable conflicts: In a situation in which any of the available alternatives will occasion profound disruption of the integrity of the self, input jamming may provide a quasiadjustment to the situation. In ordinary circumstances pervasive input from the sensory receptors intrudes into apperception, but the circumstance underlying conversion reactions are not ordinary, and the most equilibratory response possible is nonapperception.

This discussion might incline us to view input jamming as a rare and extreme phenomenon; this is certainly not so. Because of the single apperceptive channel, jamming is a continuing and ordinary process. While one input is in focus, another cannot be, by definition. If we are apperceiving the various written symbols on this page, many potentially available components—extraneous sounds, pressures, pains, and the like—are not in focus. In conversion hysteria jamming is simply more nearly complete and more permanent, but it is on the same continuum as are the ordinary reactions.

In this analysis we have tried to deal with functional disorders—those arising from an ordinary person's efforts to cope with extreme disequilibrium when no appropriate response is available. But malfunction may also be occasioned by some breakdown in the structure of the organism. When there is actual damage to neural tissues aberrant behavior can be predicted; brain damage can result in a range of symptoms varying from subtle aphasia to gross behavioral impairment. But, regardless of the degree that behavior may deviate from the norm, it still results directly from apperception, and apperception is still the most equilibratory response possible under the circumstances. If a person's behavior is unusual, it is because his apperceptions are bizarre; the grandiose delusions and hideous hallucinations of the psychotic are antecedents of deviant behavior. Regardless of how inappropriate it may seem, that behavior is actually the most equilibratory outcome of such apperceptions. All activity, from overt behavior to apperception, is equilibratory for the moment; the individual with delirium tremens is behaving appropriately to his apperceptions, and so is the paretic.

This discussion suggests that there is no clear-cut distinction among categories commonly used in classifying abnormal individuals. Psychopathy and neurosis seem to arise from different regions of the continuum of autocept fusion, but the symptoms ordinarily used to designate psychosis are simply extreme examples of those common in these other two disorders. Regardless of the general classification, symptoms are always stopgaps designed to maintain optimal equilibrium in a system (the autocept) undergoing dissolution.

Hallucinations and delusions of grandeur indicate unusual stresses in the amorphous autocept of the psychopath. They are the most bizarre symptoms, the most desperate measures in the search for self, but they are part of the same continuum as the minor impostures so common in this illness. They involve a kind of focusing reminiscent of phobia, but here the terrors of dissolution are reduced by assuming someone else's identity and affiliating the scattered segments of the person to that identity. Such delusions are most likely to occur in individuals who have had little opportunity for autocept fusion and who now find their tenuous hold on identity slipping away. Dissolution may occur as a function of traumatic experiences or violations introduced by brain damage or disease.

Delusions and hallucinations of persecution, on the other hand, are extreme symptoms of neurosis. When a rigid self-system is severely threatened, anxiety and guilt may be so intense that a hallucinated image (on which anxiety can be focused and by means of which guilt can be expiated) may occur automatically.

At the beginning of this chapter we declared our opposition to a strictly relativistic view of "abnormal" behavior. We shall now attempt a universal definition, a postulate of malfunction, in full recognition of the hazards:

Regardless of the culture of the time, malfunction occurs when the overt or internal activity that is immediately equilibratory leads to outcomes that are nonadaptive in the long run.

The individual's behavior will be nonadaptive to the extent that disorders in autocept fusion lead to distorted apperception. It will be inappropriate to the extent that input jamming (of sensory input or encodes) leads to distorted apperception. The potential for adaptive behavior will be reduced to the extent that structural alteration or breakdown occasions inappropriate apperception.

We readily acknowledge that behavior considered normal in certain cultures, subcultures, periods, and so on may be considered abnormal in others. But the critical point is that too much apperceptual distortion, regardless of the cause, will prevent effective behavior, no matter how it is defined. Certain activities must be performed effectively in all societies if we are to continue as a species. When the individual can no longer perform his own society's version of these universal activities, we have an example of malfunction.

Repair

If we wish to modify behavior so that it will approximate what is classified as normal, we must alter the processes that distort apperception—for as the individual apperceives, so will he behave. As the kind of autocept that has emerged determines directly or indirectly the degree of apperceptual warp, shifts in behavior ultimately depend upon changes in this critical system. How can the autocept be modified? It takes years to emerge and to harden into a sort of structure; how can effective alteration occur in the few months that the therapist typically has available? To be explicit, can we instigate the emergence of a more definitive self or soften an inflexible constellation that provides the basis for malfunction? These two conditions cause most apperceptual distortions that result in deviant responses, and it is on them that we must center our attack.

Fusion Techniques for the Indefinite Self

Let us emphasize at the beginning the enormity of the task confronting us. We must bring about a greater measure of autocept fusion in an adult, who has not only failed to achieve such integration during the most appropriate years but also has developed gambits that will probably interfere with such integration now. Small wonder that the psychopath resists, obdurately and contemptuously, all efforts to help him. His potential for autocept alteration is almost nil, and in order to defend his tenuous hold on the weak self that he has he must surely use the devious techniques that are available! How do we bring about a greater measure of autocept fusion in an individual who has both little potential for change and who, by definition, must resist our every effort to change him?[3]

Stratagems for Gradual Change. Although the potential for autocept emergence and alteration is greatest in the child, the possibility for change still continues, though diminishing, into old age. We may state categorically that the earlier the effort to alter the autocept, the greater the chances of success will be. Unhappily, professional help for psychopaths is so limited that few receive attention other than containment in penal institutions. And it is in prison, with its recurring rituals, that such individuals typically receive the first truly consistent inputs from which a reasonably well-integrated autocept may finally evolve. Here, then, is a grim irony: The first real chance for the young psychopath to develop a consistent autocept is in a context in which the autocept that does develop will be antisocial. The young person struggling to find out who he is receives strange material for this identification; he finds himself frequently exploited homosexually in the constant company of men who reject the values of society and extol the virtues of criminal life, and continually exploited and depersonalized by both his fellow inmates and his guards, who are sometimes equally unfortunate. Our prison system takes the individual who is desperately seeking some evidence of who he is and provides the evidence that he is deviant. There is no greater need for insight and workable procedures than in this area, and it is with a diffidence born of ignorance but inspired by this dismal picture that we offer a few.

The following techniques, we believe, can help to bring about at least partial organization in those who suffer from aberrant behavior as outcomes of indefinite selves. The basic requirement, of course, is a series of consistent and recurring experiences from which an integrated self can be derived. Such experiences must, if treatment is to be effective, correspond to the general values prevalent in the person's particular society. But how can it be done? We doubt seriously that it can be done, but here are some notions.

Let us take young psychopaths when they first find themselves imprisoned (as many of them do sooner or later) and expose them to the following regimen: regular food, sleep, and exercise; group conferences (in which they are encouraged to participate), at which certain precepts embodying basic cultural values are frequently and subtly imposed; tasks of some difficulty that require both great individual and group effort; programs consisting of dramatic and repetitive lectures on the lives and values of great men, designed to provide the basis for broader identification; continuing interest in them and absolute respect for them as individuals. These few notions contain the germ of an idea: As a man is treated and as a man behaves, *so he will become.* This principle applies particularly to that most maligned and misunderstood individual, the psychopath. There are no magic cures for him; it has taken years to make him what he is, a being without a true identity. But when he does change, the rewards both for him and for society will be great.

Techniques for Rapid Change. Although we shall discuss extreme measures here, we do not claim that they should be put into effect. There are human values the abrogation of which might more than negate any beneficial effects of such treatments. We remind the reader, however, that man has seldom been loath to endure suffering or to inflict it on others in pursuit of some higher goal.

We shall describe a technique that not only would contribute to establishment of an integrated self but also would provide a basis for disrupting congealed reaction tendencies that might otherwise interfere with emergence of such a self. It should be applied only in the most extreme instances and then only if patients or responsible members of society gave permission. Essentially, it involves isolating the individual from as much stimulation as possible, then imposing certain vital experiences again and again until their cumulative effects ensure incorporation into the structure of the emerging self.[4] If an individual were immersed in water that was neither cold nor hot, in total darkness and in absolute silence, then left until his need for stimulation became overwhelming, it might be possible to alter his autocept rapidly by constantly repeating critical precepts through earphones. Continuing this procedure day after day might result in banishment of the old identity constellations and emergence of new ones.

To abet this process punishment and reward could be used, both to emphasize critical inputs and to ensure disruption of interfering tangents. The individual could be forced to repeat aloud the messages that were continually droning in his ears and could be rewarded or punished (by shock of varying intensities) according to the accuracy and enthusiasm of his repetition. With better apparatus and more precise techniques, other appropriate inputs (tactual, visual, and perhaps olfactory) could be presented with sufficient emphasis to ensure their inclusion in the emerging self.

Why eliminate the individual's stimulation? Because it is from such continuous, though transitory, material that humans derive much feedback pertinent to the identity and continuity of the self, and the psychopath is extremely dependent upon it for he lacks a well-integrated autocept. Without background stimulation the person will be forced to use any and all input that may be made available. We must depend upon the admittedly slight tendency toward emergence of the autocept that may remain, despite the individual's age, to accomplish the rest. There is some reason to hope that this tendency may not be inoperative, as we might at first assume. The autocept emerges according to the same principles that determine organization of the perceptual field and emergence of the various constancies. Yet G. M. Stratton (1897) and others have demonstrated (see Chapter 4, note 5) that this entire organization may be altered remarkably within a few days when conditions are appropriate. Perhaps inflexibility, both in perception and autocept organization, is more a function of invariant input than underlying loss of plasticity.

At this point the reader is probably revolted by these ideas. Such treatment seems inhumane and the individual who would use them inhuman. Perhaps. But we face an unusual kind of aberration, one that has, almost without exception, resisted efforts at behavior change. We do not defend use of such measures without prior research on their effectiveness. But how are we to begin, and who will volunteer for such extreme manipulations? The Federal government could endow and support a research institution staffed by experts in psychology and psychiatry to refine techniques for altering psychopathic behavior. The most reprehensible of all criminals, the multiple murderers, who are now either killed or left to live as vegetables until they die, should be sent to this institution.

Attenuation of the Rigid Self

It is remarkable that every therapeutic technique—whether it consists of whipping people with whips or with electricity, of the ministrations of a witch doctor or of a psychoanalyst—can make legitimate claims to success. We can draw any number of conclusions: that time alone has unusual regenerative powers, that each individual who evaluates the effects of the therapy must have the same prejudice as has the person who administered it, that all such approaches have in common a feature that strikes at certain basics in the miseries of man. We do not disallow the possible validity of the first two conclusions, but any approach that demonstrates some interest in the suffering individual seems likely to have a measure of success. Talking about a problem can extinguish by minute degrees the anxiety attached to it and can, however slowly, allow an alteration of the autocept so that essential behavior can occur.

In the previous section we examined briefly some characteristics of the indefinite self and considered certain possibilities for consolidation. Now we are dealing with the opposite problem, with the autocept that is so rigid and inflexible that even the simplest demands of personality or circumstance may cause disruption and overwhelming fear. We must therefore examine possibilities for loosening the autocept that is threatened on all sides, with consequent extreme anxiety, distorted apperception, and bizarre behavior.

Let us begin with an analogy. Some years ago the author bought a sports car, one of those red ones that look as if they are going ninety while standing still, with a chronic potential for complex difficulties. Before a trip home to New Mexico to show it off, it was put in the garage with instructions that all its various workings should be tuned to a fine edge. And so they were. The car worked like a Swiss watch all through Missouri, Oklahoma, and the Texas panhandle. But in New Mexico it developed a chronic disequilbratory (to the driver) malfunction: It would hardly start, and once in motion it seized every

opportunity to stop running altogether. What had happened? What was wrong
with the car? Nothing at all, it appeared, when the car was finally placed in the
expert hands of a talkative mechanic in Las Vegas. The car had been tuned to
run at sea level, and now it was 6,000 feet above. The machine, adjusted to
perform effectively in a certain context, had been placed in an alien environment. Was something wrong with the machine? Or the environment? Hardly.

Human beings who have developed and made excellent adjustments to particular contexts may also break down when placed in unusual situations. This
point is obvious when we think of circumstances alien to all human beings:
outer space, underwater, the fiery furnace. But it seems more significant when
we consider that some environments may be disruptive to certain human beings
and not to others, even as certain cars work well at 6,000 feet and others do
not. When we speak of adjustment we must always consider the relationship
between environmental demands and the kind of autocept that has emerged. An
environment completely congruent with one type of autocept may be totally
disruptive to another. Nevertheless, when a breakdown comes, it is manifested
in apperceptual warp and the unusual behavior that it causes; the more inflexible
the self, the smaller the individual's capacity of adjustment to environmental variations will be. The neurotic individual has an autocept so inflexible that he cannot
cope easily with ordinary environmental demands: The mundane activities of
living produce so much anxiety and guilt that apperceptual warp and bizarre
behavior are inevitable. The solution is to reduce his inflexibility to permit
more effective behavior.

We do not intend to offer any novel techniques for altering the rigid autocept, but we shall mention what apparently happens in application of those
approaches that have legitimate claims to success. In all such therapies conditions have been appropriate for two interdependent processes: partial dissolution
of the autocept of the individual and incorporation of demands previously incongruent with the autocept. When these changes have been accomplished, the
disequilibrium input occasioned by threats to the autocept will no longer produce the apperceptual distortions that result in neurotic behavior.

One fundamental technique, deliberate or not, underlies all successful approaches to the treatment of the neurotic: recurrent presentation by either the
therapist or the patient of inputs reflecting the incongruent characteristics of
the autocept.

Let us consider a person who has been so rigidly indoctrinated against aggressive behavior that any impulse toward aggression results in overwhelming anxiety
and guilt. The basic therapeutic strategy involves slow but continuing exposure
of this individual to the various facets of his hostility, first perhaps in representative situations (stories and pictures) and then concrete and realistic circumstances introduced by the therapist. Along with the "extinction" approach the
patient is encouraged to elaborate on each and every circumstance of hostility
that he can recall, with particular emphasis on critical relationships with father,
mother, siblings, and so on.

The rationale for this treatment is contained in the paradigm of classical conditioning: The simple presentation of aggressive images and situations will gradually diminish the intensity of the emotion that has become attached to them. At the same time the structure of the autocept should gradually change, for, as the individual faces aggression situations and experiences anger again and again, this material slowly becomes incorporated into the self system. Then he can begin to perceive himself not only as an individual capable of aggressive impulses but also one able to cope with them. Obviously this interpretation can also be applied to sexual impulses and activity.

We should not assume that most fears and guilts can be reduced by extinguishing, however. For instance, in both phobias and obsessions the objects or situations that occasion the affect may have little to do with the actual problem. The object simply serves as the focus of disequilibratory input; even if conditioning procedures were effective, the underlying problem would remain untouched and the individual would have to resort to some other, perhaps even more debilitating symptom. In therapy it is therefore essential that the actual problem, rather than some derivative symptom, be attacked. If the patient has a phobia against spiders, it will do little good to reduce his fear of this particular animal, for the fear is only symptomatic.

It is probable that all the disparate therapies that have legitimate claims to success share some form of reliance on processes of extinction and the restructuring of the autocept. Many have also provided other ameliorative conditions. The counseling situation is typically a secure one in which fearful experiences can be more easily recounted because of the acceptance provided by the counselor. More important, the therapeutic situation represents in microcosm many of the conditions initially responsible for the patient's difficulties; it thus serves as a theater in which these same problems can be confronted and extinction and restructuring can more readily occur.

Our only quarrel with psychoanalysis is its reliance on vague terminology and tendencies toward compartmentalization. It provides the circumstances outlined and perhaps even offers dramatic—though erroneous—interpretations of an individual's problems. It is very gratifying to discover that one has something in common with Oedipus Rex.

Even neo-Skinnerian techniques have something to offer. The philosophy "as a person behaves, so he will become" and concomitant behavior-shaping techniques provide recurrent inputs: both the rewards offered as reinforcement and the repeated behavior necessary to receive them. These investigators would not, of course, agree with our interpretation of the effects of their techniques and would consider the changes in behavior per se both sufficient explanation and justification for their methods.

Actually we may be giving them too much credit, for it is doubtful that differential reinforcement of the type practiced by Skinnerian therapists in mental hsopitals can bring about more than superficial and transitory results unless they are supplemented with more penetrating stratagies. It takes many exposures to a circumstance and many repetitions of an act for the input derivatives to become incorporated into the autocept, and changes in behavior alone, without alteration in the structure of the self, avail very little. The unhappy fact is that the behavior typically affected by Skinnerian therapy is so peripheral to the basic problem that little important restructuring takes place. The Skinnerians seem to think that, once behavior has been produced by differential reinforcement, structural alteration automatically occurs. Every human being knows how to do many things that he never does and to behave in hundreds of ways that never effectively alter the structure of the self. We know how to kill people, but most of us have never done it. This behavior is in our repertories but it has no potential in the structure of our autocept. This distinction highlights the weakness of the Skinnerian approach to psychotherapy. We know of a man whose motivations and perspective were so warped that he killed seven women. If we were to follow the approach implicit in the Skinnerian orientation, we would first allow him to kill six women, then five, then four, and so on, reinforcing at each step this gradual movement toward more civilized responses until, through the magic of differential reinforcement, we had shaped him into a nonkiller. This example may seem both outrageous and ridiculous, but it is not entirely so. It suggests that crucial modifications in behavior must reflect alterations in the basic structure of the self-system and that motivations rather than superficial activities are the central problem that must be solved if we are to eliminate undesirable responses.

There is some similarity between our position and that of O. H. Mowrer. But he believes that the poorly developed "superego" causes the "sins" and "ills" of man and that every effort must be made to strengthen this beleaguered segment of personality; we, on the other hand, find this notion applicable only to the psychopath. The neurotic autocept is too rigid and must be loosened.

Summary

According to the postulate of process all activity, whether overt or internal, tends toward equilibrium; this postulate applies whether we are speaking of bizarre or ordinary behavior. All behavior is equilibratory but it may not be adaptive; when the gap between these two categories becomes extreme, malfunction occurs. If we are to understand malfunction, we must look at the circumstances that lead to distorted apperceptions, for behavior, however classified, is usually an outcome of this process. Warped apperceptions, other than those resulting from structural damage, must be traced to the emergence of the autocept early in life. If the environmental conditions were inconsistent, then an inadequately fused autocept probably emerged, and the individual commonly finds "himself" involved in repeated expression of basic urges and a compulsive search for self.

Sometimes this search may drive him past the ordinary pretenses typical of the psychopath into delusions of grandeur characteristic of psychosis.

If the conditions imposed have been both restricted and extremely consistent, the autocept that has emerged will be fixed and inflexible; the individual will be unable to tolerate incompatible input because of the flood of free-floating anxiety that will result. He will exhibit behavior typical of the neurotic; constraint and inhibition will mark his movements. If he indulges in activities incongruent with his restricted self, his integration matrix will be flooded with anxiety and guilt, and apperceptual jamming will occur. As such input is intolerable yet cannot be escaped, any of a number of compensatory jamming or channeling mechanisms (phobias, obsessions, hysterias, and so on) may operate. In every instance such devices aid in the defense of the beleaguered self and allow partial if not perfect adjustment to crises. The most extreme example of this kind of malfunction is embodied in delusions and hallucinations of persecution, in which the spectral images serve both as focuses for guilt and as instruments for its partial expiation.

If we were to try to restructure the abnormal individual, we would have to bring about alteration in the structure of his autocept. In the psychopath this effort would have to involve imposition of consistent and recurrent input under conditions allowing the emergence and integration of an autocept congruent with the demands of society. In the neurotic an essential loosening of the rigid autocept would be necessary so that the ordinary demands of life would not produce immobilizing anxiety and guilt.

Notes

[1]We have placed great importance on the process guiding emergence and development of the autocept, the tendency for all phenomena to retain holistic integrity. What is the evidence for it? There is some, but it is not as directly applicable as we would like.

The author once observed a twenty-month-old child viewing a home movie of her own antics. As she watched herself and her belongings in the movie, she became quite disturbed. When her image was on the screen she would shout the few words in her vocabulary with unusual stridence. She became more and more excited until finally it was necessary to stop the film. What was happening? Apparently the level of her comprehension and the fusion of her autocept were simply not advanced enough to allow her to endure such "schizoid" circumstances. She was just beginning to grasp the difference between self and not self, and seeing her image in the film was disrupting the tenuous organization that had developed. Obviously, more research is necessary, but some related and appropriate data are available from studies of children's reactions to their mirror images.

Several investigators (Wallon, 1947; Gesell, 1954; and Zazzo, 1948) have demonstrated that the very young child ignores his own image in the mirror, even though he can easily recognize the image of someone else. This finding is not remarkable in itself, for the child has had much more experience in seeing others than himself. But when the child does begin to recognize himself, he becomes highly disturbed, and not until he has repeated many gestures and grimaces that are familiar to him does he become more at ease.

Much more dramatic, though not necessarily more pertinent, are the data on disorders of corporeal awareness in parietal disease, when partial paralysis has resulted from neural damage. An integral portion of the body is suddenly removed from use and the structure of the autocept is immediately in terrible jeopardy. Critchley (1965) has outlined certain of the more bizarre expressions of individuals' efforts to compromise with these terrible violations. If one side of the body has been affected, the individual may literally reject the existence of that part, failing to wash or care for it. When asked about his paralysis, he may simply ignore the question and refuse to refer either to it or to the limbs involved (Babinski, 1914). If he finally accepts the fact that he is paralyzed, he may rationalize the severity of the disorder, claiming that he is a bit stiff or has a sprain; if pushed he may insist that he is not paralyzed at all. When directed to move the paralyzed limb, he may insist that it is moving when it is not, or he may move the contralateral limb and pretend that it was the one that he was directed to move. If others remark that the limb is paralyzed, the patient may develop delusions to explain the difficulty; in an extreme instance he may even insist that the paralyzed portion of the body belongs to someone else (Gerstmann, 1942). Or a partially paralyzed person may claim (Anastasopoulos, 1954) that his unaffected limbs have magically increased in power and effectiveness, so that the paralysis is essentially cancelled. Critchley (1965) has mentioned several other symptoms common to parietal disease, and all appear to be stopgap measures designed to maintain integration of an autocept under pressure toward dissolution.

2The existence of an unconscious mind has been posited by many thinkers (Plotinus, Galen, Pascal, Spinoza, G. W. Von Liebnitz, J. A. Fichte, F. W. J. Von Schelling, G. T. Fechner, and many others) before Sigmund Freud; it has been accepted by as many more since his major pronouncements.

It must therefore seem presumptuous, if not outrageous, to dismiss so cavalierly a concept arrived at over such a long period and with so much labor. Since Freud, awareness of the unconscious has come to permeate our thinking, assuming such importance that historians seek its manifestations and chart the halting efforts toward its clarification. Yet we dismiss it in a single sentence. Why?

Because many people use the term to signify the existence of a subterranean realm from which and into which processes and ideas come and go; they conceptualize the subconscious as a container into which things can be poured or from which they can be retrieved. Or they suggest that experience extrudes below the level of awareness; as if we could somehow hear below the threshold of sound or see beyond the limits of sight (when the receptors are not even activated), as in Fechner's negative sensations. We reject the notion of the unconscious simply because there is no need for it. To use the concept is parallel to saying that there is a realm of "unlight" in the flashlight when it is turned off. Certainly there are processes (from cellular to cerebral) that do not have repercussions in experience, but why call them "unconscious?" Why not say simply that most potential inputs (all but one) are not being apperceived? Why not also admit that certain inputs (both encodes and sensory components) may be jammed because of the valence (visceral repercussions) attached to them. This approach not only fits the facts, it also eliminates the compartmentalization and the contradictions implicit in the term "unconscious."

But how do we explain "Freudian slips"? We have already discussed the manner in which encodes become associated and in which the motor threshold between encode and verbal response is lowered; we have suggested that in speech there is a rapid and continuous fluctuation of apperception between encodes and the reverberations of the spoken word. The "Freudian slip" occurs when an inappropriate encode is briefly apperceived and triggers its verbal counterpart before corrective jamming can intervene. Such slips may occur because of oblique associations or because of the presence of a persistent background input, but in neither instance is there any reason to assume the existence of an unconscious mind.

What about dreams? Some people think that dreams are the royal road to the unconscious. We have already suggested that dreams may be controlled by the continuing presence of some background input and that they assume a freewheeling character because of the raising of pertinent thresholds and the loss of volitional control; but we see no reason to accept the notion of an unconscious mind. What about the studies of hypnosis in which the individual is supposed during the trance to recall materials long hidden in the "unconscious"? If we accept R. W. White's view (1941) that all that happens during hypnosis is a great increase in suggestibility and a profound need to behave as a hypnotized person (as this role is defined by the hypnotist), then the various claims become easily explicable without inferring an unconscious mind.

Although there are certainly potential inputs (both sensations and memories) that are *not* conscious and varying degrees of resistance to their coming into consciousness, the inference of an unconscious mind obscures rather than clarifies: It compartmentalizes man's mental activity and his thinking about such activity, and it introduces unnecessary complexity into a process already complex enough. It is for these reasons that we reject "unconscious mind" as an acceptable concept in psychology.

[3]Psychopaths represent an enigma to psychologists because so few behave abnormally enough to be found in mental hospitals—only 1 percent, according to one author (Coleman, 1964). But a number of studies on the specific symptoms of psychopathy have been published. The symptoms are said to include inadequate moral development, egocentricity, impulsiveness and irresponsibility, low frustration tolerance, almost total lack of anxiety and guilt, inability to profit from mistakes, exploitation of others, poor social relationships, rejection of authority, rationalization, poor judgment, a tendency to play roles, and deviant sexual patterns (Darling, 1945; Cleckley, 1959; Thorne, 1959; Wegrocki, 1961; Wirt, Briggs, and Golden, 1962; and Heaton-Ward, 1963).

The causes of psychopathy have been much more difficult to determine. D. H. Stott (1962) found evidence correlating congenital injuries to the inhibitory centers in the nervous system with this type of behavior, and H. J. Eysenck (1960) believes that psychopaths have much slower conditioning rates than do normal people, which suggests some type of constitutional disorder.

The weight of the evidence is on the side of an environmental explanation. W. C. Heaver (1943) found that a high percentage of the psychopaths in his study came from middle- and upper-class families; he also discovered that they usually had overindulgent mothers and successful, driving, critical, and distant fathers. In a similar study P. Greenacre (1945) emphasized disparities and conflicts between the parents, as well as a typical disregard for authority by the parents themselves. These parents were found to be extremely dependent upon community approval, so that great importance was placed on the illusion of a happy family. Consequently, the children learned that appearances are more important than realities. Greenacre pointed out that this condition, along with the emotional smothering of the mothers and total lack of affection from the fathers, prevents the development of normal emotions.

There has so far been little success in treatment of psychopathy. R. S. Banay (1945), however, reported fair results from intensive therapy and constant supervision of criminal psychopaths; and R. M. Lindner (1945) reported good results from the use of hypnoanalysis.

[4]There is some evidence that functional integrity of the autocept depends upon the continuing introduction of sensory materials. We have already deduced that the autocept has its origins in recurrent input and that the continuing presence of components from the various transmitting mechanisms and basic encodes help to define the individual's identity. If consistent inputs are not provided during the formative years or are suddenly halted later, the repercussions for the autocept should be profound.

S. Provence and R. C. Lipton (1963) found institutionalized children (whose relationships with adult figures are significantly less consistent and frequent than those of normal children) were less able to defer gratification of their needs than were other children and had less control of their impulses. W. Goldfarb (1943), found that adolescents who had spent their infancy in institutions were "lacking in a clear sense of personal identity" and were less capable of sustained effort.

The effects of removing ordinary sensory input have also been studied; they offer evidence of the importance of the continuing sensory monitoring to the effective integration of the autocept. All these studies place the individual in some circumstances of sensory deprivation. W. Heron (1961) had a group of subjects wear translucent goggles, separated their fingers with cotton, and cuffed their hands in cardboard; he found that sensory deprivation was significantly and *inversely* related to the individual's ability to resist the effects of propaganda; a finding directly pertinent to our view of possible approaches to changing the autocept of the psychopath. Heron also found a curious loss of volitional control on the part of certain subjects. There was even a tendency toward free hallucinations: The subjects could neither stop nor start them at will and sometimes became so disturbed by their persistence that they left the experimental situation. Many people have experienced a strange loss of identity immediately upon awakening, only to find that the indefiniteness dissolves as the familiar aspects of the environment rush into apperception. D. O. Hebb (1960) reports that pilots who are isolated on high-altitude test flights sometimes suffer from feelings of alienation both from themselves and from their aircraft. And, of course, sleep is the most common example of sensory deprivation (the sensory threshold has been raised) and involves the most obvious loss of volitional control over the character and progress of imagery.

There is thus some basis for arguing that more rapid alteration of the autocept would occur if the individual where placed in circumstances of sensory deprivation. The existing structure of the self is then threatened, which increases the likelihood that any consistent input (whether propaganda or therapeutic stratagem) will be incorporated.

References

Anastasopoulos, G. Zur Frage des pathologischen Erlebens veränderter Körperzustande. *Nervenarzt*, 1954, 25: 292-500.

Babinski, J. Contribution à l'Études des troubles mentaux des l'hémiplégie organique cérébral. *Revue Neurologique*, 1914, 1: 845-848.

Banay, R. S. *Wanted—An institute of criminal science.* Yearbook of the National Probation Association, 1945.

Cleckley, H. M. Psychopathic states. In S. Arieti (ed.), *American handbook of psychiatry.* Vol. 1. New York: Basic Books, 1959.

Coleman, J. C. *Abnormal psychology and modern life.* Chicago: Scott, Foresman, 1964.

Critchley, M. Disorders of corporeal awareness in parietal disease. In *The body percept.* S. Wapner and H. Werner (eds.), New York: Random House, 1965.

Darling, H. F. Definition of psychopathic personality. *Journal of Nervous and Mental Disorders,* 1945, 10: 121-126.

Eysenck, H. J. *Behavior therapy and the neuroses.* London: Pergamon, 1960.

Gerstmann, J. Problem of imperception of disease and of impaired body territories with organic lesions. *Archives of Neurology and Psychiatry*, 1942, 48: 890-913.

Gesell, A. *The mental growth of the preschool child.* New York: Macmillan, 1954.

Goldfarb, W. The effects of early institutional care on adolescent personality. *Journal of Experimental Education*, 1943, 12: 106-129.

Greenacre, P. Conscience in the psychopath. *American Journal of Orthopsychiatry*, 1945, 15: 495-509.

Heaton-Ward, W. A. Psychopathic disorder. *Lancet*, 1963, 1: 121-123.

Heaver, W. C. A study of forty male psychopathic personalities before, during, and after hospitalization. *American Journal of Psychiatry*, 1943, 100: 342-346.

Hebb, D. O. The American revolution. *American Psychologist*, 1960, 15: 735-745.

Heron, W. Cognitive and physiological effects of perceptual isolation. In *Sensory deprivation:* P. Solomon *et al*, (eds.), *Symposium at the Harvard Medical School.* Cambridge: Harvard University Press, 1961.

Lindner, R. M. Psychopathic personality and the concept of homeostasis. *Journal of Clinical Psychopathology and Psychotherapy*, 1945, 6: 517-521.

Provence, S., and Lipton, R. C. *Infants in institutions.* New York: International Universities Press, 1963.

Stott, D. H. Evidence for a congenital factor in maladjustment and delinquency. *American Journal of Psychiatry*, 1962, 118: 781-794.

Stratton, G. M. Vision without inversion of the retinal image. *Psychological Review*, 1897, 4: 341-360, 463-481.

Thorne, F. C. The etiology of sociopathic reactions. *American Journal of Psychotherapy*, 1959, 13: 319-330.

Wallon, J. *Les origines de la pensée chez l'enfant.* Paris: Presses Universitaires, 1947.

Wegrocki, H. J. Validity of the concept of psychopathic personality. *Archives Criminal Psychodynamics*, 1961, 4: 789-797.

White, R. W. A preface to a theory of hypnotism. *Journal of Abnormal and Social Psychology*, 1941, 36: 477-505.

Wirt, R. D., Briggs, P. F., and Golden, J. Delinquency prone personalities. 3. The sociopathic personality: Treatment. *Minnesota Medicine*, 1962, 45: 289-295.

Zazzo, R. Image du corps et conscience de soi. *Enfance*, 1948, 1: 29-43.

Glossary

Note: This glossary is limited to terms which we have coined and to those which have been given special emphasis or used in special ways.

Abnormal behavior: See **Malfunction**.

Adaptation Attribute: A widely represented evolutionarily derived mechanism which allows more effective resolution of disequilibrium states. Ex: Learning allows the organism to respond adaptively to consistencies which are peculiar to its own environment.

Apperception: The process whereby inputs from sensation and memory become automatically and sequentially focalized. Ex: If you are thinking, looking, or listening, the ongoing process of apperception is taking place and as each item (whether memory or sensation) moves into focus, it is being apperceived.

Apperceptual flooding: Occurs when an input is so prepotent that it jams out other components which might ordinarily be focalized. Ex: If a hot iron were fastened to the skin, the individual would be unable to notice anything else; the pain would flood the apperceptual mechanism so that nothing else could be focalized. Also see **Apperceptual jamming**.

Apperceptual jamming: Occurs when some component which might otherwise be focalized is excluded from apperception by a more prepotent input. Ex: The inflooding of extreme anxiety may be sufficient to keep a particular encode or sensory component from being apperceived. Freud used the term "repression" to designate this circumstance.

Apperceptual threshold: That point at which one of the many components (whether sensory or memory) within the integration matrix moves into focalization. Ex: Who discovered America? "Columbus" suddenly moved from being out of awareness to being focalized and the apperceptual threshold was crossed. A faucet is dripping and you suddenly notice it; at that moment the apperceptual threshold was crossed.

Appetite: Refers to the particular item (food, sexual partner, etc.) which demonstrates positive valence when a given drive input is present. Ex: When hungry I desire steak, while a Frenchman may desire snails.

Attention: See **Apperception**.

Autocept: A phenomenological unity arising from basic inputs (visceral, dual stimulation, mother's face, etc.) which serves as the basis for an individual's identity and much of his motivation. Ex: Whether a person indulges in volitional behavior or experiences his own identity and continuity, the autocept is responsible.

Bi-phasic behavior: Demonstrated when an organism moves in one direction to a given level of energy but in the opposite direction to a different level. Ex: Euglena will move towards a dim light source but away from more intense levels of illumination.

Compensatory jamming: Occurs when some intolerably disequilibrating (usually anxiety and/or guilt) input is either partially or totally displaced in apperception by less prepotent material. Ex: The frightened child who whistles while walking home in the darkness; the individual who fears that he may shout an obscene word while in church. Note: In apperceptual jamming, pervasive input automatically excludes other material; while in compensatory jamming,

211

such pervasive material is displaced (due to volitional override) by the inputs arising from some activity.

Concept: A generalized memory residual which summarizes and thus represents the repeated presentation of many similar percepts. Ex: Although we perceive many types of houses, all of this information is encoded under a summary memory residual which consists of a generalized visual image, sound image, word image, or "blob."

Conceptual generalization: Occurs when an intermediating encode (whether visual image, auditory image, or word image) allows a common response to two or more different inputs. Ex: A dog can be taught to salivate both to a bell and a buzzer, but it is the food encode which intervenes and actually initiates the salivation.

Cue deneutralization: The process whereby an input which did not previously affect the behavior of an organism picks up the capacity to bring about internal changes which in turn introduce secondary drive input occasioning either approach or avoidance behavior. Ex: A bell which comes at the onset of shock will develop the capacity to introduce fear which in turn causes the organism to avoid the shock situation.

Cue function input: Sensory components which in the ordinary ranges do not have disequilibration significance but which, as a function of learning, may develop the capacity to introduce secondary drive and thus occasion either avoidance or approach behavior. Ex: The sight of a stove typically becomes sufficient to produce avoidance behavior in a child.

Cue utilization: Is demonstrated when an organism responds differentially to an energy dimension which in itself constitutes neither hazard nor sustenence (may be either innate or learned). Ex: A spider responds to vibrations in the web and obtains food. A child responds to the sight of a hot stove and avoids being burned.

Disequilibrium: Any condition of imbalance within a physiological system sufficient to occasion compensatory action. Ex: That state of fluid deficit which is sufficient to initiate the drinking of water.

Disequilibrium range: The continuum of imbalance which exists between initial reaction (minimum disequilibrium) and damage to the system (maximum disequilibrium). Ex: The state which exists in a blood cell placed in distilled water between the initial compensatory action of the membrane and the bursting of the cell.

Doctrine of specific need qualities: Each type of disequilibrium input must be qualitatively distinct from all the others or the organism could not respond appropriately to a particular state of imbalance. Ex: Hunger must be qualitatively different from thirst or the organism could not respond differentially to food and water sources.

Drive: The experiential input which initiates and sustains activity. It is not (1) hours of deprivation, (2) a state of physiological imbalance, or (3) the relationship between deprivation and behavior. Drive is the literal input such as pain, hunger, or thirst which spurs the organism to react. Ex: If someone pinches you, it is not: (1) the pressure of his fingers, (2) the activation of the receptors, or (3) the tissue damage, which occasions the withdrawal response. The pain is the literal spur which produces the response. Also see both **Primary** and **Secondary disequilibration input**.

Edgeness: The sensory characteristic which is foundational to the perception of phenomena. Since it is derived from the differential response of receptors to varying intensities of imposed energy it is completely innate. Ex: If you look at a chair you will observe that it is separated from other aspects of the visual field by a continuous line which marks its boundary. This line is the outcome of a differential activation of the receptors in the retina.

Encode: Any residual of a sensory input, which either alters other memories or constitutes a new one. Ex: If you can remember what you had for breakfast, the sensory derivatives of what you ate have left residuals in the memory process. Also see **Primary** and **Secondary encoding**.

Equilibrium: The condition of balance which exists in a dynamic and reactive system during which no compensatory action is taking place. That condition which exists when a dynamic and reactive system is retaining its optimal steady state. Ex: A body cell which is in such optimal balance with its environment that no traffic is occurring through the membrane.

Evolutionary interdependence: Species which have interacted for extended periods during evolutionary development will demonstrate attributes which reflect this interdependency. Ex: Mice have acute hearing while certain owls have dampeners on their wings which greatly reduce the noise of flight.

Flare input: An almost instantaneous experiential repercussion arising from sudden and unexpected situations. It typically lasts only a few seconds and may be correlated with the psychogalvanic reflex and the startle reflex. Ex: The input which would be experienced by a person who suddenly sees a truck on his side of the road at the top of a hill.

Fluid transmitter: Any information technique which involves the introduction of input into the integration matrix by way of shifts in the proportions of certain components in body fluids. Ex: A change in the amount of glucose in the blood is apparently important in the introduction of hunger input into the integration matrix.

Focalization: See **Apperception**.

Fulcrum Phenomenon: Demonstrated when an organism moves first one way and then the other as a reciprocal reaction to changes in the level of energy around a certain point. Ex: A human being in a cold room before a hot fireplace will move towards and then away from the fire as it decreases and increases in intensity. Also see **Bi-phasic behavior**.

Homeostasis: The tendency for body systems to maintain or regain a particular steady state. Ex: Heart rate tends to remain around 75 beats per minute.

Input: Any sensory or memory component which is focalized as unity by the apperceptual process. The size of an input can possibly be obtained by first determining the speed of apperceptual shifting and then offering a variety of sensory components at that particular speed. Ex: Any item (whether sensory or memory) which can be apperceived as unity at the upper limits of apperceptual shift.

Input constancy: The outcome of three (shape constancy, size constancy, and brightness constancy) simplification mechanisms which insures that phenomena will be perceived as "the same" regardless of moment by moment changes in the retinal image. Ex: A window is seen as rectangular in spite of the fact that the image which it projects on the retina is typically trapezoidal.

Input focusing: Occurs when freefloating anxiety (guilt, hostility, hunger, or sexuality) is channeled into some particular object, animal, person or situation. Ex: A person suffering from freefloating anxiety may suddenly discover that it has disappeared but that he now has a morbid and irrational fear (a phobia) of black cats.

Input fusion: A simplification mechanism which provides that sensory components which are derived from the same general circumstance (i.e. those that occur simultaneously) become integrated into unity. Ex: We apperceive a tiger as unity even though many different cues both within and across modalities may signify his presence.

Input prepotence: Refers to a given input's relative potential for focalization. Many variables coalesce to account for the prepotence of any input. Vividness, intensity, novelty, discreteness and the degree of association with the input which is being focalized are all factors which have important influence on apperception, and thus may conjoin to account for the prepotence of any given input. Ex: An input which is intense, vivid, discrete, novel and related to the component which is presently being focalized will have maximum potential for being focalized.

Input vividness: Refers to the fact that certain disequilibration (drive) inputs are more intolerable than others. Ex: Pain is more excruciating than thirst and thirst than hunger.

Integration Matrix: A hypothetical area (corresponding to the field of consciousness) wherein the various inputs from the transmitting mechanisms and from memory may functionally coalesce. Ex: During any given waking moment many different inputs, both from sensation and memory, are available for apperception. The context of this availability is the integration matrix.

Internal locomotion: The fluctuation of apperception relative to memory encodes; has the same meaning as the conventional term "thinking." Ex: If you think about the various steps involved in the grilling of a steak you are indulging in internal locomotion.

Intrinsic dilemma: Pertains to the fact that we must use sequential categories (words, sentences, paragraphs, etc.) to explain organisms which work on contemporaneous principles, that we must deal with organs and processes separately when all aspects of the organism are actually dynamically interdependent. Ex: Learning and motivation are interdependent processes yet we must discuss them in separate sections, with words that are sequential.

Isomorphism: Refers to the manner in which organisms reflect, in their structure and processes, those characteristics of the environment which were important in the evolutionary development of the species. Ex: All land mammals have strong legs to offset the force of gravity. Also see **Evolutionary interdependence.**

Learning: See **Primary** and **Secondary encoding.**

Locus specificity: Refers to the fact that each receptor (and this is particularly true of those on the skin) has a unique quality which is characteristic of a particular location on the body. Ex: If an insect is crawling on one's skin, he knows with some precision where it is.

Malfunction: Exists when the activity (whether overt or covert) which is immediately equilibrating leads to outcomes which are persistently non-adaptive in the individual's own society. Ex: If your apperceptual mechanism is flooded with guilt and anxiety, encodes essential for effective behavior are jammed out.

Maximum disequilibrium: The condition which exists in a dynamic system when, as a function of too rapid energy shift or too intense energy application, the structure of the system is damaged. It may happen when changes occur with such speed or amplitude that the compensatory resources of the system are inadequate. Ex: A red blood cell placed in distilled water will rapidly expand until a point is reached when it finally bursts.

Memory: See **Encode:**

Minimum disequilibrium: The condition which exists in a dynamic system when, as a function of shifting energy, a compensatory reaction is initiated. Ex: If placed in an airtight room, a point will be reached when an increase in the rate and amplitude of breathing will occur in compensation for the increase in carbon dioxide.

Motocept: A phenomenological unity arising from the contiguous and recurrent presentation of inputs arising from particular movements of the body. Ex: After much practice, the various inputs derived from walking have become fused so that the process can occur almost automatically.

Motor threshold: That point at which a given apperceived input (whether sensory component or encode) occasions a motor response. Ex: A person may apperceive in input for some time before a response occurs. That point at which a response is initiated, is the motor threshold.

Natural selection: The view that variations in certain members of a species give them a slight edge in the battle for survival. They are thus selected by nature to survive and to transmit this attribute to their offspring. Ex: stockier individuals have a slightly better chance of surviving in cold climates than those with longer appendages; Eskimos have short arms and legs and stocky bodies.

Negative feedback: The condition which exists when greater deviations from balance occasion more extreme compensatory reactions. Ex: The longer a person goes without food the more rapidly he will eat.

Negative valence: The property demonstrated by a previously neutral cue when an organism consistently avoids it. Ex: A stove which is consistently avoided by a child has picked up negative valence.

Normative equilibrium: That particular range in a homeostatic system which is typical and appropriate during periods of ordinary activity. Ex: Under ordinary activity. Ex: Under ordinary conditions, the heart rate remains around 75 beats per minute.

Percept: A phenomenological unity arising from the simultaneous and contiguous presentation of sensory components which are separated from others by an edge or contour. Ex: Although a tree is a composite of many sensory components, it is still perceived as unity.

Perception: The particular unity, form and organization which raw sensory inputs come to assume, whether innately determined or derived from learning. Ex: An airplane flying over is seen as unity in the context of three-dimensional space, even though it is a composite of many inputs which are momentarily shifting in size, brightness and shape. Also see **Primary encoding.**

Perceptual generalization: Occurs when an individual automatically sees an item as the same even though it may be shifting in size, brightness and shape. Ex: A car moving towards an individual remains the same in his perception even though the retinal image is continually changing.

Positive valence: The property demonstrated by a previously neutral cue when an organism consistently approaches it. Ex: A whistle which calls a dog home has picked up positive valence.

Primary disequilibration input: The input arising from critical physiological imbalances within the organism or from traumatic energy applications. Ex: Hunger activates the organism when a particular level of depletion is reached, and pain activates the organism when traumatic energy reaches a certain degree of intensity.

Primary disequilibrium: A condition of surfeit, deficit, or trauma sufficiently extreme to occasion the introduction of input into the integration matrix.

Ex: When the fluid content of the body reaches a certain level, thirst input is introduced into the integration matrix.

Primary encoding: The learning process whereby sensory inputs become fused and structured so that the autocept, motocepts, and percepts emerge; and the constancies and three-dimensional space become manifested. Ex: The process which makes us see an approaching automobile as the same phenomenon in three-dimensional space even though it is momentarily changing in size, shape, and brightness, and is comprised not of one but many sensory components.

Primary reverberations: A hypothetical neural activity which is assumed to result when any stimulus above the sensory threshold is imposed. It apparently lasts for about one-twentieth of a second after the stimulus has been removed and is assumed to account for the lower threshold for pitch, flicker fusion, positive after images, and to contribute to the perception of movement. Ex: If one stares at a bright light for a few moments, he will continue to see a bright spot for a short period after the light has been turned off.

Process ecology: The complimentarity of functional attributes which may develop between two species which have been involved in interdependent evolution. Ex: Bats have sonar and agility for catching moths while moths have receptors sensitive to the bats' emissions and aerobatics to avoid being caught. See **Evolutionary interdependence**.

Secondary activation system: A physiological mechanism which provides disequilibration significance for previously neutral cues and occasions bursts of activity during time of emergency. Ex: The sight of a snake instigates changes which not only occasion the introduction of fear; this input in turn activates the organism so that more rapid withdrawal can occur.

Secondary disequilibration input: That which arises from the various secondary activation systems of the body and which may be broken down into (1) the various emotional experiences, (2) feelings, and (3) what we term flare input. Such input provides previously neutral cues with disequilibration significance and allows activation during emergency. Ex: Fear not only contributes to the deneutralization of the "lion," it helps provide the motivation to flee from him.

Secondary disequilibration system: See **Secondary activation system**.

Secondary encoding: Ordinary learning as distinguished from perceptual structuring (primary encoding). It accounts for the establishment of encodes, the association of encodes and the deneutralization of cues. Ex: A flashing light which occurs at the onset of shock not only becomes encoded, it also becomes associated with other aspects of the shock box and develops the capacity to produce fear.

Secondary reverberations: A hypothetical process, initiated by any sensory input, which lasts for approximately three seconds after the input is no longer being introduced. These reverberations allow the meaningful use of language and are essential for the fusion of separate input components into phenological wholes. Ex: A person who makes an error in speech typically notes the error and can make a correction.

Self system: See **Autocept**.

Sensing: The ongoing process of apperception relative to inputs arising from the various transmitting mechanisms of the body. Ex: The process involved in listening, feeling, seeing, etc.

Sensory input: Any experiential derivative arising from the various transmitting mechanisms of the body (whether specific receptor, specialized nerve ending or fluid). It is both the manner whereby the environment is represented and the spur which makes reaction within the environment possible. Ex: Pain, anxiety, sound, cold, grief, are all classes of sensory input.

Sensory threshold: That point at which a given energy change activates a transmitting mechanism sufficiently to introduce an experiential component into the integration matrix. Ex: If a feather lightly touches the skin, one may not feel it; but if the pressure is increased, a point will be reached at which the pressure will be felt.

Simplification mechanisms: Evolutionarily derived processes which help counteract the reduction in adjustment facility introduced by increasing complexity. Ex: Fusion allows the integration of multiple inputs which represent the same general circumstance.

Stimulus externalization: Refers to the fact that certain receptors (the exteroreceptors) project the experience so that it appears to be taking place at varying distances from the observer. Ex: The words on this page appear to be located several inches from the reader, although they are actually within his body.

Thinking: See **Internal locomotion**.

Transmitting mechanism: Any one of a number of techniques for feeding information concerning body imbalances and energy applications into the integration matrix. Ex: Specific receptors, as in the rods and the cones; special nerve endings, as in the receptors for pain; and the blood, as in the case of hunger.

Uni-dimensional differential behavior: The behavior which would be demonstrated by an organism which could respond in gradient fashion to only one energy dimension. Ex: A hypothetical organism which could respond only to heat, but could move faster as the heat became more intense.

Unity constancy: An outcome of primary encoding derived from the repeated information that items in the environment are typically separated from other aspects of the field by an edge which goes completely around them. Ex: An individual will tend to see an automobile as a whole even though it is partly obscured by a building.

Unnatural selection: Occurs when men select certain members of a species and promote particular attributes through controlled breeding. Ex: Horses which can run fast have been selected out and specially bred to produce the Thoroughbred.

Volitional behavior: (1) Activity which is initiated and sustained by drive input arising from threat to the organizational integrity of the autocept; or (2) activity which is motivated by some other system, but which is mistakenly attributed to the autocept, because the inputs (i.e. arising from basic memories and familiar sensations) which characterize it are more prepotent than many vague ones which may activate behavior; or (3) activity which is motivated by a basic disequilibration input (such as sex) which has become basic to, and indeed may comprise, an essential aspect of an autocept.

Volitional motivation: The input arising from the tendency of the autocept to retain and regain a particular organizational structure. Ex: When the integrity of the autocept is threatened, secondary disequilibration input in terms of anxiety and/or guilt instigates and sustains action. The behavior is volitional not only because its impetus arises from the autocept, but because the person experiences it (since the components—basic memories and sensory reverberations —which are central to his identity are always being monitored) as arising from this source.

Name Index

Subject Index